FROM FEMINIST TO RAPIST

FROM FEMINIST TO RAPIST

FALSELY ACCUSED OF RAPE

FETSUM ABRAHAM

Order this book online at www.trafford.com
or email orders@trafford.com

Most Trafford titles are also available at major online book retailers.

Printed in the United States of America.

ISBN: 978-1-4269-9317-6 (sc)

Library of Congress Control Number: 2011915428

Trafford rev. 09/26/2011

www.trafford.com

North America & international
toll-free: 1 888 232 4444 (USA & Canada)
phone: 250 383 6864 ♦ fax: 812 355 4082

TABLE OF CONTENTS

THE ROLE OF FEMINISM IN THE AMERICAN STYLE OF JUSTICE

FEMINISTS ON FEMINISM

DEDICATION

I dedicate this book to INNOCENCE PROJECT in recognition to its spiritual mission of helping innocent American victims of injustice, to true victims of rape, to all falsely accused victims of bias and all political prisoners denied the due process of justice in the world.

INTRODUCTION

Clearly, human beings are the most intelligent animals on earth, but this advantage comes at the cost of misery because intelligence has natural limitations and no one can excel in everything. Although excellence and truth in absolute form are humanly unattainable, society needs a dependable rule of law to monitor the tendency of human beings to succeed at the expense of others. It needs professionals in different areas for its very survival. Self-Reliance is therefore a derivative of illusion for no one can capture it all in one lifetime alone.

Unfortunately, governance in its broadest explication is subject to power, material and psychological greed. We rely on organized humanistic activists to check and balance social order and leadership integrity and we give contributions and free labor for the cause in exchange. A society without activism is, thus analogous to a sick body without a physician.

Progressive activism is, however, impossible without democracy, verbal and written freedom of expressions. Through these rights, activism addresses the needs of society and fights for their implementation. History shows that activism can resolve the questions of society if it has popular support but cannot guarantee everlasting result unless it overcomes the consequence of success because opportunism can interfere to reverse or complicate the end result of struggle.

What I am saying is that freedom may be partially promoted by reactionary forces to a point of victory, but opportunism sets the psychic clock back to the beginning of struggle through revisionism. Opportunism should then precede revisionism in a scenario where human struggle for freedom contradicts its mission after victory by leaders who refuse to move on. This has been the case in many parts of the world, from the Vietnamese and Cuban struggle against Imperialism to Zimbabwean and Eritrean struggle against colonialism, and far beyond to most of the struggles for freedom waged by humankind.

Wherever we stand on the question of freedom, there is one truth that we cannot breach: *any type of freedom cannot originate from the foundation of prejudice. T*he moment one trespasses or fails to defend the freedom and the rights of others, by default one has abandoned one's freedom and rights, whatever they were. Unfortunately, pseudo revolutionaries can use prejudice after victory for their personal benefit and spoil the gains of struggle, dragging us back to square one where the focus remains constant against the problem and the yesterday's activist becomes the target of resistance after choosing to be a parasite of society.

In so saying, the authenticity of activism is directly proportional to its neutrality on issues governing the activism in question; it nullifies itself, otherwise for partial activism becoming part of the problem. It is impossible to fight racial discrimination for instance, while undermining other people's sexual freedom, gender equality, freedom of religion etc. Similarly, feminism cannot liberate women from men's chauvinism through sexism.

Obviously, being is imposed but living is a choice. I happened to be a human being from the background of Eritrea who arrived to this temporary life involuntarily but choose to live it by the book voluntarily. I had neither the interest nor the tendency to write a book about my biography because the world does not revolve around my axis and I am no more important than any other person is. I was just a naturally crafted ordinary person with ordinary common sense and life style who did not have much to tell about myself. My ordinary story had to be transformed to something extraordinary because of destiny for me to get involved in this amount of work. Something had to shake my existence to induce a story worth telling for a purpose.

A crisis put me in this situation.

This book is thus, not about me but about the causes and effects that orchestrated the story into something more significant to society than to my individuality: about the fraudulent American government and the dark face of feminism in view of firsthand experience. My role in this volume is a messenger of what is supposed to be told, a transmission medium of the message from the instigators of the story to the receiving public end of society.

The question was how to reduce this contemplation to practice and take advantage of the opportunity to smuggle other important sociological issues that comprised a significant portion of my moral values into it, without stealing the show from what was to be told.

Apparently, it was impractical to transfer the cumulative message without my subjective opinion of it. The mission was impossible without exposing myself to some extent for the sake of balance and continuity because destiny delivered the experience, intelligence complicated it, the associated thoughts radiated from the brain through the mind and I own the brain. This conditioned me to begin the original material from the conditions, which I was born into and to jump directly to my teen-age years from which my life forward was built. Yet I found that the end product was about me to a noticeable extent for a reason that has to do with a human being's natural propensity to be more partial towards the self than to the no-self (the message in this context). The result was confusion. The harder I tried to stay away from the subject matter, the more I found my life history in it. The project expanded beyond my imagination to a point of having a hard time containing everything in a single volume without taking the risk of losing the point.

It took a while before I decided to settle on two books and here I go with this one (the second chapter of my original work) which eventually developed enough to stand on its own. Chronologically though, the second book (supposedly the first chapter of my original work) which will come out soon, is older by substance than this book for it reflects my life encounters until the point of my crisis.

Apparently, it was not because of economic problems that I left home in the seventies eventually to end up in the United States but in search of justice. What happened to me at the end of the day was what happened to millions of immigrants that came to this paradise to take advantage of the opportunities it offered at the expense of Native Americans. I happily became an American with Afro-American identity for life because I felt safer, although I resent being in this land without the consent of its authentic owners.

This development came with a price. It upgraded my Eritrean nationalism to Afro-Centrism and further conditioned me to experience racism and Afro American ethnocentrism directly to say the least. I started to see human beings from heterogeneous point of view. The more my youth energy slowed down in time, the less emotional and the broader I had become and the better I grew to identify myself with the universe. My universal activism is therefore a deliberate choice to stand for freedom anywhere applicable in the planet and gracefully pass by after completing my assignment of justice as impartial as I can be. To this effect, my activism started back in Africa as a feminist defender of my mother and grew into different forms in time through Eritrean nationalism finally to settle down for universal pacifism, where I socio-politically stand as a contemporary African American today.

Reality asserts that I passed through the ups and downs of refugee life to being the academic beneficiary of the opportunities offered by this beautiful country and generous people in achieving a graduate degree in Electrical Engineering (MSEE) from the State University of New York in Binghamton. I also hold a graduate certificate in Information Systems from the George Washington University in the District of Columbia, a Certificate to install, operate and program Public Branch Exchange based microwave communication systems from the MITEL Company in Florida, and commercial and residential Electrician Diploma from Penn Foster Institute in Pennsylvania.

I was blessed to serve the US Patent and trademark Office (USPTO) as a Patent Examiner for fourteen productive years. My work was in the areas of thin film and conventional semiconductor devices and fabrication methods, optical devices, active, passive and hybrid electrical circuits, communication products, all inclusive computer memory structures, adaptive and conventional feedback controlled electro-mechanical systems and all inclusive liquid crystal displays to list the least. I had the opportunity to help many examiners at conceptual rank of the discipline and procedural level of the profession, examining thousands of Scientific Patent Applications and personally issuing 998 Patents as of 2006, out of which I processed 652 applications from start to finish under completely autonomous authority as a Primary Examiner.

How my professional life ended at the USPTO is something out of the elasticity of this project that I have accepted as my next assignment, but I was forced to join the dependent members of society to the extent of struggling for survival a day at a time although staying too busy with writing to consider myself productive.

Today I am a Math teacher in a high school, shaping my future towards the end goal of teaching in college. The advantage of the obstacle I suffered professionally was certainly in terms of raised awareness on the active presence of ethnicity-based prejudice that has been safely camouflaged under the blanket of racism for so long in this country. I believe America has been singing the blues from ethnic discrimination within the black community at equal levels with racism within its society, except that racism is taken more seriously as a matter of priority.

I am what happened to me. As a materialist who believes in concrete encounters of existence, my skin color is no longer a reason for me to trust anyone from my racial group similarly to what my ethnicity in relation to my community has become as a result of the unexpected post-independence Eritrean experience. I am from here on conditioned to live the rest of it upholding equality and simplicity as my way of life and evaluating human character based on its spiritual quality irrespective of age, education, ethnic background, complexion or gender.

That be as it may, this book targets the entire world for reading. About twenty years after my legal residence in this blessed land called America, I found myself challenging the most traumatic crisis of my life. I was falsely accused of rape by a person I had known for years within the East African community in Washington, DC. It was a serious test to my feministic political identity and overall activism for all inclusive freedom and justice. It was a shocking happenstance that caught me by surprise. Apparently, I could not have resolved the consequences of the accusation without fairness from the Justice System and Feminism.

Unfortunately, they did the opposite and treated the case with partiality. I was about to become a member of the most populous prison enterprise on planet earth by the government's intentional distortion of the facts on the ground and by the sexist and discriminatory laws introduced to our Justice System by gender feminism and corrupt politicians which suffocate defenseless men accused of rape regardless of the truth. I fortunately escaped it by the help of God and people who knew me well, especially my female friends, but I was never the same.

I have suffered enough and I would hope this work will not cause me any more suffering but I have decided to expose the truth behind my academic motivation no matter what the outcome may be. I could not leave the experience untold without becoming part of the problem and taking the risk of denying knowledge to the American people whom I highly respect, needless to state without suffering from the guilt of silence. In so doing, I am not here to please or displease anybody or to benefit materially from anything related to this effort. Neither am I here to promote myself by aggrandizing facts beyond the perception of my commonsense nor to convince anyone about anything; for I care less for image than my spiritual veracity as a person.

I am only here to share what I know as a matter of exposure to what happened to me; to pursue my constructive existence for the sake of peace of mind; to inform the world that the Police and Case Detectives of the government lie at trials by professional arrangement. I am here to testify from experience and a research based standpoint that our government may have psychic and economic interest in the ever-expanding prison enterprise, which is responsible for consuming a staggering percentage of our society, destroying our family structures and rendering our children fatherless dropouts. I am here to disclose my harmony with the hypothesis that about 25% of the prison population sentenced for sexual violence is comprised of innocent victims of false accusation who are stolen from our society by the satanic gambit of the System and Radical Feminism.

I am further here to confess how naïve I had been on how feminism robbed justice in America. I had no idea that the fabulous feminism responsible for the equality of women in this society and that I fully identified with throughout my life had gone for revenge against powerless men regardless of their social awareness or contribution to the cause and personal integrity. All this coming after the movement achieved success through the united front of good men and women. I sincerely believe that the genuine struggle for equality of women has been hijacked by the rich and powerful feminist leaders and wicked politicians. The genuine cause of women has been misdirected to polarize justice negatively in terms of gender for the sake of gold, greatly jeopardizing the achievements of women in America in the end.

There is no doubt that feminism is not only important for women but also necessary for society at large. There is no question in my mind that the birth of feminism was one of the greatest achievements of humankind, without which the struggle for freedom and equality would have been incomplete. However, violence and deception are gender blind human modes of existence that affect us all impartially. Feminism traditionally defends women from violent men; a person cannot deny its positive social impact in society without being outrageous, but to ignore the fact that it does nothing to defend them and men from violent women is regrettable. It is *not* the voice of freedom for all as far as my concept of neutrality is concerned, but a powerful sexist organization that partially serves society in defense of victims of sexual violence. It is insensitive to the suffering of men falsely accused of sexual offense and in fact the basis of their incalculable suffering as well.

I feel sorry about the negative social role of feminism in general and its particular effects on children in terms of fatherless upbringing, on mothers in terms of abandoned sons and on true victims of rape in terms of misallocated public resources for the cause of false accusers. Fairness dictates that something has to be done immediately: America is in a war with itself and crying for help to detach its down-to-earth component from its pretentious alter ego.

The question is if good men should protect themselves from violent women and Radical Feminism through something called *Masculinism.* I do not know the answer yet. But regardless of my strong temptation to go for it, neither can I imagine myself being a part of such a movement nor can I suggest any other solution at this stage of the debacle. I know, however, that peaceful coexistence is a two way effort at the court of good women's political and spiritual game and I am comfortable to stick with my feminism with optimism that the struggle against destructive feminism will eventually succeed.

At the bottom line of the matter, we Americans are blessed with everything. We are kind, compassionate, culturally and ethnically psychedelic. America is the most accommodating country in the world and the greatest land of opportunity. We have relatively better freedoms, reasonable democracy and abundant material resources to cultivate and attract the best brainpower on the planet. We have the best record in materially reaching out for the needy wherever they may be and the highest potential to lead the planet efficiently. I, nonetheless, do not think we have the quality of justice and moral integrity to do the job accordingly and edify the world about freedom before we free *ourselves* from our own contradictions in the justice system. We carry the burden of proving our integrity in this regard and I don't believe we can.

For those who do not mind to know me as a person, I suggest they should also read my upcoming book *The Curse of Being and Living it.* For those who don't, welcome to this platform where I believe I have tried my best to present my thoughts neutrally on sensitive subject matters encapsulated within. Please be my guest to break the capsule and enjoy the rest without prejudgment.

FALSE ACCUSATION OF RAPE

A Flush of my Concept of Relationship

Coming from decent Eritrean parents who were successful in business in Ethiopia, everything went smoothly until my late teen-age years growing up in the country with no psychological hang up. I came out having a solid background for a bright future as one of the luckiest human beings in this planet, where the majority of humanity suffers from different forms of distress. There was one problem however, the fate of an Eritrean born into the Eritrean struggle and living it from within an Ethiopian political environment under King Haile Selassie's extremely brutal political approach to the Eritrean question.

I started to feel the pressure of my Eritrean identity in my high school years from the socio-economically comfortable grounds of Ethiopian citizenship. The intensity of my attachment to Eritrea intensified between 1970 and '74 and reached the maximum point then after when the Mengistu regime was in the process of holding absolute power in Ethiopia. It was the wrong time to be an Eritrean because the struggle was effectively challenging the Ethiopians more strongly than ever. My teen age emotional energy did not help; for it was impossible for me not to entertain Eritrean nationalism and my fascination with the struggle was too romantic for my safety in Ethiopia, where life was about to become valueless for years to come.

11

I sneaked out of the country in 1976, entered Europe a few months later and stayed there until the end of 1977. I then lucked out to arrive in beautiful America in 1978 where I have lived ever since.

Although I continued to develop my academic knowledge through hard work, my ordinary life for the most part stayed very much the same. I loved to go out and meet people. With my respect for women intact, I simply had no drive for commitment to any relationship that came along.

Looking back at my history of relationships, I tend to believe that I was not designed to conform to either monogamous or polygamous attachment with a woman. I have always been an advocate of endless self-determination with no desire either to control a person or to be controlled by one. I could not even fully discover myself until recently accepting my open-ended sensation of freedom, let alone comprehending what it was all about. For what I knew, I was blessed to be a simple compassionate person who has no intention of hurting people deliberately for any reason, but unfortunate to have been a naïvely trusting individual who paid dearly for it.

Whether I had the aptitude to use said freedom for maximum personal or social output, I lived questioning the practicality of *marriage* as defined by society to be: as a woman showed up in my life and left for another woman to follow the pattern. I was powerless to take the opportunities that arrived for me to settle down with any other woman without applying the illusion of reuniting with Bibina[1] in the equation, from the time we broke up the relationship in 1986 and at least few years into the 2000s. The question

---

[1]Bibina is my Ethiopian first love since teenage years. We spent so many good times back in Ethiopia, lived together in the States and went to college together in Atlanta and New York State until we peacefully broke up the relationship in the eighties.

was when it was going to be in effect or when it would stop becoming my reference criterion for other relationships.

In the journey, my mind temporarily focused on Bibina and convinced me to work it out (whenever I got tired of fakers and self-deception) but it also reminded me of the danger of risking my autonomy in the backdrop. Sometimes, I called her to tell her about my readiness to mend the relationship but perhaps because of my passionate attachment to the Eritrean affairs, she never took my appeal seriously enough for any tangible result to take place. She couldn't grasp the importance of openly discussing what was happening at home in Africa; she was either unable to see the benefits of mutual understanding to counterbalance the periodic antagonism of our nations regardless of interest or used it as excuse to stay at bay while simultaneously neutralizing the guilt associated with her fear of commitment.

As for me, it appears that that was my only request in the bargain as far as my recollection is concerned, although I cannot tell if I would still have settled down with her had that issue been resolved knowing that I could be pain in the butt for women. I could not succumb to her silent political position either, for I found it impractical for my freedom of expression and I did not think our relationship would last in that condition.

"That is her fault, what can I do?" sounded logical enough to get around my guilt. The guilt, however, was not going anywhere except taking a nap in my mind, saving energy for the next intensified emotional attack. It would not take long before I got depressed and lonely again waking up with an extreme urge to go back to the same person. The feeling of not being able to reach her whenever I called her for a chat was terrible, as if something was going to happen until my next chance to talk to her, but it was clear that I needed her when I felt shaky and resisted her when I felt stronger. She also behaved that way at times for she loved her freedom as much as I did.

There is no doubt that we had occasional flashbacks that sparked the tendency of reconstructing the relationship individually but the sparks never synchronized and always seemed to be out of phase for a reason beyond my reach. In view of all these, I used to feel like I was condemned to remain hostage of her metaphysical effects forever. I just could not set myself free by accepting her the way she was or move forward by closing that chapter of my life once and for all. It was a vicious cycle that went on for years of mutual affliction. At the end of the day, we went our separate ways and God gave us the resistance and understanding to remain good friends for the rest of it.

Overall, I see myself lucky to still be alive coming from a society conditioned to barely giving people the prospect of enjoying a full life. I am lucky to survive the rough and dangerous encounters of the past that many others did not. Yet, I cannot deny myself the opportunity of admitting that I have spoiled a few precious relationships and failed my friends because of my freedom obsessed ego and endless lust for solitude.

I have also gone through multiple betrayals and deceptive manipulations in my straightforward past. One came to abuse my trust and hurt my feelings for another to check in and repeat the damage with no sign in my vitality to cope up with it properly. Multiple disappointments did not awaken me to the level of avoiding negative people.

In my eventful life, I have gained much from my simplicity in terms of ecstasy as much as I have paid dearly for my naivety in terms of misery. Yet, I lived through the most productive years of my life without answers to the purpose of my existence. In that ambiguous struggle of trying to define my interest as a contemporary middle class African-American and facing the hard times coupled with the question of clearly configuring what I was as a person, the most unimaginable crisis suddenly hit home.

War between Eritrea and Ethiopia and its Effect on Personal Relationships

According to objective perception of the world, the last decade of the last century started out promising for the people of the Horn of Africa; but there was nothing except destruction towards the end of it. In 1998, the relationship between Eritrea and Ethiopia deteriorated and a bitter border conflict took place. The countries fought heavy battles and the war affected friendships and relationships on both sides. Other matters aside, ample time was created for some outraged Ethiopians to avenge Eritrea's secession in the past.

In view of my mom's deteriorating physical condition, the situation was dismal as the war complicated my family's drive to assist her. She, however, naturally passed away at the pinnacle of the trouble. The end of her suffering was like bittersweet chocolate; I accepted it with prayers, thanking God for choosing the right time to take her away.

Sad to say, the conflict took place mainly between fewer than ten million natural allies, the Eritreans and the Tigrian Ethiopians from the northern part of the country; people who share similar languages, cultural values, religions, and a common border. It was a grave mistake, a recipe for self-extinction – not to mention its reflection of African tragedy. They had struggled side by side against the brutal military regime of Mengistu, holding power in their respective countries at the end. Unfortunately, their relationship went sour and turned into the politics of hate.

As an Eritrean, I took it personally as did most people from the region, could not sleep thinking about the danger of endless war emerging over the four million Eritreans by the over sixty million Ethiopians influenced by their extremely agitated government. The obstinacy of the Eritrean government did not help but rather exasperated the situation. Between Ethiopians testing the legitimacy of the Eritrean independence and Eritreans willing to defend their sovereignty and dignity won by 30 years of blood and sweat tainted struggle, the explosion of emotions from both sides was difficult to articulate.

Peaceful coexistence is the best choice of the people for they were destined to remain neighbors; and because they are, in essence, one family having mixed their blood with one another over generations of relationship. However, chronic nationalism, dirty politics, intransigence and pride stood in the way of reason: I knew harder times were waiting ahead.

By the year 2000, the countries had already fought for two resentful years and their situation was going from poverty to desperation. It was then that Ethiopia and its distinguished friends deceived the world by exaggerating the extent of hunger in the country. Eight million people were said to have been on the verge of starvation. Meanwhile, the country kept on spending over a million dollars a day on the conflict, for the fabricated "crisis" to suddenly disappear from the news as soon as enough food and military hardware were supplied to Ethiopia (an important US ally) beyond the capacity of Port Djibouti. This was, perhaps because the Eritreans refused to accept the US-proposed withdrawal from *Badme* (the territory they occupied by force), which happened to be the direct cause of the friction. The inevitable then became reality when the third round of the war started in May 12, 2000.

Within a month, close to a third of Eritreans were displaced from their lands when Ethiopia attacked in a series of consecutive human waves, forcing the Eritrean army inward at an extremely heavy human price. Although the Eritreans were further pressured to withdraw, the most powerful nations silently approved Ethiopia's advances into the uncontested territories.

In one of the activities of the drama, U.S. envoys headed by the then Security Advisor Anthony Lake were sitting with the countries' representatives in Algeria for what seemed like an eternity. They were waiting for the result of an on-going battle in the eastern flank, where Ethiopia was trying to capture the port of Assab from within Eritrean territory. In the end, the Eritreans somehow managed to neutralize the Ethiopians at the most critical fronts, creating the grounds for the peace deal signed in Algiers in June 2000.

Frankly, I was not surprised to see President Clinton handling the situation the way he did but I was shocked to see him leave the White House desperately trying to lift the UN-imposed arms embargo ahead of the deadline. The UN peace keepers were not even completely in place yet and Ethiopia was still occupying non-disputed Eritrean territories, when he passed that questionable verdict on the self-destructive Africans to the surprise of many politicians – including the then UN chief Kofi Annan.

False Accusation of Rape by a Talented Artist in the Field

I lived through this dark time, and it was during the early stages of this horrific period that my own very terrible story took place.

I had been introduced to a woman named Hazen in Washington, DC sometime in the mid-eighties. Although she went to school in my hometown Makalle (northern Ethiopia), I never knew her when we were back in Africa. I was relaxing in my apartment when Hazen called at about seven in the evening on September 30, 1998 and invited me over to keep her company. She was from Tigrai, an

Ethiopian nation, which was in an even more bitter conflict with Eritreans at the time than the rest of Ethiopians. We had twice been sexually intimate over the past three years, though the encounters had had no strings attached.

I knew that Hazen gossiped and lied, but she was pleasant with me whenever we bumped into each other here and there. With everything mismatched, our cultural background and the absence of meaningful spirituality were our common denominators.

Michael, my Tigraian friend, well known in the community as *wedinno, (which means brother in the Tigrigna language)* was at my place in Washington DC when Hazen called and he gave me a ride to her apartment. I bought a bottle of red wine on the way. He dropped me off at about nine o'clock that evening and – oddly enough – strongly warned me to be careful. We did not have enough time to talk more but he clearly displayed his discomfort at my going there that evening through his eye contact with me. I did not take his warning seriously enough to change my mind and went to see her anyway.

She welcomed me warmly and we had a good time making random conversations and enjoying the wine. We then left her place for dinner and spent the rest of the evening at a restaurant listening to a talented artist singing and playing the guitar.

Throughout this time, she told me bad things about her own people. She said they failed to meet her hygienic and western cultural standards for a date. She talked about her plan to officially exchange her Ethiopian citizenship to become an Eritrean in view of claiming to have had some Eritrean blood on her father's side of the family. She also blamed the Tigraians in the conflict between the two countries. Her overall opinion didn't matter: it didn't interest me because I did not see that either Eritrea or Ethiopia was in any way better than the other.

We walked back to her place, a short distance from the restaurant getting silly along the way. It was nearly midnight when we got there. Inside her apartment, she left me sitting on the couch, went to the bathroom, came back dressed in a baggy T-shirt and sat down close to me. She had no underwear on. We felt each other for a while and she gently pulled my hand to the direction of her bed. She then placed herself between the bed sheets and I removed my clothes to join her for the night.

As we continued the activity, I became aroused and reached out for a condom from my pants; she ended up placing it on my penis and much more before we engaged in conventional sexual intercourse, much as we had in the past. Then she was on top.

Her demeanor changed almost immediately. After few moments, she got off me, got off the bed and started yelling at me. I sat up bewildered, recognizing with bewilderment the real rage in her voice. She was using foul language like "motherfucker" and "son of a bitch," really attacking me.

I could not understand her actions; I was confused enough to take it as a practical joke initially and expected her to return to the bed to finish what we had started. It took a moment for reality to sink in and then I tried to find out what the problem was – but that made her angrier still. After that, I kept quiet and the rest of it turned out to be strictly her show.

She continued the abuse as I sat by the bedside trying to locate my clothes. The woman had turned insane. So strong the emotion, God only knows how vigorous the internal pressure had been, as she changed her target against what she had been saying earlier, calling the Eritreans names, I could not believe. She said she hated them and that they were terrible people that must be destroyed. I knew I was about to pay for at least my trust and disregard of the effects of the war on personal emotions. I just did not know how.

I carefully did not react; I rather concentrated on getting dressed and leaving her place. All I could think of was getting out. I didn't bother looking for my underwear; I just put on my pants and shoes and was trying to locate my shirt when she started to physically push me around. She then went into the bathroom, came back with a cup filled with hot water and splashed it in my face.

Again, I didn't respond. She was trying – for whatever reason – to get a reaction from me for some agenda she had in mind.

She smashed the cup on the floor, picked up a broken piece by the handle and violently tried to stab me in the chest but I moved away quickly somehow surviving the danger. She then pulled back and came straight at me pointing the tool at my abdomen. She was completely out of control.

There I was, as this woman simultaneously spoke and acted in that totally unpredictable situation, lucky enough to have had some reflex left to escape her second attempt to hurt me. I was only there long enough to fully dress and leave, as these crazy events took place within a short time frame. Realizing how dangerous the whole thing could turn out without a "legitimate" self-defense, I stayed as alert as I could, stretching my patience to the limit.

I was caught in the middle of two choices that would each weigh against me as a man: reacting in self-defense, which would imply violence against her, and passively taking her assault and getting hurt in the process. However, God intervened and she threw the weapon away when I managed to place a chair between us. She laughed and said that I was going to see how badly she could punish me. She then picked up the phone; her posture relaxed now with one hand on her hip and called the DC Police by dialing 911.

"I want to report a rape," she said, and then sat quietly on the bed after few more details.

I have always been against violence in principle, with my fair share of relationships with different types of women including quite a few decent Tigraian sisters. Now here I was victimized by a big-time liar and skilled pretender! I have no words to express my disappointment, my sense of having been viciously betrayed, as I put on my shirt and left her apartment. On my way out, I saved the condom in my pocket and walked out to the lobby, a little concerned about how this whole situation was going to be handled. Something had been put in motion that I was not going to be able to stop by myself. It felt like crossing the junction between life and death. You are here and then there a second later when fate brutally complicates human existence.

I stood there in despair remembering Michael's warning; realizing that it was a little too late to change my earlier decision, until a sympathetic building security guard approached me to find out what was going on. He had heard much of it already standing at the lobby close to her apartment and reacted with disbelief when I told him that I had been accused of rape and that I was waiting for the Police to arrive. He and his associate had also seen us walking in together peacefully upon arrival from dinner. "I'll testify on your behalf" he promised and gave me his full name and address.

Within about half an hour, the law officers arrived at the street in front of the lobby. I surrendered immediately, walking out of the building, approaching them directly and telling them they were looking for me as soon as they stepped out of the Police car. I briefed them about what had happened and they gently instructed me to stay in the lobby and entered into her apartment.

I thought the whole thing had settled down – at least as far as her reaction was concerned – but to my consternation she received them with deafening screams that suddenly erupted as if someone was cutting her up without anesthesia. She turned the quiet environment into hell; some tenants gathered in the lobby concerned about the late hour disturbance and wanted to know what had happened.

The ear-piercing hysteria went on for a while without change in amplitude. Then she was quiet for few seconds, God bless her soul but went right back to it. Then she stopped and went on again, off and on again with machine-like consistency.

I listened to it all from the lobby, restlessly and more than a little afraid. Finally, the investigator and three more detectives, who joined him later, finished their work, including interviewing the security guard and his friend. By about two in the morning, the Officer took me to a place: where I was kept until the investigator collected my written statement and set me free without bond. I handed over the active, fluid-less condom and the Officer dropped me home at around four o'clock that morning.

The Beginning of My Defense against Two Counts of Rape

The crisis and my "apprehension" from my apartment immediately became news in the community. Close friends and acquaintances alike were calling to clarify the rumor. It then took about a month and half for me to receive a Court Order of Appearance for two charges of rape (vaginal and anal). God knows how she came up with the second offense. I went to Court and the government assigned me a public defender who, a few minutes into our first meeting and without even hearing my story, advised me to accept a lesser charge as a quick fix. I rejected his idea, exchanged numbers with him and left that day after they took my body fluids, fingerprints and pubic hair. I was handcuffed during movement in the Superior Court building.

At least two months passed before I had a chance to talk to my legal representative by phone again. In the meantime, I started to orchestrate my defense, going back in time trying to get help from people that knew me well. Everything in my life was on pause.

On the positive side, I counted on Jesus, whose picture was on the wall, as the only abstract witness to the event, the Officer and the case investigator for my respect of the law, the observation of the guard and his friend, the condom with no body fluid, the 911 call recorded on tape for her exact mental condition immediately after the "violence" took place and the fact that there were no bruises or scratches that she could use as physical evidence.

In the process of organizing my defense, it felt selfish and morally incorrect suddenly to call Alexandra, my old girlfriend for help after three or four years of no contact, but luck simplified the matter when I ran into her in U-Street by accident. It was really a pleasant surprise. To make it even better, she left a message in my voice mail the next day expressing how happy she had been to see me. When I answered that call, I told her about my situation and she turned out to be a crucial defense element that convinced me to hire my own lawyer. She said she had seen on television about innocent under-represented people unjustly convicted of crimes they did not commit.

Accordingly, I hired a lawyer named Mr. Goodman. He was a tall and handsome Caucasian. Within about a month into his involvement, he received the brief investigation report that had no record on the officers' interview with the guard and his associate. The report showed that I was saying "I love you" in the process of committing the crime, a self-importance fantasy of an attention-starved woman in my opinion; and that she had made the call after I left her apartment, a serious contradiction of the facts on the ground.

23

There was no reason for me to have stayed there that late in time and surrender to the police had I not heard the accusation while I was still at her place. She didn't seem to know that I respected the law and that I was eventually taken home by the Officer, but rather assumed that I escaped after I left her place and I was later taken to jail, a perfect match with what was rumored in the community. I couldn't help remembering then what a gossip and a liar she was.

She had also told them that we had the first and the last sexual intercourse three months before the event, rather than the truth, which was that it took place after a coincidental meeting at a friend's wedding party in the summer of 1995. Needless to say, I had not seen her for about a year before the night of the allegation. Further, she told them I called her first that evening.

Clearly, I had a reason to feel depressed about the missing testimonies of the two people from the report because they happened to be the first sign of my hope, especially considering the guard's sympathy and unconditional offer to help me out of the problem. I felt the charges were extremely dangerous and that I could not afford to be deprived of them (their testimony) by the law officers.

Despite that, however, I felt relatively optimistic, since the first fabrication was self-evident to anyone with common sense, the second not hard to challenge after some work, and the third because Michael was with me when she called.

Then we received the pictures of her apartment taken that night. Here was a woman claiming to be forced into multiple rapes, but had the bed and the overall place rearranged to a peaceful motel standard before the arrival of the Police. I received the development positively because I expected her to do the opposite.

The Mysterious Medical Report and the Inescapable Condom Theory

We then received the test result from DC General Hospital. It came out absolutely clean concerning any physical evidence on her body. However, the physician mysteriously registered the presence of semen in the vagina and the rectum. He put his signature asserting that she had hemorrhoids and rectal bleeding exacerbated by anal rape; and hysteria, trauma, fear and paranoia as their associated psychological effects. Amazingly, he also indicated the absence of any detectable injury on the assailant's body, when in fact I had not seen him at all. It took him about half an hour to reach these conclusions before sending her home seemingly unattended.

I nearly had a heart attack when I read the report. There had been no anal intercourse between us ever – not during the other two times we'd seen each other and certainly not that night. It could have taken place accidentally or intentionally caused as part of her setup from the top position where she was in relatively better control: I just did not sense the existence of any anal penetration if it ever did. In any case, it became an independent criminal count. Absent a mistake by the doctor, where had the semen come from?

The only reason I saved and gave them the condom was to show that there was no ejaculation or finished sex. I knew something was terribly wrong somewhere, as I found myself in a complex situation where no one was going to believe me against an expert's claim. My lawyer suspiciously looked me in the eye when I challenged it and strongly told me that he did not want to discuss that any longer. He eventually insisted that I must accept the semen and the anal intercourse regardless of the truth or find another lawyer to deal with it. He said that was how it was going to be unless I was willing to pay for the DNA analysis to prove my innocence.

I argued again for the last time on their burden of scientifically relating me to the semen, but he said that "feminist interference" in the rule of law had changed that procedure. That was the first time feminism came to my awareness in relation to this type of case.

I probably should have engaged an independent laboratory at that point but I did not. What I had been going through was too much for my emotional capacity. I was also getting tired physically. Therefore, I resentfully decided to accept what I did not do and build my defense around it as if it took place consensually. Yet, I was still in trouble, as the condom became my worst nightmare and a source of unexpected problems. No matter how I flipped it around, I could not see any way out of the mess in which my naiveté had trapped me.

It was startling to think of how they could use it against me: as if I had had it for some time during the intercourse but removed it to ejaculate on her body parts. This sounded like something I would give serious thought to as a Juror and a theory good enough to stigmatize an accused as a perverted rapist.

The Beginning of My Psychic Disintegration

I almost lost it between the ambivalence of forced acceptance and endangered innocence, as I silently cried for the first time in years outside my Lawyer's office. I have no words to describe my feelings about facing my siblings, especially my born again sisters, nephews and nieces, on the developments of the day. It was morally crushing and characteristically embarrassing to articulate in the least, cornered like that by an expert's declaration and my compulsory decision to accept the anal rape part of the accusation.

Insomnia and despair started to eat me alive. The anger and the drive to do something terrible were unbelievable. The worst time of my life had just arrived.

I also heard that a Crisis Center had placed my so-called victim under psychiatric treatment, a situation that would better crystallize the claims in the Criminal and Civil Courts.

Bad as it was, even worse, she started to stalk me in my neighborhood.

I was drinking coffee outside the Starbucks Café at the DuPont one summer day in 1999 when my accuser came to my table, pulled up a chair and sat there. I jumped over the short fence and ran away petrified about her mental condition.

A few other times, she stood half a block away from my apartment and watched me from a public telephone stand. Each time I turned around and waked away despondent about the extent of trouble I was in.

Then she started occasionally to wait at the DuPont-Circle Metro Station where I got off after work, staring at me while I went up the escalator. As predictable and annoying the pattern had been I eventually avoided it by getting off at a different platform and walking home the rest of the way.

My telephone was ringing constantly at weird hours and when I answered it, someone breathed and whispered on the other end.

To aggravate the situation, the prosecutor twice asked the judge to stop me from bothering her and sending her mediators to negotiate out of the crisis. As a result, he repeatedly warned me to be careful of an illegal practice, which they had no evidence I was doing. My lawyer, Mr. Goodman protested the allegation but nothing changed. We neither had any concrete evidence against it nor had the prosecution team anything beyond her verbal accusation but they contemplated an arrest warrant for obstruction of justice before the judge gave me a final warning to stop the practice.

During one of my appearances, the prosecutor indicated interest in DNA analysis. She said "not immediately" though, when the judge asked her when she might have thought of having it done. It was unclear why she chose to go that way, especially in the absence of my denial to consensual sex. Irrespective of what happened to that effect, I was surprised to see the limitless freedom prosecutors enjoy to legally abuse public funds compared to the accused that are conditioned to fully carry the burden of defense expenses.

I was concerned about my future but then there was no future about which to be concerned. I was often talking to myself or lost in deep private thoughts in the presence of others. I had become quieter and humbler. As the situation dragged on, people could tell that something was wrong with me. I repeatedly promised myself that things might turn around for the better just to make it through the day but I did not like myself enough to take my words seriously. My internal conflict was so obvious that I started having a problem staying alone. I developed the urge to be around people in order to feel as important as and to detach myself from my accuser but I was unable to relax because the case had already adversely modulated my emotional stability. It had psychologically dropped me to her type of personality, effectively changing the relationship between my self-perception and myself. I was simply rendered inferior below my worst demarcation of character. Though my friends were supportive, I found it hard to freely enjoy their proximity at their level of freedom and integrity.

There was no room for self-deception, for I could not forgive myself for associating with Hazen knowing the type of person she was. It was impossible to hide from the notion that my life was a mess. With all that menacing guilt, I still managed to have lunch with Bibina one afternoon and told her about my plan to shape up if I ever made it through the crisis. I was releasing the words with very weak self-esteem in the background. She just listened and reminded me that life must move on, and the future was uncertain.

My activities changed significantly. I lost interest in my hobbies and stopped exercising and playing the guitar. Instead, I was constantly spending my money in bars looking for people who knew something about her that might help me win the case.

I also started making mistakes at work to the point of telling my supervisor about my situation.

The case was more complicated than I had thought it to be. Who knew what would come next?

In those challenging times of my life, I depended on two of my friends for company. Abisha is a long-time Ethiopian friend I came to know in the early eighties. He is a multi-talented artist who paints, acts, writes, and plays the guitar. My friend is also blessed with comfortable voice range covering about three octaves but he has not patched it for exposure to the public yet. With all his universal qualities, my dear friend loves his Ethiopia with chronic nationalism. I saw Abisha almost every evening then.

Michael (wedinno) was a generous and compassionate man who had taken my problem to heart. He was also a creative person with boundless patentable ideas and quick thinking with about 60% success rate on the quiz show *Jeopardy*.

Something that made the accusation particularly difficult for me was that I had been sympathetic to women since I was a child at home. My obsessive love for my mother was the foundation to this attitude. I cannot swear that I am absolutely free of chauvinistic tendencies should the natural character of a man be considered chauvinistic. However, I can swear that I am a human being who cannot hurt women by innate outline and a humanist who cannot stand human or animal suffering in general. I believe in materialism, in something that exists concretely such as the emotional and physical difference between men and women, but I do not believe one is better or worse than the other. Nature balances out opposing polarities of anything and I see men and women as any equal and opposite duality pairs at the equilibrium point of the scale.

Violence against any living thing is terrible. I do not brag about my consistent stand against violence against women for I cannot imagine standing for otherwise. How are we supposed to treat each other then . . . beat each other up? Striving for peace is not achievement at all but a moralistic choice within. Physical abuse against women has no place in my imagination leave alone in my practical life. I have done it before and I will do it again when it comes to involving in a situation where I confront a man abusing a woman physically. I cannot inactively walk away from it and face my moral values. Among the biggest role models in my political life were women like Angela Davis and Martha Mebrahtu, an Eritrean activist in Emperor Haile Selassie's era of Ethiopia. I lived highly personalizing and respecting women's significant participation in the Eritrean struggle. I had even been directly involved in battered women's issues in northern Minnesota through the Head Start Program.

Unbelievably, I wished the charges were about murder! I believe anybody can commit one if pushed to the limit but acts as the ones I stood accused of were something for which my political experience, social awareness and upbringing had not developed me into a person capable of committing.

It was at that traumatic psychic state that I learned my teenage sweetheart Bibina was pregnant. The information was a solid uppercut to my deteriorating condition. I called her and confirmed the information the day I heard the news.

We had been apart for a long time but in the back of my mind I had not given up the thought that we might be able to get back together some time in the near future – after all, she was my first true love.

That evening, I had an appointment with my friend Chris but he was not available. I needed someone to talk to immediately. I could not stay in my apartment alone nor could I tolerate it for the short time needed to change my clothes after work. It seemed like a haunted place in which my mind and the body were choking each other and dissecting me in between.

What fate it had been, being accused of raping a broken woman who has no moral and intellectual substance while missing the opportunity of fathering a beautiful child with the extremely attractive, intelligent and ethical Bibina! It was very hard to justify my being there for whatever I was as a person. It felt like my existence was meant for nothing more than being a case study of society about a man who seemingly had everything going for him but who ended up falling apart a piece at a time. It seemed I was condemned to suffer it all for lack of determination to finish it off the way my selfless brother did (my younger brother had committed suicide in New York).

I went to a local bar where I found my friend Charles drinking beer. I joined him but my restless mind, randomly swinging like a pendulum without focusing on anything, was forcing my soul to react restlessly, like a crack-head. I briefed him about the overall situation with Bibina when he asked what had gone wrong. He was not even agitated, but rather was reassuring. He said nothing would stand in our way if Bibina and I were meant to be together, and that I shouldn't worry about things I couldn't change.

Nothing he could have said would have made me feel better. He made it so simple at a time when I needed simple reassurance. With that state of mind, I went back to the apartment. Then I listened to her new message on my machine, I called her back, told her that I still loved her; and that we could always work it out and raise the baby no matter what had taken place. The idea of not considering the father of the child in the equation was that of a desperate man's nonsense; Bibina patiently listened without response.

The stability of my professional career seemed small compared to where I was standing. It paid well and I liked the routine examination of patent applications; the ones I worked on mainly focused on micro-electronic innovations and occasionally in other areas such as on memory structures, display and optical devices, electronic circuits, etc. I stayed the course at work but my heart wasn't really in what I was doing.

It was as if I had become a walking zombie; my mind was nowhere to help nowhere to be found or not able to help. The strength that helped me survive in different countries and environments was gone, as I felt the terrible effects of my rapidly diminishing fortitude and resilience. My ego was nothing but a self-created bluff. Rather than assisting me when I needed it most, it was out of touch – like most of my childhood friends who suddenly disappeared from my life.

No matter what I did, my fragility was thrown back in my face. The more I thought I could deal with the situation, the more I realized there was nothing left inside. I knew I was vulnerable to anything.

I reached my apartment one evening to find it vandalized and the door left open. Surprisingly, I was not upset: I welcomed it as opportunity to hurt myself and get it over with. I rushed in to find nobody there and started to throw whatever was left against the walls until I cooled off and stopped.

It was difficult to make it to work considering that I was also in the middle of a program for my promotion to a higher level and that there was tremendous pressure from what was expected of me by upper management.

My demoralized siblings were likewise sustaining much anguish regardless of my pretension that I was in control. My sisters were confused and my brothers consumed with unhealthy quietness any time the issue was discussed. However, it was easy to tell what was going on from their facial expressions: it seemed like they could strike at any time if something was to go wrong, especially considering their experience as Eritrean fighters during the hardest times of the liberation struggle. I denounced myself for affecting other lives. I was taken aback when I heard one of them saying that she must have been crazy to expect living a minute after I was taken away; but there was nothing I could do about what my brother had in mind. My first and last attempt to deflect the thought angered him instantly, as he told me to shut up and stay away from what had been none of my business.

The suffering without something meaningful to lean on was like the earth spontaneously spinning out of orbit in the absence of the sun, the center of its balance. Of course, I had to keep on moving a day at a time until a Jury trial would decide my destiny. But it was inconceivable for me to count down time in confinement and watch my life slip away in a claustrophobic environment should I be found guilty of something I was not capable of doing. Compared to what I paid for my misadventures in the past, this was a hard pill to swallow and might as well be the end of it. The solution I was contemplating then was suicide – heading on to see what happens in the next life – although it was difficult to imagine the degree of pain I would leave behind as a result, a moral responsibility that weighed more in my mind than did my determination to do what I had to do in that situation.

At that desperate moment of my life, I started avoiding myself and could no longer resist my condition. My damage controller overloaded, the effects were overlapping with everything I did. I had to capitulate humbly to something I did not know. Something had to happen before it was too late.

I turned to books and came across some ideas on how to reshuffle life and my environment from a universal point of view, but I could not see my role without securing my life first. I then focused on the volumes affiliated with self-help and spirituality. Nothing changed. I was running out of steam and patience.

In the meantime, the prosecutor offered to drop the criminal charge down to misdemeanor on the condition I pleaded guilty but I declined because I did not want to be dragged through the Civil Court system by this woman, which was the obvious corollary to such a plea. I was also aware of how some feminists use the rape stigma to suffocate those who plead guilty, even after they served their time.

One evening, I met an Ethiopian man from Seattle, a city I had been visiting the previous week, which opened the door for conversation with the generous and candid gentleman. We ended up at a Reggae club together and eventually settled in my apartment for the night. When he woke up, he used my phone to call his relative; he told me that he was ready to visit her and asked me if I knew her. She turned out to be my accuser. I was troubled by the coincidence and didn't say anything more than that she was a friend but I felt she might use the call to prove her false accusation of bothering her. Fortunately, nothing like that ever happened.

Consistent with my normally active social life, I used to flirt a little with one of the clerks at my work before the crisis took place. Jinna came to my office one hectic day and was pushing me to do something about a case I was examining at the Patent Office. I was already in the middle of writing an office action but she kept on pushing and she would not stop no matter how many times I told her to. I then accidentally said something in the exchange that I cannot even remember, to express my frustration with the way she was acting. She told me what I said was sexual harassment and walked out with an attitude. Luckily, I got away with this too but she could have blackmailed me for anything.

The experience was another lesson about how much this country had changed without my awareness. It certainly made me even more afraid of women, effectively changing my social life and routine entertainment choices. I knew I would never make a similar mistake to aggravate the situation through another episode of accusation because I stayed away from women and environments that could bring me closer to them all together at that stage in my life. Yet, the effort was not good enough to help me overcome the paranoia about something beyond my control still miraculously taking place.

Glimpse of Hope

At the point of the impasse, my sister Abi advised me to discuss the hospital report with my doctor, which I did. He quickly noticed the absence of microscopic process in it and informed me about the practical impossibility of detecting semen with human eye. He also knew the doctor who did the examination and informed me that he was African. He then advised me to ask for a guideline as to how the test was performed.

My lawyer requested and received a FBI lab report – one that we did not know existed! It could have been because of his incompetence or something else beyond my understanding but he did not know it existed until the request was made. On the other hand, I am not sure if the prosecutor knew of its existence either, because it does not seem to me like she could legally have kept the information to herself without sharing it with my lawyer.

The report was a properly conducted DNA based lab analysis of Hazen's blood sample, vaginal and rectal swabs and smears, my body fluids, the condom, my underpants and pubic hair, which were transferred to the FBI laboratory on the eighth of April, 1999 and released on the fifteenth of July, 1999. The result detected no blood and semen in the swabs, smears, underpants, and the condom; and no foreign hair in her private areas.

What a feeling it was to hear the perfect emptiness of the report! It was as if a spiritual force had lifted my bent down state free from all pain. I told my loved ones immediately to save them from another second of suffering.

It was unclear whether the analysis was made format the request of the prosecutor after indicating a strong interest in one of the appearances. She might have expected similar results to that of the doctor's and probably went ahead with it to strengthen her evidence. That is what I would have done in her situation had the doctor's report been independent of government influence. If that was the case, my common sense tells me that she missed the opportunity of easily winning a simple and direct case by yet another divine intervention. Because all she had to do was, consolidate the charges based on the defective report from the DC General Hospital alone, which was still a valid expert's conclusion irrespective of the doctor's professional capacity.

Can you imagine what would have happened? I thought we could challenge most of the issues no matter how difficult and earn the benefit of the doubt; but the condom in relation to the semen theory and the associated perversion disgrace, was a powerful point that would neutralize the integrity of defense and change my life forever.

The scientific truth re-illuminated the end of the tunnel and significantly reconstructed hope. The most complicated and strongly vindictive issue was out of the way, thanks to God, my sister Abi, my doctor, my lawyer and the FBI in the condition it functioned independently of prosecution interference.

I certainly had learned to stay ready for more surprises until it was over and I had no idea how the rest of the case would unfold, but it was a special moment in the darkness for me to celebrate my freedom from the condom theory that had the potential to make the jurors suspicious of me being a pervert.

An awakening social agenda, at least it seemed to me could be deduced from why in the planet the African physician reached for the fatal conclusion without proper examination in just a few minutes. As a matter of information, the assailant had been reported as Afro-American, needless to mention the "victim" was African. It did not require integral calculus to assume that the ridiculously malicious physician could have been biased against Black Americans. Although I don't know whether he was part of the prosecution conspiracy, he could have been one who stereotypically accepted the distorted notion that they were all criminals to have signed the report without the slightest concern about the accused.

I do not think he would have fabricated the presence of semen in her body parts without proper procedure had he known I was either White or African for that matter. I cannot see how he could lie about his direct examination of the assailant without something in mind. Not in America where time and resources are wasted on unnecessary litigation, unless he thought he could easily get away with his remarks. For that, I think the profile had to be Afro-

American from a poor background. Unfortunately, what reflected by his improper conduct could have been the perception of some immigrants of that social group. My hypothesis aside, I wondered how many innocent people he could have possibly smoked in the past.

On the other side, with all of this information at hand, I could not grasp why, at that point in revelation, the prosecutor did not consider at least dropping the second charge, which had lost all credibility. A misdemeanor offer to begin with, the absence of physical evidence, the contradictions between facts on the surface and Hazen's testimony and the ultimate DNA-based vindication... and still none of all that helped to change her mind.

I went to meet my lawyer one afternoon only to find him lurking outside the building waiting for someone to let him in. He had earlier told me that it was normal for him to receive negative responses from feminist lawyers in the building whenever he defended people accused of rape: that the tension had been going on for quite a while. This time, he said, he had locked himself out and none of them would let him in. We went to a bar to do what we had to do, but the experience was unexpected feminist slap in the face.

My Relationship with My Lawyer

Although I was lucky to find a considerate lawyer, communication between us was terrible. He was one of the most impatient people I have ever met in my life. Initiating any previously discussed topic instantly annoyed him and he expressed his feelings clearly. Whatever I thought important was apparently useless to him, as I helplessly watched him reject my ideas outright; and for heaven's sake, I had not lost my sanity yet to be that nonsensical.

We had different strategies for the trial from the very beginning with no ground for compromise. He was angry at my failure to understand the defective system and the role of feminism in the case but I felt the same for his persistent use of the "Rape Shield Law" to have it all his way. He had the tendency to decide alone as to how to go about it without allowing me to be involved at an equal level of participation.

About five months before the trial, the misunderstandings reached the highest point: we simply could not stand each other. I thought a recent car accident might have impaired his judgment when he decided not to consider the importance of the 911 tape and the investigation report with all its contradictions because he thought they could undermine them on the basis that she was traumatized. He also warned me not to expect something from the testimonies of the law officers for "they always tend to support the prosecution team." I was confused about what was going on. It simply did not make sense to me for the government to have been that partial and reckless against a clean taxpaying citizen in such a life-threatening situation.

While I wanted to demolish their case by dealing directly with the facts on the ground, my lawyer disregarded the events of that night and rather concentrated on my good character witnesses as a better approach. I understood the quality of his approach to the case but wanted to place it in the second order of priority. Seriously speaking, I did not believe him when he told me that I could not legally inform the Jury about the misdemeanor offer; but again, I was at fault for not doing my own research to verify the information.

We started separating without saying good-bye after heated arguments. The friction worsened so much at one point that my friend Chris started to play the role of middleman and did it efficiently. On one occasion, Mr. Goodman called Chris for a meeting and had to call back again to remind him not to bring me, "that man" to the place of appointment. The gentleman showed a serious lack of confidence in my mental condition to sustain cross-examination.

My Spiritual Transformation

At a moment in all of this, my friend Alexandra gave me a healing massage that triggered a significant mindset reversal. Her spiritual hands on my back felt good enough to wish having them every day but I had no idea about the extent of their magical gist on my state of mind. I went home relaxed and slept well to wake up fresh the next morning for the first time in a long while. I felt good the whole week and felt even better when I started using my sister Abi's natural capsules. I then accidentally came across a book called *The Light inside the Dark*. The title instantly attracted me because it hit a nerve.

I opened it immediately as if there were something precious waiting inside for me. After I finished flipping the pages, something profound but obscure had transmitted into my soul; it turned out to be my dark life's candlelight and the anchor of my transformation.

It was a special moment when I started to notice that I was living with my rival in myself. For the first time in my life, I happened to suspect my mind as my most perfidious enemy. In fact, it seemed like a good friend giving me ideas, somewhat temporarily teasing me only to end up systematically navigating me full speed ahead to the source of my problems. Although I didn't know how and why, at least I found a clue about my defective orientation in relating to things and dealing with emotions.

So magnetized to recovery through this briefly grasped spiritual means, I found myself one Saturday evening at the Buddhist Vihara Temple in Northwest DC with three Sri

Lankan monks getting ready to meditate. They asked me questions and gave me a brief introduction as to how to participate and I went on to my first long and difficult practice that lasted for about an hour.

I perused this path of enlightenment trying to answer my emotional dilemma and to spot the missing link in the discovery. It seemed like the mind alone could not have been the source of all my problems without assistance from something else obscure to me at that time. It is a reflection of the brain after all that cannot cause its own existence. The brain being a physical entity incapable of producing emotions on its own, the question was what that mysterious catalyst responsible for emotional distress had been in the backdrop. I could not answer the question independently and had to go back to books for answer.

In the course of the journey, I found out that I possessed a disjointed system without feedback control: the reason for my deep emotional suffering. I discovered the root causes of my affliction to be the self-ego and the mind at primary and secondary levels of the matter. Hungry for more of this knowledge, I went from book to book spending all my free hours from that day on with great spiritual scholars from all over the place.

I was even capable of touching my guitar with a relatively peaceful mind and make songs with lyrics that reflect my situation. One of them goes like this:

SATANIC FLUKE

Here I am, Here I am
I have been hurting for a long time
That Satanic fluke in September
Vicious betrayal I hate to remember
Hard times hit home full-fledged ahead
Splintering my soul distressing the mind

Everything changed upside down
In the dark season of a despaired man
Pushed to the limit life in a shadow
That fictitious charge was too bitter to swallow
Here I am, here I am
I have been hurting for a long time
Living the days lost in the jumble
Hope falling apart melting in the rumble
I had nowhere to run, no place to chill
Except feeling the pain, that came here for a kill
Then I saw the light inside the dark
That made me suspicious, of my destructive mind
Am now waiting for that decisive day
To gain my freedom and enjoy it everyday

I did not know how far it would go but I knew it was about time to start breaking away from my ego. To expedite the process, I had to open my mind to any spiritual knowledge from any form of spirituality. This honest submission to something beyond my might made it possible for wisdom to sneak through the fences of ego into my soul a piece at a time.

I learned that resolving my internal conflicts was a choice I had to make about my condition. Once I understood that, I started looking at things more clearly and developed a different way of dealing with my problems by choosing to relate to rather than comparing myself with the innocent victims of society.

While putting in enough time for my case, I refused to let it control me any longer and decided to enjoy my life without personalizing the psychological dent. My tolerance and patience improved radically and the effects showed: I started to walk around alone with smiling faces like an idiot.

I needed the lift, as it turned out. That season was by far the gloomiest of them all. I was simultaneously confronted by three distinct challenges.

The issue of Bibina's pregnancy might have been the end of my dream to mend a very important relationship in my life: it was a terrible setback and a threat to my psychic stability.

The war at home was psychologically devastating and its consequence too catastrophic for humanity to stand. It was also a threat to my national identity as a person. It is difficult for outsiders to imagine the impact on Eritreans going to war with a nation twenty times greater in population.

The accusation clearly threatened my freedom at large.

My condition in the last few months before my trial for all of that, however, was peaceful. The crisis taught me humility, an asset I could not have bought for millions of dollars.

I came to terms with Bibina's situation by accepting the yet-to-arrive baby as an extension of our family. I knew I could only take the missed opportunity in the ordinary past, as a lesson for how I should behave better in the future; that attachment and happiness were mutually exclusive and time non-recyclable. Then, I decided to detach myself by trying as hard as I could.

Concerning the war, I was in San Jose airport waiting for my flight home from a business trip when I read about the Ethiopian offensive of May 12, 2000 in the *New York Times*. The paper disclosed Ethiopian advances deep into uncontested Eritrean territories. I stopped everything and meditated for about ten minutes. It was clear that no matter how difficult the test had been, a person's resolve heavily depended on his or her capacity to restore adverse and negative encounters to auspicious and favorable conditions. I welcomed the crisis as a golden springboard for another psychic renovation. I was disappointed but not disturbed as I used to be in such situations. The feeling was along the lines of, "let us get it over with once and for all." I envisioned a gain in terms of spiritual development for Eritreans and Ethiopians in general as a result of the barbaric bloodshed to which they were exposed. I thought the ugliness of killing one another would install compassion, humility and forgiveness in our egocentric souls. I felt that the harder the strong feel about their competence to turn things around, the more they find themselves one step below their objective.

The experience further solidified my spiritual development.

As for my accuser, I accepted the possibility that she could've been driven to despair by her low self-esteem and anger about the war between our peoples: that attention and material compensation might have teased her greed to cross the lines of virtue the way she did. I chose to see the woman as a wounded soul and a universal threat that has been attacking and will continue to attack society because of her miserable life. That I happened to be available to drain her eruption at the very moment she snapped. It became clear that I needed to relax cautiously without being complacent. Most of all, I acknowledged her piercing internal disarray and felt sorry for her. I then ended the source of my negative emotions by simply forgiving her.

Unfortunately, the woman was possessed by Satan, no wonder she invented the rape allegation trespassing the warning of Jesus as posted on her apartment wall with a finger pointing to the sky. The devil did not like my approach as he kept on trying to penetrate my spiritual field through the woman under his possession. A messenger indirectly approached me about her interest in settling the matter for $10,000 but I told him I had nothing to settle for.

I went to my favorite coffee shop one day to find the normally unfriendly and politically biased Ethiopian cashier turning into an angel. Kifat strongly insisted on going out with me and told me that she had dropped by my apartment for a visit in my absence. She had never been there before. Her change of attitude was mind-boggling and very hard to accept without being suspicious.

Not only was I careful at the time about getting involved with women but the possibility that Kifat, a lady from my accuser's hometown in northern Tigrai could have been her relative did not make the situation any easier. To my surprise, she also told me private things about my family. This person who had had limited contact with me knew about my roots in depth. I did not have to be a psychologist to avoid the "date" with this person but kept wondering what might have been going on until I saw her with my accuser another day in the coffee shop.

Evil people do anything to hurt others. Their comfort is a function of how much suffering they cause to others. It is simply their nature to remain sleepless looking for ways to control other lives because they have no control of theirs.

In the meantime, Hazen continued the stalking, though it no longer had such an effect on me. I was beyond caring, becoming a person capable of supervising my actions and emotions with reasonable degree of success. Many things had changed at that point and I had already started writing about my experience and the spiritual question of existence in general, attentively trying to explore the instinctual factors of human character. I had no better choice than to use her as my informal psychopathic patient who appears in my clinic periodically to be psychoanalyzed. Frankly, she turned out to be a perfect case study for my research on evil minds and life-less ordinary souls, a subject matter detailed in my pending work on *spiritual engineering.*

As far as the stalking was concerned, she once came close while I was sitting at the DuPont-Circle Park waiting for a friend. A little nervous but attentive and careful, I moved away when she was about to sit on the same bench. On another day, I was reading in a café when I saw the troubled woman looking for a chair close by my table with a cup of coffee at hand but I collected my things and calmly left the place.

Then she started running in Swann St, NW by my apartment (between 18th and 19th street) a narrow and inconvenient street for what she was doing. The Meridian Park, known by the community as Malcolm X Park, a couple of blocks away from her apartment was certainly a better place for running in my opinion. The choice was up to her but my responsibility was cautiously walking in the opposite direction without allowing the athlete a chance to create problems.

One nice summer day I had a sudden eye contact with her sitting outside a café. She smiled, looking at the sky arranging her hair as if posing for a camera. I did not let that heinous individual steal the moment though, but rather transmitted the stress back to the source and slowly continued my way ahead.

Feminism

The origin of prejudice goes back in time to the origin of humankind. My understanding of society assumes that earlier human beings should have been in fierce economic competition individually and collectively within their randomly distributed communities. The fittest minority should have ultimately excelled to the top through force at some points of the chaotic struggle, while the submissive majority only had to obey the words from above that were to become cultural and traditional norms of society. Morality was ultimately defined by the most powerful who had the superior muscle and sufficient drive to dominate.

By instinctual design or not, the fight for dominance in society has traditionally been exclusively between men. Based on this direction of thought, it seems to me like the original cultural and traditional values of any society represented the fittest men's concept of communal ethics. It was therefore natural for them to have fallen short of defending all members of society. The majority of men were reduced to slave labor and most women to sexual objectivism, motherhood and domestic servitude.

Although the setup was bad for men *and* women in general, the top class's capacity to mold culture and tradition according to its interest should have given mankind the tendency to believe that the male gender in general has had the edge to control the economy because chauvinism was approved to be the legitimate and natural moralistic order of society.

The strength of women did not only come out of normal experience but also out of extreme oppression from men throughout history. Women had an issue with society at the most fundamental scale of existence. Man created the problem and accelerated it beyond the horizon of his comprehension. The damage inflicted on women by men was too humongous to wrap their minds around. As a result, no ideology has been as complex and diverse as feminism.

How would you face man's definition of God in his own terms? What do you do when man assumes his word as the word of God? Once *masculinity* was accepted as God's choice of gender, a case permanently closed on the feminine to carry the burden of sexual difference for eternity. In other words, God envisioned as the masculine head of nature justified the perception of a father as the leader of the family and the male gender as the only legitimate authority in society because the Supernatural masculine God relative to nature attributed to the power of men relative to women. Whether the Adam and Eve story was told accurately or not, it is known to establish divine based discrimination of women globally. From the many verses in the bible that undermine women's equality to speeches made by prominent religious figures of the world, women were simply denied equal participation in society ever since the onset of creation.

Consider Confucius's, "One hundred women are not worth a single testicle," And the Hindu tradition's belief that, "In childhood a women must be subject to her father; in youth, to her husband; when her husband is dead, to her sons. A woman must never be free of subjugation." Can you imagine the number of Asian women that suffered for ages by remarks and traditional attitudes as these?

Now think about the effect on society of Tertullian's ("the founder of Western theology") remarks in A.D. 22: that a "Woman is a temple built over a sewer, the gateway to the devil. Woman, you are the devil's doorway. You should always go in mourning and in rags." And, "Do you know that each of your women is an Eve? The sentence of God - on this sex of yours - lives in this age; the guilt must necessarily live, too. You are the gate of Hell, you are the temptress of the forbidden tree; you are the first deserter of the divine law."

Men wrote the bible and interpreted it at will to dominate women by "holly instruction." The way they did it was not even through a suggestion but through order such as, "Wives, submit to your husbands as to the Lord. For the husband is the head of the wife as Christ is the head of the church, his body, of which he is the Savior. Now as the church submits to Christ, so also wives should submit to their husbands in everything." Ephesians 5:22-24

How do you describe father St. Clement of Alexandria's ridiculous teaching in, "Let us set our women fold on the road to goodness by teaching them . . . to display . . . submissiveness, to observe silence. Every woman should be overwhelmed with shame at the thought that she is a woman" and that of St. John Chrysostom's (Patriarch of Constantinople), "Among all savage beasts none is found so harmful as woman"?

48

What sense do you make out of father St. Augustine's hatred in "Any woman who acts in such a way that she cannot give birth to as many children as she is capable of, makes herself guilty of that many murders ..."?

Imagine what people who could not even forgive their mothers could have done to their wives and other women!

How could an oppressed woman control her emotion on what took place in Lyons, France in the year 584, where at the Council of Macon, "forty-three Catholic bishops and twenty men representing other bishops" voted on "Are Women Human?" and that the result was "thirty-two yes and thirty-one no." Women were saved from being categorized as animals by one vote.

How do you face the Old Testament's (Deuteronomy (22:20-21) verdict on a woman found non-virgin during sexual engagement that instructed men to ". . . bring the damsel to the door of her father's house and the men of the city shall stone her with stones that she die"? Is not this still going on in some backward cultures of the world?

How do you confront the teaching in Exodus 22:16-17 "And if a man entice a maid that is not betrothed, and lie with her, he shall surely endow her to be his wife?" Was not this blessing a rapist with divine authority to marry his victim? I know man practiced this terrible guideline at least in East Africa until recently by cultural orientation but I am not sure if he still does.

Where do you start to repair the psychological poison injected into man's mind by distinguished Christian teachers of the likes of Martin Luther who declared that, "Women should remain at home, sit still, keep house and bear and bring up children." and that, "If a woman grows weary and, at last, dies from childbearing, it matters not. Let her die from bearing; she is there to do it."

These biblical verses and remarks are few of the many good examples that serve to prove that man was a menace to humankind. Whether the holy books distorted the words of God by intention or by misunderstanding, the entire foundation of religion renders women inferior to men. This was the situation all women faced in society when they started to fight for their rights and this was the reason for their extreme emotional response in their diversified struggle for equality. Unlike overthrowing an oppressive system by means of armed struggle, the question of equality for women involved countless complications from society and requested unflinching dedication to secure equality by law and to neutralize the psychology of men polluted by centuries of traditional and cultural fixation.

Apparently, there was no reason for women to accept creation as understood by man for that meant to deny their own humanness. Therefore, feminists had to go as far as challenging the bible, at least partially to signify their existence as human beings. They had to weed out its chauvinistic contents to guarantee equal representation by the Holy book.

I tend to believe that as unfair as men have been to women, maternal love may have been the most effective factor in stopping them from inflicting even more tragic damage to women. But, how much more damage could they have inflicted?

In the flip of the coin, man trapped himself in a No-Exit situation. By exasperating his innate chauvinism to oppress women, he created a contradictory formula for himself as well as his nature. He made a big mistake classifying his gender as sexually active and the other as sexually passive. It backfired in terms of the psychic state of having to prove his masculinity as regards to sex. In some setups, man considered his sexual handicaps such as impotence, endurance, genital size and premature-ejaculation as threats from women's sexual supremacy and tried to resolve his complex by imposing sadistic practices such as genital mutilation and infibulation as integral part of cultural and traditional norms of society. It strongly seems to me that these practices reflect man's disappointment in his sexuality.

Apparently, the struggle of women for freedom was a multi-faceted phenomenon that involved economical, sociological and psychological aspects of life to say the least. Men had to be confronted on all intellectual grounds to leave women alone. Considering that Freud, the father of psychology in the areas of the "unconscious mind and the mechanism of repression" focused on "male development, implying that female development either mirrored male development or was inferior", his classical psychoanalytic theory states that, " . . . the child's identification with the same-sex parent is the successful resolution of the Oedipus complex[2] and of the Electra complex; his and her key psychological experience to developing a mature sexual role and identity genital. Sigmund Freud further proposed that girls and boys resolved their complexes differently — he via castration anxiety, she via penis envy; and that unsuccessful resolutions might lead to neurosis, pedophilia, and homosexuality. Hence, men and women who are fixated in the Oedipal and Electra stages of their psychosexual development might be considered "mother-fixated" and "father-fixated" as revealed when the mate (sexual partner) resembles the mother or the father."[3] This male oriented

---

[2]"In psychoanalytic theory, the term Oedipus complex denotes the emotions and ideas that the mind keeps in the unconscious, via dynamic repression, that concentrate upon a boy's desire to sexually possess his mother, and kill his father." Oedipus_complex/Wikipedia. (n.d.) Retrieved from: http: //en.wikipedia.org/wiki/Oedipus_complex

[3]Oedipus complex/Wikipedia. (n.d.) Retrieved from: http://en.wikip edia.org/wiki/Oedipus_complex

psycho-assumption had to be negated and academically confronted as part of the struggle in the psychological front.

Karen Horney[4] was one of the prominent intellectuals in the field who departed from the most basic level of ethics that "it is inadmissible to equate the term 'male' with sadistic and on the same line women as 'masochistic.'"[5] She then challenges Freud stating that "Penis Envy[6] was not the only cause of women's castration fantasies [such as] revengeful attitude towards men . . ." but also that ". . . men's fear of women could have contributed to the 'male oriented fear of penis concept'" and that ". . . the penis envy concept might also have roots in men envy of the women"[7] in the areas of pregnancy, childbirth, motherhood and breasts.

Psychoanalytic feminism originated in the 1970s to the same generic end because its followers noticed a void in why women still pamper masculinist approach to gender relationships in spite of their intellectual and political commitment to feminism. Do biological factors have something to do with women's acceptance of patriarchy or are there other explanations to the pattern? One of the best

---

[4]"Karen Horney . . . (16 September 1885 – 4 December 1952) was a German psychoanalyst and psychiatrist of Norwegian and Dutch descent. Her theories questioned some traditional Freudian views, particularly his theory of sexuality, as well as the instinct orientation of psychoanalysis and its genetic psychology. As such, she is often classified as Neo-Freudian." *KarenHorney*/Wikipedia. (n.d.) Retrieved from: http://en.wikipedia. org/wiki/Karen_Horney

[5]Horney, Dr. Karen. *Feminist Psychology* (1967)

[6]Freudian sexual development theory built on the assumption that all little girls instinctually crave to develop a penis of their own.

[7]Horney, Dr. Karen. "On the Genesis of the Castration Complex in Women," *Feminine Psychology* (1967)

contributions to this effect was done by Juliet Mitchell's[8] *Psychoanalysis and Feminism* in 1974, where she appeared to defend the hypothesis that there is a content of the unconscious mind rather than biology to this situation. As a socialist she taught about the potential role of Marxism in women's liberation from psychological point of view stating that it ". . . may provide a model within which non-Patriarchal structures for rearing children could occur [such that] . . . lack of the 'family romance' would remove the Oedipus Complex from a child's development, thus liberating women from the consequences of Penis Envy and the feeling of being castrated which Mitchell contends is the root cause of women's acceptance that they are inferior. According to Mitchell, children are socialized into appropriate gender roles. Therefore, women grow to be equally socialized into becoming the caretakers of their households."[9]

In all this, I wonder if Sigmund Freud considered the social condition of women in relation to men with his analysis, which certainly considered the difference of the sexes from biological and inherent roles in society and in a family structure in particular, when he developed his *penis envy* theory. I can understand why girls of his time would wish to be boys if this theory took place in society, assuming the condition of women was worse in his era and

---

[8]"Juliet Mitchell is a British feminist. . . [She] is best known for her book Psychoanalysis and Feminism. Freud, Reich, Laing and Women (1974) . . . [which] tried to reconcile psychoanalysis and feminism at a time when many considered hem incompatible." *Juli et Mitchell*/eNotes. (n.d.) Retrieved from: http://www.enotes.com/t opic/Juliet_Mitchell

[9]*Juliet Mitchell*/Wikipedia (n.d.) Retrieved from: http://en.wikipedia .org/wiki/Juliet_Mitchell

considering the negative effects of discrimination on women would reflect on the psychic condition of their young girls.

Feminism is a highly philosophical movement that progressively developed according to the elements of the challenges women faced in different stages of society. I loved it with passion, given my little knowledge of it, because it opened the door for the mind to explore many academic areas of survival. However, I thought I could have missed the bigger picture by not putting the effort to know it better, especially after sensing my lawyer's attitude towards it and briefly tasting its influence in the justice system through my experience. In line with that, I decided to learn about what made the Criminal Justice System biased and how feminism might have contributed to that end. I moderately studied its development specifically after the sixties, the time it secured universal importance as one of the most influential socio-political philosophies. It's worth recapping the history here.

Feminism as a concept probably originated in Europe considering that "'the first scientific society for women was founded in Middelburg, a city in the south of the Dutch republic, in 1785 [where women had their own journals as well]."[10] "Mary Wollstonecraft's *A Vindication of the Rights of Woman* (1792) is one of the first works that can unambiguously be called feminist."[11] In the 1850s, it became apparent here in America when the hypocrisy of denying half the population its right to vote and keeping them as second-class citizens became uncivilized for society to ignore. The movement then found greater stimulation in the

---

[10]*Feminist movement*/Wikipedia (n.d.) Retrieved from: http://en.wikipedia.org/wiki/Feminist_movement

[11]*Mary Wollstonecraft*/Wikipedia (n.d.) Retrieved from: http://en.wikipedia.org/wiki/Mary_Wollstonecraft

1960s, probably at different intensity levels in different parts of the world.

Encapsulated within the Civil Rights movement, its earnest global upshot, at least in the US, was to achieve equal rights and status for women in all aspects of life, while the ultimate goal was to guarantee equal educational, financial and employment opportunities, sexual freedom, the right to choose abortion and women's full involvement in politics.

In time, the assumption that the movement represented women in general did not pass the test, for it was proven to have practically represented the stereotypical interests of Western white middle-class women. Many feminists started to come out with new ideas to challenge the notion that women have identical problems and activities. Women from different backgrounds started to be organized according to their experiences. Contemporary feminism therefore diverged to various sub ideological branches under the umbrella of the liberation movement in what is sometimes called the "second wave of feminism."

Lesbian feminists viewed the perception of heterosexual gender roles as a reflection of the overall gender tasks in society. Their position targeted the norm that established the unconditional acceptance of heterosexuality as a partial factor for creating favorable grounds against homosexuality.

Liberal feminists primarily promoted women's unconditional inclusion into the existing sociopolitical structure. Their approach was the most reasonable in my opinion in that it focused on building women's confidence to compete in society and carry their burden of achieving equality with men through compatible performance. They believed in achieving gender equality and transforming society via healthy personal and academic communication with men rather than relying on sympathy from the underdog position. Their philosophy was built on the foundation of dignity where every woman was individually capable of gaining equality by choice through active participation, which did not require the change of existing social structures. It particularly considered abortion rights, equal educational and voting rights, economically manageable childcare and health care as important questions of women and monotonously raised the issues of sexual and domestic violence in public forums as its normal mode of struggle for gender equality. One of its most eloquent agendas was *equal result for equal performance*.

The Marxist-Leninist sect approached the oppression of women from economic point of view, pointing at class distinction in society as the root cause of its actuality. It viewed "prostitution, domestic work, childcare and marriage" as patriarchal system's means of economically exploiting women. This sect in essence welcomed the involvement of men in the all-inclusive class struggle of mankind through which women's equality would naturally evolve by default of successfully ending class distinction in society. I assume the European sect was ideologically stronger than the American sect was in this regard because of direct access to communist literature and strong East European leftist socio-political influence.

Material feminism relates to this sect, at least in respect to the doctrine that material conditions in society were a key factor to the development of gender hierarchy that traditionally undermined women.

Radical feminists focused on the political substance of domestic heterosexual relationships in relation to power distribution between the genders. They considered the western capitalist system as a male maneuvered sexist mechanism of oppressing women or as an ordinary patriarchal political system that inherently discriminates against women. They considered utopian social structure as the only way of attaining women's equality in society. Anarchist Feminists like Emma Goldman may belong to this group in a way for developing the thought, ". . . that the hierarchies in businesses and government and all organizations need to be replaced with a decentralized ultra-democracy." They literally extended the struggle beyond the question of gender in society.

Although black feminist scholars were actively engaged in studying the issues of women of color and especially their survival under the brutal conditions of slavery and institutionalized racism, *Black feminism* came to existence a little later than expected in the 1970s. It quickly identified mainstream European American feminism's failure to address the simultaneous oppressions of all-inclusive women of color in the areas of racism, sexism, class and homophobia. It recognized that matters of particular concern to Black women, especially lynching and sterilization abuse could not have been derivatives of gender discrimination but of something alien to the experience of white women. As a result, they rejected representation by the white middle class women's movement because of the desensitized race factor in its program. They criticized the feminist leaders of the time for overlooking the class-based contradictions of colored women in society. They specifically included Europe into their overall strategy of struggle mainly because of the Third World women's condition under European colonialism. American feminist Gloria Jean Watkins behind unflinching support of prominent feminists such as Angela Davis[12] and Alice Walker[13] was

---

[12]"Angela Davis has been an activist and writer promoting women's rights and racial justice while pursuing her career as a philosopher and teacher at the University of Santa Cruz and San Francisco University. Angela Davis is often associated with the Black Panthers

one of the most critical black women of the era who blatantly disqualified the white middle class based feminism for leaving "the issues that divided women" (i.e., the issues of racial orientation) untouched in its agenda of resistance.

Apparently, some black feminists with a broader view of the matter did not appreciate the ideological confinement implied by black feminism. They saw the inextricable binding of sexism, class oppression and racism and went for Womanism instead to address universal issues of women on the ground. This all-inclusive philosophy was first initiated by the notorious black feminist, Alice Walker.

---

and with the black power politics of the late 1960s and early 1970s. She joined the Communist Party when Martin Luther King was assassinated in 1968. She was active with SNCC (Student Nonviolent Coordinating Committee) before the Black Panthers. . . she has published on race, class, and gender issues and Angela Davis ran for U.S. Vice President on the Communist Party ticket in 1980." *Angela Davis*/About.com. (n.d.)_Retrieved fro m: http://womenshistory.about.com/od/aframerwriters/p/angela_d avis.htm

[13]"Alice Malsenior Walker (born February 9, 1944) is an American author. She has written at length on issues of race and gender, and is most famous for the critically acclaimed novel The Color Purple for which she won the Pulitzer Prize for Fiction. She was born and raised in Georgia." *Alice Walker Wins Pulitzer Prize for Fiction*/Tim elines. (n.d.) Retrieved from: http://timelines.com/1983/alice-walker-wins-pulitzer-prize-for-fiction

Post-colonial activists like Chandra Talpade Mohanty[14] were openly critical of Western feminism's ethnocentric tendency of dealing with the issue of women. They argued that colonialism and Western feminism marginalized postcolonial women without succeeding to render them voiceless; meaning that postcolonial women could talk about their experiences and needs confidently and that they didn't have to be represented by Western feminism. Western feminism's misunderstanding of the Asian society is reflected by the concept of "Orientalism" where an imaginary replica of the Orient is wrongly created to serve as the comparative opposite of western civility and superiority. These feminists believe that Western feminism highly signifies the "problem of veiling women" in Islamic societies in order to amplify its illusive self- perception as the best.

According to an article, "Western views of women in Islamic countries"[15] Chandra Mohanty suggests, "the universal image of the "Third World woman" is constructed by adding Third World's differences to gender relation. This image is predicted by the assumption of western woman as secular, liberated, and in control of her life in contrast to the

---

[14]"Chandra Talpade Mohanty is a prominent postcolonial and transnational feminist theorist. She became well-known after the publication of her influential essay, "Under Western Eyes: Feminist Scholarship and Colonial Discourses" in 1986. In this essay, Mohanty critiques the political project of Western feminism in its discursive construction of the category of the "Third World woman" as a hegemonic entity." Chandra Talpade Mohanty/Wikipedia. (n.d.) Retrieved from: http://en.wikipedia.org/wiki/Chandra_Talpade_Mohan ty

[15]*"Islamic feminism": compromise or challenge to feminism?/*iran-bullitin.org (n.d.) Retrieved_from: http://www.iran_bulletin.org/poli tical_islam/islamfeminismedited2.html

makeup of the Third World woman. Yet not all women in the West are in fact secular and liberated, just as not all women in Islamic societies match the pre-made image of "Muslim woman . . . Also, not all Muslim women have the same idea about Islam. Their ideas are influenced by their class status, cultural background, education, and position in society." Mohanty points out that "many feminists write about Muslim women being powerless and oppressed, and about their needs and problems. But there are few feminists who write about their choices, freedom, or power of action."

Third-world feminism is mainly related to African feminism, motherism,[16] Stiwanism[17] negofeminism,[18]

---

[16]Womanism as a concept has been employed by a number of African feminist writers as the tool for development. The western concept of feminism therefore on the surface appears to be disclaimed by many as foreign concept. It also has served to alienate male support, as it seems rather confrontational while womanism seems to be conciliatory. But as these concept really different, the paper explores writers who have espoused the womanist tradition in contrast to feminist American writers and conclude the womanist tradition and feminism are different faces of the same coin.

[17]Stiwanism is feminism in African point of view developed from the hypothesis that third world feminists need to check and balance white feminism's tendency of superiority over other feminists in social issues. It advocates the unity of black men and women against white all-inclusive white hegemony in general. The concept is discussed in detail by Molara Ogundipe-Leslie in *Re-creating ourselves: African women & critical transformations.*

[18]Nego-feminism is African feminism that tends to set feminist ego aside for compatible negotiation on gender equality with the male gender.

femalism,[19] transnational feminism,[20] and Africana womanism.[21]

African feminists certainly found a gap between their brand of feminism and Western feminism, developed a new approach to the ideology and called it *Motherism*. This Afrocentric feminism considers motherhood as the center of gravity of the African family structure, meaning that the African woman is a mother first. They argue that motherhood has always been the black race's most basic support system of survival and unity and believe that the concept of mother is deep in African society to the point of

---

[19]Femalism seems to be a different name to feminism which "refers to movements aimed at defining, establishing and defending equal political, economic, and social rights and equal opportunities for women"

Feminism./Wikipedia (n.d.) Retrieved from: http://en.wikipedia.org /wiki/Feminism.

[20]"Transnational Feminism is a contemporary paradigm. The name highlights the difference between international and transnational conceptions of feminism, and favours the latter. As a feminist approach, it can be said that transnational feminism is generally attentive to intersections among nationhood, race, gender, sexuality and economic exploitation on a world scale, in the context of emergent global capitalism." *Transnational feminism*/Wikipedia (n.d.) Retried from: http://en.wikipedia.org/wiki/Transnational_feminism.

[21]"Africana Womanism is a term coined in the late 1980s by Clenora Hudson-Weems intended as an ideology applicable to all women of African descent. It is grounded in African culture and Afrocentrism and focuses on the experiences, struggles, needs, and desires of Africana women of the African diaspora. It distinguishes itself from feminism, or Alice Walker's womanism." *Africana_womanism*/Wikipedia. (n.d.) Retrieved from: http://en.wik ipedia.org/wiki/Africana_womanism

greatly influencing African art, literature, culture, psychology, and spirituality. At the simplest expression of the philosophy, a Motherist is a man or a woman committed to welfare of the Mother Earth as a unified element through "love, tolerance, service and mutual cooperation of the sexes"[22] without a drop of sexism. The philosophy is said to be active in former British colonies of Africa and especially Nigeria, Sudan, Zimbabwe etc. Catherine Obianuju Acholonu of Nigeria states, "African women are "the spiritual base of every family, community and nation. . . Women are represented as the rebirth of "the last hope for the restoration of the natural order in life and in every sphere of life" and departs from the school of thought that colonized African soil "has been totally dominated by men, is coloured by wars, civil strife, hunger, famine, tyranny and genocide . . . calls for a return to the mother essence, in other words women and motherist leaders." Further, Naima Alu Kolbookek, of Omdurman, Sudan seems to have fused African motherism and "modern Black American womanism" according to a source of information about her work. Other popular contributions to this art include the distinguished work of Ayako Mizuo on Post Feminism and Trans-nationalism.

One of the most touching statements on the subject matter was delivered by Ayi Kwei Armah's notion that ". . . female figures [are] suffering because of the colonization of their houses, conquered by their husbands. Women seem only to be wives, enslaved by a chain of many unwanted pregnancies. Motherhood is depicted as an unnatural condition, for which women are allowed to work, because "to be a mother" is the best possible job for them or, more

---

[22]Acholonu, Catherine Obianuju. *Motherism: The Afrocentric Alternative* (n.d.) Retrieved from: http://www.ishmaelreedpub.com /articles/CatherineAcholonu.html

often, it's just the only way to exist. This condition marks women with an identity that they try to refuse, looking for another female status and a different social role."[23] The expression hits home and blends very well with the most fundamental role of our mothers in Africa.

Clearly western women were doubly oppressed politically and domestically, but African woman and black women in general were three times oppressed: politically, domestically and by white colonial slavery. Setting the colonial effect aside, Armah's description of a woman vis-à-vis domestic structure as the mother (to my understanding), "is a symbol of a patient suffering. She represents the millions of Ghanaian women betrayed by husbands who have failed them and politicians who have exploited and then destroyed them."[23]

Christina Ama Ata Aidoo (1940, Abeadze Kyiakor – Ghana) has represented the saddest face of another country where women are far removed from the western female model of oppression. Aidoo "depicts primarily female characters who live in poorer urban and rural sectors of Ghana."[24] Aidoo's *Certain Winds from the South* is focused on the female condition in rural areas of Ghana: "We hear such women usually go to their homes to die . . . I had told myself when you were born that it did not matter you were a girl. All gifts from Allah are good and anyway he was coming back and we were going to have many more children, lots of

---

[23]*Postcolonial Motherism: A Brand New Woman in the African Novel* (n.d.) Retrieved from: https://www.postcolonialweb.org/africa/godona1.html

[24]Behrent, Megan. *Ama Ata Aidoo: Independence and Disillusionment in Postcolonial Ghana*/Post Imperial and Postcolonial Literature in English

(1997) Retrieved from: http://www.postcolonialweb.org/aidoo/independence.html

sons" (13–15). These homeless women [appear] very similar to the mothers of *Bones* (1988), the first English novel published by Chenjerai Hove (born in 1956, in a rural area of Zimbabwe)," says a critic. [23]

In view of this, there existed obvious conflict between western women and African women for one to conclude that the western style of feminism was not only an unsuitable solution but was also a problem to the African woman's mode of survival. Colonialism in Africa exasperated the condition of African women to another level of oppression that western women were fortunate enough to escape; similarly slavery on the condition of colored women in the west, relative to the experience of white women in general.

Chicana feminism focused on the situation of Mexican American, Chicana, and Hispanic women in the United States within the generic concept of multiracial women of color.

Cultural feminists went for either equal status or the overthrow of men's roles and customs in society. Their position emphasized the uniqueness of the feminine makeup responsible for directly influencing women's thoughts and creativity. The concept of "female nature" or "female essence" according to these feminists only differed from the psychological nature of men as a matter of cultural orientation. Other sects like *Amazon feminism* took it from there and radicalized it to the point of rejecting the biological differences between men and women.

Standpoint feminists argued that feminism should be heavily involved in the examination of women's experience of inequality in social environments involving racism, homophobia, classism, and colonization.

Atheist feminists suggest that religion in its absolute form is anti-women and that the women's movement can only succeed by defusing the influence of religion in society.

Secular feminists argue that the dominance of the liberal or patriarchal view of Islam in society dictates the relationship terms between Islam and feminism. Without assaulting religious beliefs, they tend to believe that women's emancipation cannot be achieved under "a theocratic government or a religious movement."

Sex-positive feminism believes that women are in control of their bodies and therefore can experience sex with more freedom than ever before because their sexuality is better understood and more accepted today in developed countries. They argue that women should take advantage of this change of attitude to satisfy their sexual needs and enjoy sex with men from an equal standpoint. This sect supports pornography because it "allows men and women to share sex equally."

Separatist feminists believe that men and women have irresolvable differences in that all men naturally carry some sort of patriarchal values that cannot be filtered out, even by honest choice. Therefore, men cannot contribute positively to the question of women. They seem to completely reject heterosexual relationships and inclusively remove men from the solution as the natural problem of women and society at large by default of their gender. At the rest point of their agenda, this group supports the absolute cultural separation of male and female in society.

Evangelical (Christian) feminists argue that monogamy is the answer for egalitarianism in sex compared to other alternatives such as polygamy, and prostitution. This notion is contradicted, however, by other feminist sects such as sex-positive feminism, which believes that unrestricted sex would also promote egalitarianism since it is performed freely and equally with men. This view is in a sense similar to what was projected by Friedrich Engels's *Origins of the Family, Private Property, and the State* according to my source of information, in that monogamy was understood as a norm designed by men to control women.

Individualist feminists stand against the interference of government in the choices of women to do whatever they want with their bodies, probably because the government is generally considered a man's institution. Yet, it seems like one branch of this group is only concerned with women's rights while another stresses everybody's rights in this regard.

Anarcha-feminists to my understanding encouraged women to reject all forms of political power in society in respect to inborn feminist obligations.

Existentialist feminism arrived from Simone de Beauvoir's[25] background of philosophy. This feminist is remembered for building her philosophy behind the saying that "When we abolish the slavery of half of humanity, together with the whole system of hypocrisy that it implies, then the 'division' of humanity will reveal its genuine significance and the human couple will find its true form." She was certainly a person that had no illusion about the

---

[25]"Jean_Paul_Charles_Aymard_Sartre (French_pronunciation: [saʁtʁ], English: /ˈsɑrtrə/; 21 June 1905 – 15 April 1980)_was a French existentialist philosopher,_playwright,_novelist,_screenwriter, political activist, biographer, and literary critic. He was one of the leading figures in 20th century French philosophy, particularly Marxism, and was one of the key figures in literary and philosophical existentialism. His work continues to influence fields such as Marxist philosophy, sociology, critical theory and literary studies. Sartre was also noted for his long polyamorous relationship with the feminist author and social theorist Simone de Beauvoir. He was awarded the 1964 Nobel Prize in Literature but refused it." Jean-Paul Sartre/Wikipedia (n.d.) Retrieved from: http://en.wikipedia.org/wiki/Jean-Paul_Sartre

controversial issues of heterosexual relationship as she once said, "I am too intelligent, too demanding, and too resourceful for anyone to be able to take charge of me entirely. No one knows me or loves me completely. I have only myself." This school of contemplation advocates prostitution as the best alternative for a woman to achieve an immediate solution from economic dependence on a heterosexual relationship, should it fail to respect equality and freedom between the partners.

Ecofeminism linked the domination of women with men's domination of the environment. It saw a direct connection between the destruction of environment and oppression of women by men. As I grasp it, Ecofeminists tend to think that the reason men of power exploit the environment and oppress women is that both were taken by men as passive and helpless entities of their aggression. At the bottom line, they thought they could repair their oppression by, "working towards creating a healthy environment and ending the destruction of the lands that most women rely on to provide for their families." This is philosophically farfetched compared to all other sects of feminism in that it tends to equalize women to environment and to target men on both accounts of destruction.

I like unique outlooks and I classify Ecofeminism in this category but I am not sure how women in this mind set approach the reality that women contribute to the destruction of environment as much as men do. They eat animals, and wear their skins in terms of cloth and shoes and use them for many other purposes such as belts, hats and purses as well.

Meninism is "a global organization of men that believe in and support the feminist principles of women's political, social and economic equality."[26] This group believes in active participation of men in feministic causes in order, "for feminism to benefit men and continue progressing towards equality of everyone. . ."[26] it believes in the theory that feminism cannot achieve its goal without support from men, though it can achieve some of it alone. These are men who support the cause of women for absolute equality but believe that the term feminism is reserved only for women.

Other feminists based their struggle on the condition of women as a derivative of social and traditional conditioning.

Yet, others utterly denied the existence of the natural difference in gender identity and sexuality by defining them as something fabricated by society and looked at feminism as a struggle for the freedom of all inclusive mankind

Clearly, there were a few other feminist movements of different types and approaches beyond those I managed to list that came and went in the past. I do not know how many sects are still active, how many could have evolved as new comers and how many of those in the list have ceased to exist in time. I have learned, however, that although feminism scrambled into diverse ethical, socio-economic and political theories, all sects have been working for their respective objectives under the common denominator that *every human being has equal rights by birth; but there exists better opportunity for men and that women suffer from the norms of masculinity that have conventionally constrained them.*

Apparently, as in anything else in human experience, one or a few of the sects had to dominate in the final analysis of the fierce ideological confrontation; and it seems to me that the extremists are in the driver's seat today. As a

---

[26]*Meninist: Men Supporting the Women's Movement*/feminist.com(n. d.) Retrieved from: http://www.feminist.com/resources/links/men. htm

result, the movement in the US gradually shifted its focus from their original program, somehow losing fairness in the generic meaning of equality.

I do not deceive myself that I can get away with this accusation without proof and multiple facts will be presented hereafter to that cause, but I believe that my analysis has it crystal clear that feminism has failed to balance all the social effects of "violence." It has fallen short of strategic thinking, becoming violent women's arsenal of revenge.

The media often shows convicts, their innocence proven after serving time in prison. Nothing ever happens to their accusers. Throughout the experience of convicts, being exonerated based on DNA, silence has been the choice of today's powerful feminists who decline to address the irreversible predicament of their victims for the sake of gold.

The Journey towards My Trial

As time passed, my communication with my lawyer significantly improved as a function of my growing awareness of the Justice System. Cafés replaced bars and intensive reading persisted as my priority of activities.

I was opening my eyes to anything relevant to my case including Hazen's movements in the community because I had been terribly maligned by her lies to the point that I heard new things about me everywhere I went. One of the issues of concern happened to be my Eritrean activism.

There is no doubt that I have fractionally lived my life as an Eritrean activist in favor of peace. I cannot control how people take this and I have no suggestion to that effect because it is none of my business, but I am here to stay as an Afro American individual from an Eritrean background and continue to live my life without excitement or resentment about it. I certainly remained supportive of the nation's self-defense against Ethiopian aggression before and after the country's independence from Ethiopia as much as I remained critical of the Eritrean government's actions whenever necessary.

Some Ethiopians certainly did not like my political position. I do not know how else they expect me to have been.

Taking advantage of this ominous situation, I heard that Hazen approached few anti-Eritrean organizations to politicize her case based on the lies that she continued to spread about our encounter. I also heard of her request to publicize her version of the situation through personal interviews on their radio stations to "counterbalance the cooperation I was getting from Eritreans," which was another lie.

Days go quickly and so does pain and it was February 8, 2000, when I was peacefully sitting inside the Starbuck's café looking out through the window. As an alternative to suicide, I used to wonder if musical instruments and computers were allowed in prison when I sometimes entertained the worst of my fears. But those types of thoughts had disappeared as I considered myself internally and externally comfortable at that point in time. My volatile mind was no longer the terrorist it had been and it had no more space for negativity. It felt as if I might have reclaimed it from my ego to feel the result in terms of relative emotional freedom. I had done the best I could in favor of my defense and there was nothing more I could do. On February 22, 2000, I would be tried for the two criminal counts of rape at the DC Superior Court. I was about to face it the way it was supposed to be faced: neutrally positioning myself at the spectral center of the duality comprising *guilty and innocent* without expecting anything from the trial. By all accounts, I was set to welcome the trial knowing that it would mark the beginning of my detachment from my accuser. Whatever would be would be as I was conditioned to open a new chapter of my life soon.

In the meantime, I was feeling better as a reward of extending my hands to the needy homeless and panhandlers at the rate of about 10% of everything that was spent on the case. I went out of my way to assist the needy as if there would be no more opportunity for it. I felt they very much deserved their legitimate share of my money at the time the case rendered it vulnerable for an all-around abuse.

Clearly, there was no freedom in sight until the curtain was lifted, but I refused to worry about the unknown as I was patiently counting down time for the decisive day. The skies had become more beautiful and I was blessed to be in a situation to see how precious a free life could be. I would be one of those walking freely in the cold and beautiful day if nothing but the truth mattered.

With only few days to go before the start of the trial, I was informed that I had passed the program at work and secured my promotion. I became a Primary Patent Examiner with full authority to independently examine and decide the status of patent applications. Although I participated in the traditional gathering for the occasion in my boss's office, it did not mean anything to me.

My Defense Structure and Mysterious Loss of Evidence from My Apartment

My defense was structured to address every point the prosecutor could possibly raise. Besides the key witnesses who had experiences indirectly related to the case, four good and five bad character witnesses were on the line.

On the physical evidence level, we expected the physician from the Hospital to be consistent with his report and planned to use my doctor and the FBI DNA analysis to tackle his distortion.

Should the prosecution discuss the fabricated traumatic effects on the accuser, I was prepared to use the 911 call taped by the Police to demonstrate how relaxed and normal Hazen had been when she reported the offense in my presence.

To provide a remote idea of when we might have had our first sexual contact, I had the wedding videotape that showed how close she had stayed to me that evening. I also had few of her past associates ready for other things if necessary.

Three days before the trial, on Friday evening, the 19th of February 2000, some of my witnesses and my lawyer held a final meeting in my apartment to crystallize our mutual understanding. The meeting went well and we had most of the issues discussed. As reluctant as Mr. Goodman had been to use the 911 tape at the trial, it seemed as if he was finally convinced that it might have contained something important based on my constant appeal to give it a chance in our previous meetings. Therefore, playing it for him for the first time was part of our plan for that evening.

Unfortunately, the discussion took more time than expected and he had to postpone hearing the tape to the next day.

The cassette was in the tape player at the time we called off the meeting and stayed there thereafter as far as my recollection was concerned. That was also the only copy I had since it was encoded and could not be duplicated. I had carefully preserved that crucial element for all that time; yet, it was displaced from the tape player and mysteriously disappeared after that meeting. The loss of that powerful evidence was a serious psychological blow that suddenly disarmed me from challenging the "crime's traumatic effect" on Hazen. It was even more frightening to think of how much information could have leaked to the opposition if there indeed was some sort of internal sabotage.

All that in place and no matter how hard to understand it had been, I had to shut off my mind from wondering who could have been the *Rat* among my friends who at the time used to stay in my apartment. There was simply no appropriate time or psychic space for more disparaging feelings in my already cornered mind. At least I knew that when I tried my best to move ahead of the disturbing obstacle.

There was nothing else to do except to inform my lawyer to have it replaced by the Police. Unfortunately, at least two weeks' notice should have been given in advance for its replacement, which was impractical within the time frame remaining for the start of my trial. I was speechless and teared up a bit in privacy but refused to succumb; I strongly needed my relative stability for a few days, just for a few more days until the end of the trial.

The Beginning of My Trial and the Effect of Rape Shield Law on My Case

The weekend passed by relatively fast and the showdown started in the early hours of February 22. The first day was spent on Jury selection and the process went on from there, consuming half of the second day. By coincidence, one of the potential Jurors was a friendly coworker at the Patent Office. The judge announced the charges to the Court as I was sitting with my lawyer grinding my teeth, especially when he proclaimed the second count as "anal rape."

By the afternoon of the twenty-third, the Jury was selected and pretrial arguments conducted as to who and what were eligible for admittance from the list of witnesses and circumstantial evidence that the defense submitted.

The prosecution side did not have to go through that same process.

To my distress, three of my strongest witnesses Danny, Michael and Rachel were eliminated because of the dehumanizing Rape Shield Law. That was the first time I tasted its brutality. Sadly, my whole defense was structured around them; no wonder why my lawyer had excluded some of my ideas regardless of their importance to the case. It was not because he was the lunatic I thought but rather I was naïve for being unaware of how feminism had stolen justice in America.

They took my right to defend myself by informing the Jury that she once called the Police when her former boyfriend, Danny, was in her apartment bathroom. He discovered that when he opened the door for them a little too early for her plan to work. She said she called them because she was scared he was going to hurt her but he saw the whole thing differently and thought she was about to frame him up for sexual violence by synchronizing an episode with their arrival at her place. He based his conclusion on how peacefully things had been going that evening and particularly at the time he decided to clean up for the anticipated romantic evening. It fortunately took longer than she expected.

She had further accused him of stealing about $30,000 worth of money and antiques from her place, yet she returned to the Courthouse a few days later to officially cancel the charge by writing (on the report) that she changed her mind, maybe after she discovered she could not carry the burden of proof. The records were properly filed at the Courthouse. I was going to use this testimony to show the Jurors Hazen's instability, irrespective of how they were going to take it.

Danny was also ready to expose her unstable conduct and unconventional sexual interests including obsession with anal sex. This was an important defense weapon to challenge her association of the practice with supposedly fatal cultural consequence in her country. Although anal sex was considered abnormal in Ethiopia, there was no such punishment for practicing it in so far as my knowledge was concerned, but that was apparently what she "told the prosecutor" according to a dependable informant.

By excluding my friend Michael (wedinno), I was robbed of the opportunity to expose that she had kept his money in the past and refused to give it back using a false accusation of rape as a weapon to scare him away. That was his punishment for refusing to help her "establish a false sexual harassment charge against a Police Officer at her hot dog stand, in which she promised him to be the partial beneficiary of material gain from winning the case with his support."

By sidelining Rachel, they stepped on my rights once again, denying me the opportunity to inform the Jury that my accuser Hazen "knew that Rachel was not fully qualified for Financial Aid as New York State resident at the time she met her at the State University of New York in Oneonta. She used the knowledge to blackmail her into sitting for a pre-calculus exam in her name before she dropped out of the University." Further, she was ready to testify that Hazen had "stolen at least once in her presence during that time."

God's Magical Work in Favor of My Defense

After the legal terrorism effectively crippled my defense, the prosecutor changed the misdemeanor offer to felony and unsuccessfully tried to negotiate with my lawyer on that account. She then informed the judge that Hazen was convicted of a minor shoplifting charge, which she said had "nothing to do" with the case. This admission was an assumption that we had done a full investigation and

75

already found the public information. It was by all accounts a clever idea in view of the fact that it only required one to stay in line at the relevant office in the Superior Court building to extract it, but it was also a risky move on the condition of a wrong assumption.

Fortunately, the coin hit the ground in my favor as it gave us the chance to look for more facts ourselves, since my investigator obviously had failed to do this assignment efficiently. As a result, my friend Chris, my sister Abi and my brother Esaw promptly produced her records, which became the last pretrial agenda, while I was inside the Courtroom with few minutes to go before the Jury came in for the opening statements.

The happenstance passed as one of the major gifts from the prosecutor making a momentous impact on perfect timing in my mystifying life. Nothing could better prove to me of the verity that God sees from a distance when the restlessness of his good children puts them in jeopardy as he justifies the price they must pay for their own transformation. However, he also gives them another chance by reaching out to fill the vacuum at the most critical time of their lives. I had the opportunity to experience this blessing in person.

We found Hazen's folder polluted with two shoplifting charges, a second-degree theft and a simple assault charge. The stealing counts took place within seven years between 1983 and 1990; and I think she was found guilty twice after pleading innocent. That means she might have routinely practiced the habit for the entire decade, at least to my way of thinking. Another issue was a Restraining Order[27] against

---

[27]"A Restraining Order is a court order intended to protect you from further harm from someone who has hurt you; to keep the abuser away from you, or to stop harassing you, or keep the abuser from the scene of the violence, which may include your home, place of work, or

her from one of her former boyfriends. I also noticed that her last name was spelled differently on different occasions. The judge admitted the first two after fierce resistance from the prosecutor to reject them all. I accepted the development with grace because it was like dancing in paradise to win a portion of the truth from the Feminist Justice System.

Before getting into the gut of the confrontation, we had to protest her Ethiopian interpreter from an anti-Eritrean political organization because of bias. The judge ruled and replaced him with another interpreter.

Finally, the trial began the afternoon of February 23 and I could not frankly have been in a better mindset, given the hurdles.

Pre-trial Speeches and Court Proceeding

The prosecutor introduced the case to the Jury first. She talked about the physical attack to a point where any person would expect severe injury as a result. The Jurors must have been stunned by the description of the brutality.

Throughout the ordeal, she repeatedly pointed her finger at my face and said anything she had wanted to say about me. She defined me as a manipulative rapist and went on painting me with characteristics alien and opposite to my record and self-understanding. In return, I calmly witnessed the truth being murdered without personalizing the offense and feeling sorry for the way she made a living. I gave her the humblest eye contact for the repellent terms she was throwing one after another. I circumvented the messenger

apartment. It is a civil order and it does not give the abuser a criminal record." *What is and How to Get a Restraining Order*/About.com. (n. d.) Retrieved from: http://divorcesupport.about.com/od/abusiverel ationships/a/restrain_order.htm of deception by focusing on the root cause of the problem: that some human beings do anything for money.

I even felt more touched for the young intern in that team in training for a licensed killer. Her cheeks had turned as red as if I slapped her on the face. A time bomb already exploding by acting devastated, she was practically manifesting what the prosecutor had taught her in Human Destruction 101. It was important for her career to score a professional point by winning the case behind the prosecution, an opportunity for just another line in her resume.

To me, it was an introductory class on the fraudulent American government's role in the Justice System and the dark face of feminism, as I peacefully took notes without worrying about the immediate future.

The way they assassinated my human values was too agitating for some of my friends to continue listening to and they left the Courtroom.

The prosecutor protested that I put a condom on and pushed my penis into Hazen's vagina. I did not know that I was in a feminist planet where regular intercourse had become a crime, as my lawyer hissed an aside wondering if she had seriously expected me to put it in her purse instead.

My lawyer on his part smoothly told the Jury that the case was about deception for personal advantage. He said the Jurors would learn about clear-cut inconsistencies as the confrontation progressed and the defense presents facts on the ground and credible witnesses to that effect.

Government Distortion of Events

Then the Officer from the scene took the stand and testified that they arrived few minutes after assignment and apprehended me at the lobby "before I escaped."

It was troubling to hear him bend the truth. That was not what I had in mind until that point in time. Never in my wildest imagination did I foresee hearing an Officer of his responsibility lying under oath. It was inconsequential to point out that he knew that I stayed in the lobby until I saw the Police car that brought him with his companion. He knew that I walked out and met them at 16th Street, NW, facing north. He knew I saluted them gently, surrendered and briefed them about the event before they even asked. There indeed was ample time between the call and their arrival for me to travel from the west to the East Side of the City had I intended to run away from the scene, but I did not do anything wrong to cause me to do so. I would have gone to their main office down town and surrendered there had I known how they handle their business of justice. Unfortunately, my naïve confidence in the system took me to the cleaners.

I felt like a rock had dropped on my head when that happened, considering my dependency on his testimony as a neutral law officer. I instantly felt its effect on my ethics and intelligence; I was never the same person again. For the man I thought of myself to have been and taking into account the amount of suffering I had sustained through the process, that duplicity changed my purpose of sitting there from seeking justice to protesting injustice by sacrificing myself for the cause; I craved to be victimized. No longer was my safety an issue to me. I cared less for being caged or killed for that matter compared to how I lost reason for defense after I heard what I heard.

Of course, that state of mind was a brief insanity I could not avoid going through, but was certainly my immediate reaction to what was going on in the Courtroom.

The situation had already provided answers to the questions of the moment. The truth was right there for them to decide: to use it or to misuse it. They chose the second option but for the choice to be valid they had to twist the truth and they did. It was not about the man on the stand, but about what had happened to him that caused him to be what he was that bothered me most. It was about what happened to America to misrepresent itself in such a disgusting way. I always saw myself protected by the government until that point in time but I found myself floating with nothing to lean on then after. If my government does not protect me who will? If it cannot be neutral, then why is it here?

Common sense tells me that he wanted neither to look ridiculous nor intentionally to hurt me as a person. In fact, he appeared sympathetic when he transported me to their station downtown and back to my apartment the night the accident took place. But, it seems like he *had* to act that way as a Policeman in this situation. He had the professional obligation to protect the prosecution's side of justice from contradiction by neutralizing its difficulty in explaining my voluntary surrender vis-à-vis my accuser's recorded misinformation that she called the Police after I left her place. They did not want the Jury to know that I surrendered immediately upon their arrival based on my awareness of the accusation, a scenario that would disqualify the case by labeling my accuser a liar. Apparently, he succeeded in helping the prosecution team get away with the contradiction; a case was manufactured to deceive the Grand Jury, and the government purposely plundered public trust and resources at the expense of pending social priorities and my life.

As much as I grew up glorifying America since my childhood back in Africa, I felt ashamed of being part of it by necessity. Confronting the real face of this beautiful country was a difficult experience that stained my hope about the situation of society both nationally and internationally.

My Accuser in Examination

It was frightening to see how they handled the charge of violence, whether real or fabricated. After the Officer, Hazen came to the stand holding ball shaped objects to stabilize her nervous system, which she claimed was "crushed" by the experience. She was delicately escorted by and physically leaning on a woman from the Crisis Center, as if this very fit exercise freak could not walk on her own. They also supplied her with a pack of napkins to dry her tears of deceit intended to gain the sympathy of the Jury.

She introduced herself as a college-educated, taxpaying professional hair stylist and testified that I initiated the call that evening. She was probably advised to give that testimony because local phone calls appeared to be unrecorded for lines from the carrier companies of the time unless one paid for the service.

What was confusing was that the "college-educated" Hazen had a translator back and forth between English and her native language, aside from the occasions she accidentally communicated in English. Her new profession in my judgment was a cosmetic cover acquired a few months into the trial by the help of the Crisis Center to balance out my professionalism, either by pure fabrication or by a crash program.

Today, prosecutors can modify the personalities of accusers any way they want without being legally challenged by the accused. They could have made her a scientist and get away with it uncontested. They do not have to prove anything. The Rape Shield Law not only gives them the authority to hide life styles but also the freedom to restructure events. The ambiance is similar to the way a lawyer and an "accident victim" sometimes consolidate a case by pretending injury. Therefore, there is no secret about her new personality beyond the government's interest to win the case by any means necessary. Unfortunately, the gambling here was on my life.

Hazen had made her living selling flowers and hot dogs on street corners in her productive past. Then she was known in the community for claiming to be an import/export agent of an undefined commodity for the years thereafter.

Hazen was not limited to being a college educated professional cosmetologist but by some miracle, she also described herself as a *Civil Rights Activist* in that tragic miscarriage of justice where a liar and compulsive kleptomaniac can acquire any title, thanks to bad feminism. I believe she had no capacity to understand what she was told to identify with.

Nothing could have better manifested the racist nature of the Caucasian prosecutor and her disrespect for the Civil Rights movement than the way she stepped on the natural quality of activism to represent the contrary character on the stand. I do not think she would have coached her client to be an activist had she been white or had the Jury been of Caucasian majority simply because the duplicity would not have had an impact on the outcome. The Jury was, however, in the majority black and she saw something in coloring her project through activism to soften the black Jurors whose intelligence she racially underestimated: to make it more appealing by presenting an upgraded "product," the product herself most probably had no idea of what her "activist" status was all about. Activism requires intense reading and participation at minimum that my accuser could not have achieved with the help of a translator alone.

Then my accuser came to the center of the Courtroom to exhibit how the incident took place with the prosecutor simulating the victim. They stayed there for about half an hour wrestling and looking confused in staging their rehearsal because the "victim" at times entertained the role of the "assailant" from the opposite conceptual position.

According to the demonstration and their overall description of the "crime", I must have hit her all over her body, including her face and breasts, carried and then threw her on the bed after "asphyxiating her to the point of unconsciousness", and then "forcefully opening her legs" to commit the "crime." They continued the drama as if she could have remembered anything after what she said happened to her.

There is no doubt that the prosecutor had a better chance presenting the case as date rape in my opinion. Instead, her mediocre common sense got in the way by getting her into that level of embarrassment without the slightest evidence to support the ludicrous exaggeration.

This self-defeating concert might have scared my loved ones in the Courtroom to death, but it was the best they could have provided me within that critical situation for two important reasons. There was no counter-reasoning burden on defense in the absolute absence of anything to substantiate the narrative and I believe the action compromised their decency and credibility in the eyes of the Jury at the expense of short-term impact. These advantages were not given, however, but were achievable on the condition my lawyer took care of business appropriately, which was too early in the confrontation to judge.

My accuser surprised me when she restructured her original statement recorded by the Police as, "the first sexual activity took place three months prior to the incident" into the truth that it happened after a wedding party in 1995. Although the statement was worthless vis-à-vis the prosecutor's power to nullify it as something not written by the accuser, I was still expecting her to stick to the lie assuming that she was incapable of telling the truth and that she did not know I had the wedding tape in my possession. However, she did the opposite, another episode I left behind with Zen state of mind. Once again though, this was another defense opportunity should my lawyer use it to expose the contradiction to the Jury.

To pick points here and there, she testified that she had the first and the only sip of wine in her life that evening because of passionate pressure from me. Interestingly, that magical sip forced the woman to forget her keys outside the apartment door as pointed out by my lawyer in cross-examination. Further, she did not pay attention to the half-full bottle of wine (not the one I brought) in the picture of her apartment taken that night by the police officers.

She said our first and last consensual affair ended up with rough sex, the reason why she did not want to continue that type of relationship with me but she gave me a "friendly hug" that night on the way to her place after dinner.

It seems like the lethal offense of cruel offenders somehow counterbalances the errors they make as if a divine force renders their formula unbelievable for ordinary coherence. I was not impressed by the prosecutor's rational thinking ability at all. People in her class of intelligence try anything to convince others to believe their lies but the intense pretension they go through practically denies them the projected goal by taking away a big chunk of their reasoning potential. At the end of the day, they fool themselves just because they think they were smarter than their audience. It is not so much how they react in public that amazes me, but the mystery that they believe that they can get away with it.

Then the cross-examination took place and my lawyer first confronted her with the two counts of theft, which she admitted right away. The prosecutor fruitlessly called several times for the judge's interference in the smooth flow of examination. He then went into her Grand Jury testimony in contrast to her current testimony. "Telling the truth is like hitting the right key in a musical instrument," says one blessed Buddhist: she was not in tune as there were too many twists and inconsistencies to put in detail.

My lawyer did well challenging her testimony in the process but he did not take advantage of the two opportunities offered to us by Hazen and there was nothing I could do about it.

The Testimony of My Accuser's Physician in the Trial

Eventually, the doctor who examined her appeared and testified on the absence of any detectable bruise or scratch on any part of her body except on the anus and failed to give a single conclusive cause for it. He said she suffered from "protruded prolapsed hemorrhoid" and indicated constipation, pressure, trauma or penetration by anything as a probable reason for the detected alteration. I found him a little more careful than I expected him to be when he avoided going into the "semen in her body parts" theory; maybe because he discovered I was not the authentic African-American he thought I was and/or he probably knew we had the truth (the FBI test result) at hand that told otherwise.

Based on his testimony, the absence of blood on my body suggests a different scenario from the speculation that "I caused her such an injury." Furthermore, the fact that the condom was absolutely free of a single blood cell shows that any detected blood in that part of her body (her anus) found during his initial physical examination, (where he wrote a report asserting that she had *hemorrhoids and rectal bleeding exacerbated by anal rape)* could neither have existed during the intercourse nor could it have suddenly showed up out of the blue. I cannot be certain, but I seriously think she inflicted the damage on herself to devise the second criminal charge as part of her overall objective before the officers arrived at her apartment the night of the accident. It seems as though said bleeding might have occurred after I left her place, since there was no scientific probability for at least the condom to have been completely clean of said blood on a single cell level of its chemical composition even though it was only limited to vaginal contact with Hazen.

The Testimonies of Witnesses in the Trial

My good character witnesses were waiting for their turn and this seemed to be the right time to introduce them briefly.

One of them was my friend Bibina who was always present in different stages of my life. From my teen-age love to my adult life soul mate and from my classmate in college to a dependable friend after the relationship, she is definitely one of the most important people in my life. We are destined to support one another for life no matter what the situation may be. My dear friend was in labor the weekend before the trial and could only join me in prayer from home with her newly born baby.

The true feminist Peggy Landin is a Caucasian social scientist blessed with a loving heart who earnestly used to serve the northern Minnesotan community. We have worked together with kids, battered women and many other socially under-privileged people in the region. She drove for three and half hours from her town down to MPLS and took a flight to DC at her own expense to attend a rescheduled trial. I had to be fair to let her stay home with her kids, though she was ready to come again for the active trial. One of the testimonies she was going to give in the trial according to my knowledge was that I worked under her supervision with vulnerable women in northern Minnesota and that I did not take advantage of my position to exploit any one of them sexually. Peggy is a person who took her feminism seriously not to have given me a chance had I been that type of person. Having her for a friend means to be fortunate.

Other friends were important to me. The list includes Alexandra, an attractive and mentally stimulating African-American software engineer. We had a relationship in 1989 but separated when I went to Eritrea for personal reasons. Although I do not get the chance to see her as often as I want, my dear friend always remains an important part of my life. Having her on my side was simply a blessing from above.

Then there was the very sharp, humorous and lovely Sandy Harrison, also an African-American Computer Scientist, who I have known for years. We went out on many occasions without strings attached and the mutual respect for each other was so deep, we are simply inseparable. I love Sandy for how she navigates her life and for how down to earth she has been. My friend has proven to me time and again that she really cares for me and I will do anything to safeguard her in return.

In this group, I include my Eritrean friend Zakk (a chemistry teacher) who is an exceptionally peaceful man. The strong advocate of "happiness by choice" is simply deep in the heart and was truly the origin of my relaxation and hope throughout the dark season. It was a pleasure to come home despondent and listen to his messages every evening that went on and on assuring me there was nothing to worry about. The support he provided certainly reflected the quality of his character. I thank God again for bringing me to his circle.

Another gentleman in the group was Jack, an Eritrean Real Estate Agent who had been close to me for almost three decades. I could talk a lot about him based on years of experience but I prefer to be reserved because it is irrelevant to the subject matter at hand. My brother recently passed away but he knew how I felt about him and that is where it stops. He used to drive a long distance from Maryland to meet me in DC whenever I needed his company. I respect his consistency and devotion to friendship and deeply appreciate his everlasting presence in my life.

The last four testified about my character in general and my peacefulness in particular. Although they were disappointed to not have the chance to say more (because my lawyer designed it to be as short and to the point), they were outstanding in telling the Jury what they thought of me, using powerful and persuasive expressions.

The next person in line was my most down-to-earth Ethiopian friend Michael (wedinno) who was allowed to be there for only one issue. He told the Jury that he was in my apartment when Hazen called and that he gave me a ride to her place with a bottle of red wine in hand. Then he went on, saying that he warned me to be careful when he dropped me off that evening but the prosecutor aggressively objected and stopped him at that point because he was restricted from saying that by the Rape Shield Law. But, the damage was already done. Michael did his job well considering his emotional involvement in the case, which had made my lawyer reluctant to use him as a witness. To have him around was simply like hitting a jackpot.

The opposition did not risk of challenging their views and my supporters left one after another without any contest.

Then the West African security guard testified about what he saw us peripherally doing and left without a word from the prosecutor.

At that point in the trial, the defense had an edge against the prosecution team by a score of six to one (the one being that of the Police Officer's testimony in favor of the government). I do not think they expected such an offense after what they had put me through. The situation agitated the prosecutor to restlessly sit, stand and call out "Your Honor!" a few times without any point to address.

While this was going on, Emilia, one of the "bad character" witnesses was waiting for her turn outside the Courtroom. Her boyfriend showed up and not only did he try his best to stop her from testifying against Hazen but also was in Hazen's room discussing matters beyond my reach. Soon, another witness, Rachel, innocently agreed to be interviewed by the same Officer and the case investigator for over ten minutes behind closed doors.

My Cross Examination

Finally, I took the stand for direct examination. Then I was in cross-examination. The prosecutor dehumanized me in a futile attempt to test my temper in front of my terrorized siblings and friends. However, I managed to stay peacefully in control. Aside from manifesting rudeness and abhorrent moral fiber, she did not score anything significant against me.

We were released that Thursday afternoon for a long weekend. We remained relatively relaxed and I went to my office on Sunday, February 27 to complete a pending assignment – only to find my boss in the building. He informed me that some people had visited on Friday, meeting with the Group Director and interviewing the Clerk Manager to try to ferret out anything unethical they could use against me. He could not tell me if they were allowed to access my desktop computer – which would have been illegal as it contained hundreds of confidential patent actions and applications.

That evening, I bath, meditated and phoned my dad in Ethiopia to ask for his blessing. I also talked to my born-again Christian sisters in Queens and Oklahoma City and we prayed together over the phone for my safety and my accuser's freedom from herself. Then I rested well to wake up fresh the next morning.

I started Monday, the 28th of that month with a peaceful mind. My lawyer had instructed me to be at the Courthouse earlier than usual to meet with my doctor. It was about eight o'clock in the morning when I stepped out of my apartment on Swann Street, heading to the DuPont Circle Metro Station. Walking down 19th Street, I made a right turn at Q Street NW and saw Hazen in front of me also walking in the same direction. I slowed down to avoid catching up with her and she made a left turn at the west side of Connecticut Avenue by the subway entrance – contrary to my expectation. Then, I stood at the escalator going down to the metro platform.

All I said was, "Jesus!" when I saw her on the opposite side of the subway entrance about forty feet away from my position facing north and staring at me. She was certainly the last person I wanted to see that morning! I avoided the eye contact and walked hurriedly down the long escalator. I caught the next train and reached my destination. As I was taking the exiting escalator at Judiciary Square terminal, I saw her again four or five steps under my position. How she managed to do that from that far behind was beyond my capacity to understand but I ignored her evil presence and walk-meditated to my destination.

I continued with cross-examination that day being confrontational at times deviating from my lawyer's original plan. I somehow needed to address the misdemeanor offer and the importance of the 911 call without limiting my answers to "yes" or "no," as I had been advised to do.

When the prosecutor asked about the "non-provocative nightgown" my accuser was wearing that night, I said what I saw then was a T-shirt, consistent with what she told the Grand Jury.

When she asked if I had ever seen that nightgown in the past (it was being displayed to the Jurors), I took a calculated risk and said that I had seen it the day she offered the *lesser charge*, which was true, indicating my uncertainty about legally specifying what the actual offer (misdemeanor) had been.

When she asked about Hazen's hysteria at the time of the attack, I challenged her to hand over the 911 tape to the Jurors for them to sense if that indeed was her state of mind. I thought anyone who heard it would nullify the incident's "traumatic" effect on the accuser. Obviously, she bypassed the idea.

When she said I physically hurt the "victim" during the event, I responded that she could not prove what she was accusing me of because the horrendously exaggerated violence could not possibly have taken place without any marks on her body.

When she asked if I had touched her breasts and penetrated her vagina and anus, I responded affirmatively to the first two and flatly denied the last. She told the Jury that the Ethiopian cultural consequence for a woman found in anal sex practice was death and that I had indirectly destroyed the "victim." I grew up in that culture and knew nothing of what she was told by her client, not to mention her passionate broadcast of the fabrication in the community without the slightest concern of said consequence.

When she asked if I constantly dined at Hazen's place, I answered "not even once."

When she asked if I regularly accompanied her to the gym, I said, "only once when we accidentally met on the way."

Something interesting happened when my sister Abi went to the rest room in the middle of the Court procedure. She was alone there by coincidence and while washing her hands, Hazen suddenly showed up and stood by her side. My sister "was shocked and left the rest room immediately."

Feminism's Hypocrisy

In the meantime, the pretentious attention the Crisis Center woman had offered Hazen showed a qualitative twist after her role was dramatized in front of the Jury, as she spent the rest of the trial inside the Courtroom away from her. Nobody knew what had suddenly happened to all the crying that was done on the stand and to her so-called fragility that seemed to have required her undivided attention. A miracle seemed to have healed her immediately after she testified. The maximum attempt was made to deceive the Jurors; the "victim" had been used enough to the point she could no longer generate income and that was the end of the game.

Defying logic with illogic is nothing new to feminism but a modus operandi with no legal consequence. Feminism disclosed its hypocrisy in classical fashion in President Clinton's ordeal. That gentleman, whether guilty or innocent, was accused of countless violations from improper sexual conduct with Kathleen Willey and Elizabeth Ward to the cases involving Paula Jones, Monica Lewinsky, Jennifer Flowers and the sexual assault charge by Juanita Broaddrick.

With women coming forward one after another, while humanity watched the endless puzzle with disgust, most prominent feminists did not come forward in support of the "victims" defined by their own specifications. In fact, they tainted their images rendering the accusations unbelievable in view of their past sexual and personal history. They were the ones that made a victim's sexual life inadmissible in Court through the *Rape Shield Law*. Yet they turned around and violated the same standard, which became the nightmare by which their socio-political substance was practically considered.

There is no question, however, that they have sedated the male gender, as well as decent feminists, to a point that they easily get away with anything they wish to. Feminism has always been against men of power, but it fumbled terribly in Clinton's case by choosing to stand behind the "powerhouse of powers" and against women with critical issues of its very ideological principles.

According to the statement of NOW (National Organization of Women), "While women are angry and do not condone his conduct, women want President Clinton to remain in office. We believe, and the women of the nation concur, that Mr. Clinton's actions are not impeachable. His misdeeds are not of the nature of high crimes and misdemeanors required by our Constitution for impeachment of the president." [28]

What a mess! An organization that is just an accusation away from destroying a family would not even consider his actions as misdemeanors.

Further, the then President of NOW, Patricia Ireland, was said to have stated that, "Ms. Jones's lawsuit was unworthy of support because it is backed by 'disreputable right-wing organizations.'"[29]

I found this statement very hard to believe to the extent that I think it accidentally came out of the person who said

---

[28]"Then and NOW-What a difference a decade makes" a piece of material from NOW's official press release (September 24, 1998)

[29]Quotation by Juliette Cutler-Page, Editor-in-chief of Feminista! Retrieved from: http://www.rightgrrl.com/1999/feminista.html

it. I cannot imagine the President of NOW revealing that the organization's position on victims of sexual harassment depends on who supports them rather than on their direct experience of the crime. This is a clear-cut betrayal in that the question of women was sacrificed for politics through NOW's conformist position on the case of Paula Jones.

This tendency of deviation from the authentic position of the movement was duplicated in the last presidential campaign when NOW, the axis of American feminism, endorsed Barack Obama over Hillary Clinton to the most powerful political position in the world. It is no longer about gender equality but politics as usual.

The Continuation of My Cross Examination

The prosecutor at one point protested my trip to Minnesota without notifying my accuser or something to that effect. I apparently did not have anything to say about the clear invasion of privacy. In one way, I was a "rapist," on the other, something like a boyfriend in that difficult-to-comprehend ambiance. I could not understand why I should have informed that woman about my movements just because we shared two spontaneous sexual episodes. Although the occasion might have passed as another present from the prosecutor in view of the Jury, it was indeed a sad revelation of how far bad feminists had gone in standing in the way of men's normal activities.

In another instance, her picture with naked belly posed like a *Playboy* model was shown to the Jurors and I was asked if that was how she looked like at the time of the "crime." I agreed and kept quiet but I did not think the picture was necessary for them to see how "attractive" she had been after they had seen her live on the stand; considering her looks could not have faded in such a short time because of me.

Then the prosecutor asked me if I was attracted to Hazen and I shamelessly lied for the first time in the trial by answering affirmatively to avoid a trap. She would have been surprised though, had she sensed how the answer made me feel inside.

My Doctor and Bad Character Witnesses on the Stand

My doctor was the next in line to give his opinion on hemorrhoids as mainly caused by constipation and sometimes by alcohol consumption.

Three witnesses took the stand against her character thereafter.

Rachel, a very bright Eritrean/Ethiopian and long-time friend from New York was part of the team. We had spent good times in upper west side Manhattan during the 1980s. She was there for a limited testimony that did not include her knowledge of the woman as a thief and a manipulator based on her blackmail-induced calculus test experience at the State University of New York in Oneonta. This true friend was dedicated to meeting my lawyer at any time for the sake of my wellness, as she had considered my case her priority at the time. I thank her very much for her concern.

Emelia was an intelligent and eloquent professional paralegal friend from an Eritrean background. As an activist conscious of the need to do more to protect women, she was balanced enough to see the other side of the story. She knew Hazen very well as a person who was capable of taking advantage of the existing partial laws against violence. Having this considerate and brilliant individual on my side was added pressure on the prosecution team. I love everything about my friend and I feel blessed to know her as a person.

My buddy, Abisha knew Hazen well enough to have developed a clear cut opinion about her. I love him and he knows that. I must thank him for his consistent proximity, moral support and for his resolute resistance to the immoral pressure of some Ethiopians to abandon me because I was an Eritrean activist. Clearly, it was an opportunity for them to finish me off once and for all for the person I was; but my friend stood loyally throughout the struggle.

Three of them described the woman in terrible terms and left without challenge from the prosecutor.

Another Government Lie in the Trial

It was at that point in the process that the government took a desperate turn to win the case at any cost. In their anxiety, the Police Officer and the case investigator (detective) tried their best to interview my friends for anything they could use in the trial, but they failed.

They, however, managed to fabricate a story as a last attempt to help the government forge a criminal out of an innocent American citizen. In so doing, I heard the case investigator testify that they arrived at the building lobby, caught me before I ran away, and took me to her place where she identified me as the rapist. He further testified that I confessed to engaging in rough anal sex with my accuser when he conducted a lengthy interview at his downtown office.

He would of course have pressured me to put the "confession" down in my written statement for the record and I could not see myself resisting complying had that been the case, because I was at his mercy that terrible night.

I could not help relating his conduct to why the prosecutor changed the offer from misdemeanor to felony. Apparently confident of winning the case with the help of the so-called law officers, especially after they crashed my defense using the Rape Shield Law, it seems like the "rough sex" issue raised by Hazen and this witness could not have been coincidental. It was unpleasant even to look at the morally challenged man, although I was staring at him without receiving direct eye contact in return.

He had also used the situation to form a close relationship with Hazen, according to an informant, but I was not in a position to do anything about it.

In any case, my justice-paradigm had already shifted for their decadence to surprise me anymore. Yet, it was scary suddenly to lose confidence in the system after living in this country for over twenty years all the while believing in the absolute opposite. The fear was inductive of another caused by the extent of my ignorance about what had been going on in this society. I was ashamed of paying taxes to such a corrupt structure that dehumanizes its own citizens. I wished to have had other means of survival rather than helping it with my money to operate legally in such a way. My taxation did not guarantee my representation. It is a puzzle to me how one can survive a lynching from the malicious, immoral and inhuman institutions that pretend to serve justice. Unfortunately, it took personal experience for me to find out the truth. Most of all, the situation pressed me to change my ways. It also challenged me to do something about the problem as a concerned citizen of the country. Besides reconfiguring my perception of feminism and the system, a demoralizing task for a person of my age, the minimum I could do was to expose the tragedy through this thesis.

I found the system to be more terrifying than cold-blooded murderers, as I found myself regretting my past judgments made without knowledge of all the facts: Lord have mercy! However, I convicted a young man for drug possession and did it again to another man for car theft based on the testimonies of law officers when I twice served as a Juror in the District.

While Jury trials reflect justice in a civilized society, government distortions manifest the opposite as far as our Justice System is concerned. I see our Jury trials in their independent form as solutions; the absurdity of the government, however, renders them mere pretensions of civility rather than real time answers. What can a Jury do other than convict the accused in light of the government's absolute freedom and determination to obscure the truth against defenseless citizens (a typical scenario in America)? Who would ever imagine that the government intentionally lies to win cases? The setup sadly tells me that no Jury can guarantee fair justice, at least not here in Washington, DC, the capital of the planet based on my concrete knowledge of how my past judgments were influenced by the way the cases were prosecuted.

A friend suggests that Court proceedings without Juries, in a manner similar to the European model might solve the problem and specifically pointed at the English Justice System as a case in point. Nonetheless, the idea would be destructive in America. Assuming the information was correct; Europeans may at least have a relatively neutral law enforcement culture to depend solely on the verdict of judges, a privilege we do not enjoy here in the States. But, life teaches a lot and there I was living for decades strictly by the rule and suddenly blessed enough to directly experience the ugliness of gender feminism and biased justice.

Despite the outcome, I was thankful to have gone through the extreme limits of suffering and to be in a practical position to feel the pain of innocent victims betrayed by the government. I am not sure if our non-homogeneous composition was the cause of such recklessness but I came to understand the fragility of our superficial unity as Americans from this terrible experience.

The history of injustice in this country continues to keep going changing faces from generation to generation as if we cannot do without. It was slavery back in the days, racism to the extent of justifying the presence of Buffalo Soldiers within the American Army of yesterday and this mess in today's America by deliberate choice of the government.

Statistical Data about American Prison Situation

The US has the most lawyers per capita standing at one lawyer for every 265 Americans based on Internet based information source.30 We also have the highest Number of Prisoners in the world. According to public information,31 the nation's inmate population increased by 1,122 a week in 1999. This figure indicates a significant decrease, although the prison population had reached 1.86 million and was heading to exceed 2 million by 2001. As of 1999, we have had one in every 11 blacks, one in 25 Hispanics, and one in 65 white Americans in confinement. Federal prisons were also 27 percent over capacity at the end of 1998 despite a construction boom. In general, six blacks and three Hispanics went to prison for one white person during that time. Obviously, Blacks and Hispanics are poorer than Whites on the average. Their incapacity to finance defense expenses might be one of the causes of the biased justice.

30*What country in the world has most lawyers per capita?* /Answers.com (n.d.) Retrieved from: http://wiki.answers.com/Q/W hat_country_in_the_world_has_most_lawyers_per_capita#ixzz1RKqjfs mi

31Slevin, Peter. *Growth in Prison Population Slows*/The Washington Post. (April 20, 2000)

According to the Bureau of Justice Statistics,[32] our inmates reached 2.1 million in the year 2002. About 10 percent of Blacks in the age group 25-29, 1.2 percent of White men, and 2.4 percent of Hispanic men were incarcerated that year. Although a good portion of them could have been drug-related, there is no doubt that the record includes innocent victims of bias.

Based on another source of information,[33] "One in 36 adult Hispanic men, one in 15 adult Black men and one in nine Black men between ages 20 and 34 are behind bars. While the rate of violent crimes has fallen by 25 percent over the last 20 years, prison population has tripled. Overall, the U.S. imprisons more people than any other nation. Second is China, with 1.5 million people in behind bars." Further, "2.3 million people are incarcerated in state and federal prisons and local jails . . . 1 in 100 American adults are behind bars" and that "it costs $25,000-$30,000 of public money a year to incarcerate each prisoner. The cost increases significantly with older prisoners and those who need medical care."

I am including different sources of information with slightly different statistical data about our prison situation in order to approach the subject matter objectively. While the sources may not have presented identical ratio of inmate population per racial group, they seem to be substantially the same as far as our prison population was concerned.

Once America allows big corporations to benefit from private or federal prisons and stockholders invest in our inmates, our prison population will increase irrespective of

---

[32]*US Prisoners Increase, Crime Drops*/The Washington Times (July 24, 2003)

[33]"USA-Prison Nation," University of Michigan based research (April 03, 2008)

the drop in crime. This guarantees the United States to stay ahead of any other country permanently in the world in prison population per capita. Our economy seemingly fluctuates up and down but the number of our inmates consistently elevates year after year and for relatively longer terms than prisoners elsewhere,[34] a unique American profile in the face of global reality.

Although I hardly exculpate the system from practicing racial partiality, I find it important at this occasion to indicate that it may not necessarily be a color issue when it comes to domestic and sexual violence. My experience allows me to get into the justice issues without coloring them racially. In my case, the Policeman and the investigator were blacks. In so saying, there is no doubt that the foundation of the US government has always been white oriented, even today in the Obama administration. And I do not think the gentleman can change the situation just because he is partially black, for there is no such thing as black justice drafted to serve society in history. I do not think the white man alone is the cause of this situation entirely anyway, since I know there are inhuman blacks around as well. We blacks after all hurt each other probably more than any other racial group can hurt us. I would not have been here to begin with had the black leaders back in Africa done their study of justice well. Thus, I no longer consider skin color as a prerequisite of substance more than humanity at large. Whoever is responsible is immaterial; the scale of injustice practiced in today's America is too deep in political culture and historical roots for anyone to repair. Needless to state, I am afraid we may all be unfairly

---

[34]*U.S. Has Highest Number of Prisoners*/Online Lawyer Source (May 13th, 2008) Retrieved from: http://www.onlinelawyersource. com/news/us-prisoners-rise.html

polarized against each other by the intentional design of our system; God save America from itself!

Closing Statements and Jury Deliberation

In her closing statement, the prosecutor told the Jury to remember how confrontational I had been during cross-examination; she had no idea how blistering the chair was. She looked at my people in the Courtroom, pointed her finger at them and angrily told the Jury that their solidarity could not rationalize my innocence – this in contrast to there being no one on her client's side except the woman from the Crisis Center. The prosecutor appeared to be more interested in increasing her professional productivity by messing up my hard-earned life than the extent of my family's suffering as a result. The displayed appetite for human life at least told me, if not others, how addictive the sin could be. One could see her physically reacting like a hungry hyena losing a chunk of meat from its salivating mouth.

To my judgment, the prosecutor had been unconsciously assisting my defense throughout the trial. She came up with one more assistance when she closed her show by saying that she could not imagine a "good looking professional" to mess around with a "hot dog lady." Although I may reserve the right to contain my thoughts about my looks, it was an unconscious revelation of her deceptive performance. How the "college educated beautician" suddenly dropped to her actual livelihood aside, the confession indeed disclosed her client's intellectual incompetence for a "Civil Rights Activist," a stigmatized title with her "college education."

I think such contradictions take place because lies are easily forgotten but frankly, the problem was not the "hot dog lady" as a person but the twisted human being in the package. I do not believe material and academic success should excuse the rejection of human beings in the opposite side of the duality, as I have chosen to live simply in this life without intentionally hurting or undermining anybody despite what I did in school. The prosecutor's professional status does not vindicate her immoral execution of justice that emasculated her productive role in society. I personally consider pure common sense to be more important than destructive intellectual substance; and I would rather be with a normal hot dog stand worker than a professional explosive sufferer of her type. Beyond that, I prefer being homeless to making a living behind fabricated cases at the expense of innocence.

Finally, we rested our case after four days of squabbling and handed it over for Jury deliberation. My lawyer closed his statement by stressing that; the "petty criminal" who habitually steals some one's property would not hesitate to take anyone's pride and life away.

The Verdict

We finally arrived at the most important moment of the trial where the judge took the stage while the rest of us quietly listened to him. He solemnly instructed the Jury to maximize fairness. He repeatedly warned the Jurors to consider each law officer as any other witness and to avoid the mistake of giving their testimonies more weight than the testimonies of other witnesses in the trial.

That is what I call impartial justice from a subjective point of view and the reason for my relative optimism about the justice system because it endorses the equality of citizens and law officers by law. I left the Courtroom thinking that the justice system would be better off at the hands of society without government interference after he freed us for a break.

There was tremendous pressure on my friends as we all waited for the unknown. Visibly absent was my super-sensitive buddy, Michael (wedinno). He said he could not handle the emotions associated with the verdict. In any case, my crew stayed together until the end and we all sat around refreshing ourselves in a nearby café outside the Courthouse until we were instructed to return to the Courtroom for the verdict, sooner than we expected.

As it turned out, that the Jury took about forty-five minutes to decide that I was "not guilty" on both counts of rape in the late afternoon of the twenty-eighth day of the month.

Justice was served and it was wonderful to calmly sit down and watch my siblings and friends hugging each other and celebrating the victory. I then congratulated my lawyer and joined the group after the judge officially announced my freedom. Some of the crowd left and some decided to enjoy the moment together at the Dahlak Restaurant in Adams Morgan. Michael heard it too, and joined us there where Kelly, the charismatic manager, opened champagne for everyone to start partying that evening as if it were the last, while I enjoyed it as if it was the beginning of everything.

Friends, well-wishers and relatives all over the world were thinking of me that day, as I found out later from the messages on my answering machine.

As terrible as the entire experience had been, it was also instrumental in squeezing the best out of me. Each development in the struggle was good enough for artistic expression that generated in my mind to reflect its associated emotion. It was after I discovered the moral vandalism of extreme feminism that I came up with the following song.

COMPASSION

What's going on, why is it so hard
Giving peace a chance, I can't understand
    It ain't violence fairness is the deal
    Productive existence, ain't how much power you pile
    Freedom is okay, if you don't let it steal your mind
    Over-stretching it exchanges you for your pride
    Respect for every life is harmonic substance
    Guarantee for safety peaceful coexistence
    But too much suffering affliction and strife
    Had I had known that, I wouldn't come to this life
What's going on, why is it so hard
Giving peace a chance, I can't understand
    What you do in this life is what comes back around
    Obstruct your ego from taking you for a ride
    Without forgiveness solid spiritual ground
    Ecstatic existence is an illusion of your mind
    Existence is imposed; you are here for a while
    Living it is a choice you can rap it with a style
    Succumb to compassion accept humility
    All you got to do then is enjoy your sanity
What's going on, why is it so hard
Giving peace a chance, I can't understand

105

Freedom and the Aftereffects of False Accusation

Although freed at last, I had to be careful not to spoil the victory. I did not want to waste energy giving credit to myself for exposing the importance of the 911 tape, indirectly telling the Jury about the misdemeanor offer from the prosecutor and on being blessed with people who cared for me, etc. I could have related my joy to her distress and lose momentary presence attached to the meaningless personalities and thoughts that stole two good years of my life.

I could have gotten involved in revenge, further complicating my life.

I could also have injured myself by going over the things I could have done. I had resentment, for example about not informing the Jury that I would not have returned to the United States had I really committed the crime, especially in the absence of bond for my release. I was out for the Winnipeg Folk Music Festival in Canada while I was waiting for my trial and had the entry visa on my passport.

I could also have challenged the prosecutor when she said that Hazen had long hair when we first had sex by inviting the Jury to see her short Afro of that time from the wedding tape I had in my possession. That would have been the best time to hand it over.

I could still have investigated the mystery behind the 911 tape's disappearance, ending up pointing a finger at someone in the defense team and creating serious internal and external problems. Frankly, whatever happened then had already happened, and I believe it happened for a reason. For however much the suffering had been, I am sanctified to have experienced it because I would never have known the effect of such a dilemma in human life without it.

I, however, wished it would stop right there, at that level of my suffering for I resent my incapacity to either ignore or avoid its permanent impact on me in view of my relationship with my friends who might have had nothing to do with it. The consequence was and is beyond my control, although I would do anything to change the situation if it was feasible. It is sad that something comes in to complicate human life when least expected. It is unfortunate that I cannot change what I want to change all the time as a human being. I wish we had the ability to selectively forget what happens to us for then would have been the right time for me to apply the privilege and continue trusting forever. Regrettably, that too was not possible because we have been individually cursed with a powerful memory system that records things and events out of our command. The best we can naturally do is forgive, because forgiveness minimizes the pain of the wound, though it would not change the damage done to the relationship. But, I didn't even know who to forgive except myself in the absence of concrete knowledge about the person responsible for the problem; needless to say that moving on can hardly take place without transformation.

Like anything else in life, the happenstance was a function of cause and effect. As far as the cause was concerned, it was okay whether it was intentional or accidental and regardless of the target; and sincerely, it is not my spiritual business but the effect happened to be mine since I suffered it hard. Still, I would not hesitate to erase its relevance to friendship, to psych myself back to my old state of trust before the disappearance of the tape: if only I could.

I had to move forward, disappointed, without anger. I found learning from the overall experience and sharing the truth of awareness to be the best choice for my interest as I tried to confront my next piece of life without immediate threat in the way.

107

It felt as if I reclaimed my life to better enjoy the world with new mentality, but reality is different from illusion that I could not shake the crisis off and proceed. The weeks following the verdict were strangely uncomfortable; I just could not sleep the nights through, as I spent them arguing with the prosecutor in my imagination. My frustration was so much more magnified after the crisis was put to rest that I could hardly smile for a long time.

I started recollecting my responsibilities and hobbies and picking things up from where they had been paused irrespective of how challenging the process had been. Positively, I had no hatred or anger against Hazen. She was out of my life one way or another and was not even an issue throughout the ordeal once the case became a federal matter at the Court. I was angry, however, about something I could not quite identify. Though the unpleasant sensations gradually faded away and the healing process went without external intervention, I could not enjoy my freedom to the point of considering therapy.

I had been with people throughout the impasse. I went to places I would not normally go to find anyone that could help me and met with individuals I wouldn't normally meet. I went to bed with thoughts in my mind and barely made it to work, as exhausted as a person in a labor camp would be. In the brief absence of thoughts, there was the telephone ringing every few minutes denying me the rest my body was craving. Coming back from work meant the starting point of work for my defense. I did not have the chance to enjoy my solitude throughout the ordeal.

Now that it was over and I had been going through the process of mental transformation quite a bit, I wanted to be alone to regain my psychological balance and to have the opportunity of introducing my new self to myself without the pressure of feminism, Hazen and the government.

As I was slowly getting used to being by myself with relative ease and freedom, I tried to figure out the exact nature of the aftereffects of the matter from a personal perspective. It was time for me to filter out the negative effects from the positive effects of the experience.

I knew my record would stay active for a while and left it for time to resolve the issue because I was not ready to be around the Courthouse immediately after the case ended. I also knew that I was too hurt to sustain any more suffering. I felt like I could not afford to socialize with women in this country until I regained my trust, if I ever would.

I realized within a few months after my freedom that I had lost few personal qualities and acquired new ones. Some of the changes were apparent: I for example have been living in seclusion away from my active social life of the past. I sensed that bars and clubs were no longer my favorite places to be. It seemed like I had developed the art of being alone and working on this book and other materials tirelessly. I traveled outside the US alone at times and enjoyed the prospect of developing my dissertation from different social and environmental perspectives of life.

The longer I stayed with my thoughts, the more I found original ideas about things that spontaneously came across my mind. The extent of work I put myself into and the amount of time I dedicated for it gave me the chance to discover hidden creativities that I never knew existed. The harder I pursued this direction the more diverse the topics grew and the stronger I was convinced to divide my work into different categories (this and others). I felt good about this development.

In the artistic front, I do believe that the crisis enhanced my capacity to articulate feelings lyrically and to create songs accordingly. I am not sure if there is enough time in my life to share this portion of my experience with society, especially with the shaky vocal chord in my system, but it is something I will find out in the future.

Some of the effects are nevertheless still hidden. They have been working on me in the backdrop and I left the challenge for time to play its role of educating me about them. Living with some obvious and some obscure effects, neither could I precisely tell the resultant effect of all the outcomes enforced on me by the horrible experience nor could I tell how my unconscious mind has been reflecting it in my personality at different stages of my life. Whatever it was, it had very little to do with Hazen, a melancholic victim of her sins, but rather with the government, feminism and human character in general.

My Last Jury Duty

Nevertheless, I served my third Jury duty as Juror 001495 in the District for about two weeks since October 22, 2001. It took place after the crisis taught me a lot about the Justice System. The case was about two black teenagers, each accused of dozens of criminal charges over an extended period of time in Maryland and DC counties. Unlike in the past two duties when I convicted the accused without questioning the prosecution's integrity, it was completely different this time. I was dedicated to be responsible but only by allowing the facts to dictate the final terms of my judgment.

There is no doubt that the situation offered an important opportunity as far as the consistency of government distortion was concerned. Whether I was about to confirm this theory one more time or not, it came at the right time for me to judge my integrity on the merit of neutrality despite what happened in the past. Just because the government habitually behaves unjustly does not vindicate criminals and I was not that naïve to breach the public trust imposed on me and impair my rationality in this regard.

Moreover, I was not about to write a book for adventure. If that was the case, I should have written a novel but I am not good at that. I am on a mission of exposing the truth here, not for the sake of material advantage but for my own spiritual satisfaction, well aware of the implications of my statements and ready to take responsibility for them. I have to be honest about my thoughts and feelings if I intend to raise public awareness through the magnitude of work like this.

I therefore accepted my jury duty with this clarity in mind. I listened to every detail of the opposite sides with extreme concentration and interest to end up sensing multiple twists and turns by the law officers. Alas, all Jurors were as naïve as I had been; it was scary to see them giving the officers the benefit of the doubt just because they were in uniform but I gave them their burden of proof.

Among other inconsistencies, the government should have told a more rational story than the mockery of "[locating the defendant's shotgun about two feet away from the place of his apprehension not by the immediate officer waiting for help at the spot but by another who showed up at the scene to enforce about half an hour later]." You probably can see the possibility of this happening in the day light for that long a time but I could not imagine a human being with average sight doing so.

The question was how the accused managed to put it there (about two feet away) in the process of his apprehension by the law officer who by some miracle missed noticing its presence. I wish I could answer the question affirmatively because of *a fluke* because the term is a powerful tool that people sometimes use to obscure the truth. And frankly, I like the way it sounds. But, my

111

commonsense did not accept it to be so in this circumstance. It rather went in favor of *invention*.

This was how the system underestimated our intelligence and tried to cage the poor kids for the permanent destruction of their future. It almost succeeded but God placed me in the way. I could not help but to smile sarcastically about what was going on, with deep sorrow inside thinking about what we can do to children of the world under the cover of fighting terrorism. I focused at the gloomy faces of the kids' parents whenever I caught the government cheating and telepathically gave them the comfort of hope and optimism without eye contact.

It turned out that intense discussions and arguments took place at times; and all the other Jurors stood against my position, with few of them openly showing their impatience and bitterness about the way I was legitimately trying to save the kids from the hungry mouth of the system. We were definitely on the opposite sides of justice. A few days into the experience, I was alone. After the first week was over, they could hardly stand even to exchange greetings. I just came in the mornings and sat down quietly in the Jury room without any contact with anyone but my newspapers, while the rest of the jury talked to each other. I cannot forget the tension when we were voting and especially when my hand was the only one raised against their judgment because that happened to be the time when the mumbling started, making me nervous at times and wishing I was not there.

The environment grew progressively more uptight and an unhealthy relationship matured between a young Juror and me to the extent that I regretfully went through unfriendly verbal exchanges with him. I just got tired of his agitation against my position on the charges. I told him about my intention to inform the judge unless he stopped the practice. Then the other Jurors stepped in to pacify the hostility.

The pressure of seclusion from the rest of the Jurors was terrible but neither was it enough to taint my spirituality nor did anything else matter more than the menace against teenage lives from the unethical system that had a problem being pure and impartial. The situation went on for two weeks without me yielding from my grounds. The judge sensed the hopelessness of resolving the stalemate and he could not have it continue beyond the second week in view of cost, and thankfully sent us home; and that was the end of it.

To complete my recollection of it, I ended up "convicting" them each of two or three well-substantiated offenses but found them innocent otherwise (approximately forty criminal charges).

In conclusion, I advise falsely accused people to make no mistake by waiting for law officers at the site of the "crimes." You can minimize government distortion in your trials by voluntarily surrendering at their headquarters.

FROM FEMINIST TO RAPIST

THE ROLE OF FEMINISM IN THE AMERICAN STYLE OF JUSTICE

Undeniably, the crisis involved multiple aspects of life and specifically amplified my awareness of Radical feminism in contrast to justice. I want it clear that I am not talking about true violence, which unfortunately takes place every few seconds in America. I feel honored to acknowledge the excellent performance of feminism in this regard and thank it for the positive social role it has been playing in boosting women's awareness of their rights and in directly and effectively dealing with the problem.

My work here is based on my understanding of genuine feminism as being a movement against all forms of bias: one that has no illusion about the fact that no individual or group with a tendency of bias at *home court* can achieve, deserve or justify asking for total freedom from any form of bias in society. Home court in this context implies to an individual's or a group's most direct social issue of concern such as women on the question of gender equality and colored people on racism. Women cannot genuinely defend or guarantee gender equality while being sexist correspondingly to black people not being able to genuinely defend or guarantee racial equality while being racist.

Human experience is impossible without deception, and false accusation falling into this category. It happens every day everywhere. False accusation can be innocently composed and one must feel sorry for innocent victims in

115

this case. It can also be crafted for personal reasons. One dark motivation is vengeance. It can be provoked by the tendency to cover up consensual sex with a stranger especially after being intoxicated or drugged. It can be used to attract attention or to be rewarded with compensation. It can also take place because of a woman being conditioned to think that she was raped as a result of feminism's intricate definition of the subject. I do see violence here and expect justice without bias.

Regrettably, there is no justice.

Although the focal point of this project is feminism, I find it important to mention the government's negative social input through the experience of Donald Eugene Gates (an innocent District man who was recently freed after suffering 28 years of injustice) for the crime (rape and murder) he did not commit. This is not because his experience is unique but because it happened to come out to the public recently

According to public information,[35] "A 1997 review by the Justice Department discredited the work of that FBI analyst, Michael P. Malone, and 13 other analysts, finding that they had made false reports and performed inaccurate tests." Apparently, "The analyst incorrectly linked two hairs from an African American male to Gates. The hairs were found on the body of the victim." It is hard to believe all of them making the same mistake simultaneously, but let me excuse them at the maximum stretch of fairness assuming that it was accidental.

However, I don't have words to describe my feelings about what was revealed: "the authorities had relied on more than testimony about hair when they asked a Jury to convict Gates. *A government-paid informant who said he*

---

[35] Keith Alexander, Staff writer in Washington Post, December 16, 2009

knew Gates . . . in the District in the early 1980s testified that Gates confessed to him. Gates told attorneys that he had never heard of the witness."

The tragedy was further presented in the Post[36] with important information about the role of the lead prosecutor of the case who "said later that it was the first time he had put a paid informant on the witness stand during a trial" to tell ". . . authorities that Gates admitted to killing Schilling during a botched robbery. Gates told lawyers that he never met the informant to whom he supposedly confessed."

Something came to my mind after I finished reading the article: considering this took place about 28 years ago and my case about 10 years ago, the government must have consistently practiced its business of distortion at least between 1981 and 2000. I cannot fully understand why, but I am frightened of it to the point of respect.

Setting aside the experience of the country vis-à-vis Native Americans and slavery, injustice continued its norm in different styles to the time of the Civil Rights movement without any honest sign of change. Chances are it may never change. America appears to be comfortable with being the cause of suffering to its people who have been dying for its cause all over the place.

In the international arena, we know how the case of Saddam Hussein was presented to the public in order for the Bush administration to do what it had to do to his regime and material resources of Iraq. I believe the man was too cruel to his people and his neighbors for me to have the slightest sympathy for what happened to him. I am only touching on this here before moving on to my main topic because it is still fresh in the memory of Americans as one of

---

[36]Alexander, Keith. Prosecutor reflects on wrongful conviction in D.C. Killing/The Washington Post. (March 6, 2010)

the most recent political misadventures of our government outside its own turf.

This is consistent with the history of American political misbehavior in other societies in the name of freedom and justice, which goes as far back as the era of Patrice Lumumba,[37] (this opinion of course is with recognition of the partially positive results of our intervention internationally). I let it remain to be seen if its image in view of the universe is in contrast to its self-perception as the role model of freedom; but I do not take it seriously for that.

The consistency of our performance in this respect makes me question my intelligence to the point of suspecting that I might have missed something important somewhere.

I could go on about our government's sometimes sham style of justice in more detail but enough has been said and written about it nationally and internationally by many activists and writers through the years. Although I am sure it will occasionally pop up in my discussions ahead, I don't think I can be as productive as I want to be by prioritizing the subject matter in this forum without taking the risk of being monotonous.

Nevertheless, I do find it more imperative to discuss thoroughly the effects of feminism in society today, since I

---

[37]"Patrice Émery Lumumba (2 July 1925–17 January 1961) was a Congolese independence leader and the first legally elected Prime Minister of the Republic of the Congo after he helped win its independence from Belgium in June 1960. Only ten weeks later, Lumumba's government was deposed in a coup during the Congo Crisis. He was subsequently imprisoned and murdered in circumstances suggesting the support and complicity of the governments of Belgium and the United States." *Patrice Lumumba*/Wikipedia. (n.d.) Retrieved from: http://en.wikipedia.org /wiki/Patrice_Lumumba

felt betrayed and saddened by how unfair it was to me. I say this because I have always supported the struggle of women and I was the true victim of the crisis by a negative woman who neither had respect for feminism and the true victims of violence nor had the capacity to respect herself.

I have a problem with feminism's negative role in society of giving accusers the benefit of the doubt and excusing them from carrying the burden of proof. I feel sorry about this sexist choice of staying away from the larger scope of the human struggle for freedom. We have a respectable justice system that treats the government and the public equally but I resent its convergence to the most effective way of launching gender crimes in America because of paralyzing pressure from bad feminists and corrupt politicians.

I had never questioned feminism's sincere social role in any of my most naïve socio-political positions, but I know now that it has endorsed a different political idea: that it no longer belongs in the progressive camp of society only but also in the materially more comfortable regressive camp. It has practically decided to swing between opposite camps at will, depending on who brings the most money to the table.

First, I formally apologize to all feminists for my new stand on today's feminism. I know I may be mistaken for a chauvinist or labeled as revisionist. Whatever the result of my work may be, I have decided to come forward as openly and honestly as I can be on the issue, as I from here on declare my withdrawal from the NOW style of feminism that I followed and fully supported in the past.

I believe Feminism is in crisis: I call upon good feminists to pay attention to what I have to say in this opportunity and do something to save it from the sellout divisive enemies within. I am humbly asking this from the angle of modest coexistence.

For all practical modes of operation, the relevant elements of American justice appear to be interdependent. Feminist leaders generate ideas one after another and their powerful lobbies exert pressure until the politicians succumb to their demands because of the money and the power they guarantee through women's votes. They take a strong position against violence by committing high-level crimes; laws are passed and cases established accordingly. An accuser becomes their source of income and psychic gratification in exchange for possible job training, bonuses through the Crisis Centers and of course for the eventual big stake from the accused.

The more cases they take on irrespective of the people involved, the better feminist leaders can financially exploit the public, the firmer their job security, and the more intense their psychological stimulation from human agony.

Here may be where the trauma experts come in, to work hand in hand with them and benefit for their assistance and time from the same source of income, which is the public fund.

While money is generated left and right from public funds and innocent men rusting in prisons, today's wealthy feminist leaders take advantage of former victims of violence or activists to serve them freely at the Crisis Centers in the name of the cause. These are innocent victims of feminist leadership hypnotized to assist accusers of sex crime unconditionally.

Prosecutors unfairly punish the accused for professional success, upward mobility and career stability because the quantity of convictions raises their productivity. Lawyers then get busy making taxable income that benefits local and federal governments.

An article in the Washington Post of March 8th, 2001, page B5, by a staff writer discloses the District Council's concerns about the staggering "overtime abuse" of public funds by the DC Police Department, through which some Officers doubled or tripled their base salaries in the year 2000. Testifying in Court during off-duty hours was reported to be one of the sources of overtime dollars according to the Washington Times (July 16, 2003 and May 5, 2004). This could have been the reason why there were multiple distortions by the law officers assigned to my case. If the Police Officer and Case Detective had the tenacity to misinform the Jury in support of prosecution, I do not see why they could not have done that at the Grand Jury to safeguard their material advantage.

I have nothing against Police Officers and Detectives and in fact, I sympathize with them for what they go through every day, although I cannot take any one of the jobs in its current spiritual form. They are after all underpaid for their stressful profession and they may welcome extra income here and there whenever the opportunity is offered. I, however, find it hard to see them going as far as they go in this regard without pressure to bend the truth from authority. I doubt if they can keep their jobs for long without substantial obedience to the system, no matter how resentful they may be about the setup. They must help prosecutors win cases for survival by filling in the gaps as crucial sub-systems of the bomb composed of two powerful and caustic elements, bad feminists and greedy politicians.

The following direct pieces of information from the Police community give me reason to partially and only partially vindicate law officers for being the circumstantial victims of something unfortunate because reality points to the government and feminism as the root causes of this gross American injustice.

According to Paul Elam's *On Jury Nullification and Rape*, Sunday, August 1, 2010, "just recently the Orlando Police Department made the public proclamation that false rape allegations have become an epidemic." and that Baltimore,

Louisville and Pittsburgh reported similar numbers of false accusations (30%).

The question is how they deal with false accusers.

As infested as America is with innocent prisoners of false rape accusations and with the Police openly producing concrete statistical data of the horrible gender crime, there is hardly any news about the government challenging the accusers. In fact, it seems to aggravate the situation.

Stephen Baskerville et al teach in *American Gulag – Feminist Laws Persecute Men,* that, "Forced confessions were common in Pennsylvania and that men are incarcerated 'unless they sign forms stating, "I have physically and emotionally battered my partner."' The man must then describe the violence, even if he insists he committed none," meaning that they help him fabricate his crimes after they force him sign the document.

"Eddie Lowery lost 10 years of his life for a [rape] crime he did not commit. There was no physical evidence at his trial for rape, but one overwhelming factor put him away: he confessed." He said, ". . . he was just pressed beyond endurance by persistent interrogators." The article further states that, ". . . more than 40 others have given confessions since 1976 that DNA evidence later showed were false, according to records compiled by Brandon L. Garrett, a professor at the University of Virginia School of Law."[38]

How can this take place in a civil society without instruction from central command?

Warren Farrell reveals the following statistical distribution of the Innocence Project that tells where we

---

[38]Schwartz, John. *Confessing to Crime, but Innocent,* The New York Times, (September 13, 2010)

stand as society in today's America in view of police misconduct.[39]

Police Misconduct (a factor in 37 of the first 74 DNA exonerations)

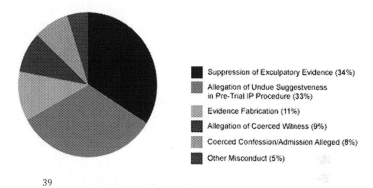

Suppression of Exculpatory Evidence (34%)

Allegation of Undue Suggestveness in Pre-Trial IP Procedure (33%)

Evidence Fabrication (11%)

Allegation of Coerced Witness (9%)

Coerced Confession/Admission Alleged (8%)

Other Misconduct (5%)

39

I relate my experience to these statistics in the following manner.

Police Related Suppression of Exculpatory Evidence

The law officers' elimination of the long interviews they made with the two men at the site of the "crime" (the building security guard and his companion) from their final report belongs to this category of the problem.

Police Related Evidence Fabrication/Other Misconduct

There is no doubt that the false testimonies of the two law officers belong in "Other Misconduct" category, but I believe they also belong in the other category, though no material proof was submitted at court to that effect.

---

[39]Elam, Paul. *On Jury Nullification and Rape*/Men's News Daily (August 1, 2010) Retrieved from: http://mensnewsdaily.com/2010 /08/01/on-jury-nullification-and-rape/

Here comes the question of prosecutorial misbehavior that detrimentally affects the fate of the accused. A classic example of this problem is what took place in the Duke University lacrosse case where the prosecutor was said to have prosecuted the cases by suppressing exculpating evidence knowing that the accused men were innocent.

According to the author of *Maine - False Rape Witch Hunt,*[40] victims of prosecutions in Maine's Bar Harbor region describe the situation as a modern day Witch Hunt. Further, "Court documents suggest that numerous men are currently facing charges of sexual misconduct in a small county of little more than 50,000 people. At the center of these prosecutions is a 44 year old Assistant District Attorney Mary N. Kellett, who has a reputation for prosecuting men on questionable evidence and questionable probable cause. As in the Salem Witch Trials, these prosecutions are often based solely on accusations with no physical or corroborating evidence."

"[I]t is most important for law enforcement to believe the woman, act on her report, and do exactly what she wants them to do if a woman falsely accuses a man of rape," according to the article. Apparently, prosecutors work in this frame of thought (men's lives are worthless compared to questioning the integrity of women's accusations).

According to Paul Elam's *On Jury Nullification and Rape*, August 1, 2010, former Colorado prosecutor Craig Silverman once opined, "For sixteen years I was a kick ass prosecutor who made the most of my reputation [by] vigorously prosecuting rapists. I was amazed to see all the false rape allegations made to the Denver Police Department."

---

[40] *False Rape Witch Hunts Gone Wild*/MND. Retrieved from: http://mensnewsdaily.com/2009/10/23/false-rape-witch-hunts-gone-wild/

Warren Farrell presents the following Innocence Project statistics on the magnitude of the mess in today' sexist America.

Prosecutorial Misconduct (a factor in 33 of the first 74 DNA exonerations)

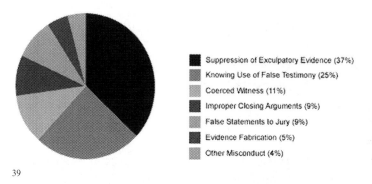

- Suppression of Exculpatory Evidence (37%)
- Knowing Use of False Testimony (25%)
- Coerced Witness (11%)
- Improper Closing Arguments (9%)
- False Statements to Jury (9%)
- Evidence Fabrication (5%)
- Other Misconduct (4%)

39

Relating my case to this, I came with the following analysis.

Prosecutor Related Suppression of Exculpatory Evidence

This is based on the prosecutor's elimination of at least three highly relevant witnesses from my defense structure, my accuser's two counts of violence against other people, a restraint order filed against her by a former boyfriend, and a false accusation she filed against someone, which she later retracted.

Prosecutor Related Evidence Fabrication/Other Misconduct

I relate my experience to the first category when it comes to the prosecutor's disclosure to the Jury of a gown that I had not seen the night of the "crime" as the one my accuser was wearing, then to imply that it was not provocative. Likewise, I connect it to the second category because the prosecutor's presentation of my accuser as a college educated beautician and a Civil Rights Activist was misleading.

Improper Closing Argument

I relate my situation here to being addressed as a manipulative rapist by the prosecutor and her refusal to drop at least the anal rape allegation, since there was no DNA evidence to support it, and asking the Jurors to convict me on it.

Another vigorous catalyst that plays a nasty role behind the scandal is a group of private prison contractors that economically benefit from prison enterprises. One example that supports the theory is the appearance of a ". . . gentleman . . . in Benson, AZ to pitch a plan to the city manager", the plan being "the private prison industry" to "draft a piece of "model legislation" and use its powerful lobbyists and political money to get the bill passed . . ." in the name of "Support Our Law Enforcement and Safe Neighborhoods Act." The law would then "send hundreds of thousands of illegal immigrants to prison in a way never done before. And it could mean hundreds of millions of dollars in profits to private prison companies responsible for housing them."[41]

---

[41]greendem. *NPR: Private Prisons behind Arizona's Immigration Law* (Oct 28, 2010) Retrieved from: http://www.dailykos.com/story/2010/10/28/914400/-NPR:-Private-Prisons-behind-Arizonas-Immigration-Law

Feminism's Indirect Promotion of Slavery in American Prison Systems

Aside the fact that private businesses provide prison infrastructures and material supplies, prisoners may be forced to work for as ridiculous a wage as "25 cents an hour"[42] for manufacturing businesses. Corporate stockholders may also benefit from this cheap labor to be motivated into lobbying for longer sentences and the prison population increase to that end.

Evidently, it becomes important to talk briefly about labor camp economics in order to address this issue with reason.

Keeping in mind that I have learned my lessons the hard way for conclusively stating something without evidence, my research says that labor is highly exploited in some of our prison systems.

Traditionally, a labor camp is defined as a punitive institution for confining political prisoners and using them in forced labor. It is also defined as a "detention facility where inmates are forced to engage in penal labor."[43]

On the flip side, slavery is defined as "a system based on enslaved labor: the practice of, or a system based on, using the enforced labor of other people" or "condition of being enslaved laborer: the state or condition of being held in involuntary servitude as the property of somebody else" or "hard work: very hard work, especially for low pay and

---

[42]Paleaze, Vicky. *The Prison Industry in the United States: Big Business or a New Form of Slavery?*/Gramma International Havana, Cuba (October 13 2005) Retrieved from http://www.gran ma.cu/ingles/2005/octubre/juev13/42carceles.html

[43]*Labor_camp*/Wikipedia (n.d.) Retrieved from: http://en.wikipedia.org/wiki/Labor_camp

under bad conditions" or "state of being dominated: a state of being completely dominated by another."[44]

The source of information says that the US is doing "exactly what the U.S. has been lambasting China for" in California and Oregon prison enterprises, which is said to be similar to "slave labor." The information is based on comprehensive University of Massachusetts study, which also states, "If prisoners don't work, they serve longer sentences, lose privileges, and risk solitary confinement."

Based on the definitions above, Wikipedia, the encyclopedia declares that the United States of America practices labor camp style human exploitation that has roots in slavery. The practice fits into the definition of the outrageous mode of production.

The allegation is serious and requires serious public attention to be realistic. Slaves did not have to be accused of anything to become slaves (at least in the west) as long as they look different from their masters (in most cases), but prisoners are accused of breaking the law and convicted to serve time for their actions. This is the only difference I see here, in how a slave is characterized in terms of forced labor and how America does its business with some prisoners.

In view of this difference only, one may controversially argue that slavery does not exist in the American prison enterprise. The question is how do you reconcile the system's behavior in relation to innocent prisoners conditioned to be in labor camp? My answer is affirmative here in favor of slavery in this country, once again strictly on the question of innocent prisoners exposed to labor camps.

---

[44]*The Enslavement of Americans by their Government*/Good Sense Politics (March 2, 2011) Retrieved from: http://goodsensepo litics.blogspot.com/2011/03/enslavement-of-americans-by-their.html

Whether we like it or not, this is where I think we stand as a nation irrespective of how we see ourselves. We send people to prisons for cheap labor and considering the staggering number of innocent prisoners in America, not only did I find Radical feminism to be one of the criminal organizations that contribute to this delinquency through false accusations but also suspect its leaders to have a hidden conspiracy with the beneficiaries of labor camp for material advantage.

The Effect of False Accusation of Rape in American Society

By making anything a controversy, public and private resources are embezzled by a few individuals in the lucrative sexual harassment industry. What is going on among other things is organized scandal against Americans and their economy. The accused does not stand a chance without fully financing defense bills and far beyond. Those who can afford must pay lawyers' fees, investigation expenses, for the service of medical experts and any other costs associated with witnesses at minimum. Of course, the expense can escalate taking DNA and other scientific support systems into account because prosecutors may no longer carry the burden of proving crimes in this country. In practice, the accused must prove their innocence. A case in point to this hypothesis is Washington State Supreme Court's shifting of the burden of proving innocence to the defendant in 1989.[45]

---

[45]Baskerville, Stephen. *Feminist Gulag: No Prosecution Necessary*/New American (January 7, 2010) Retrieved from: http://www.thenewamerican.com/index.php/culture/family/2705-feminist-gulag-no-prosecution-necessary

Even then, one has to be super-lucky to make it because many analysts say that Crime Laboratories have the tendency to falsify results in favor of convictions. In my case, the Physician from DC General Hospital who first examined my accuser certainly falsified facts though I cannot confidently put his performance and laboratory results in this category because of insufficient information; but not the FBI, which did a good job that strongly contributed to my freedom.

In most practical scenarios, the accused are forced to plead guilty to get a more lenient sentence on their first contact with their overworked public defenders, and chances are they will if they cannot afford to defend themselves. I certainly went through this process and I am lucky to have had the resources necessary to hire my own lawyer for my defense.

As such and more, the US confines innocent men for no more reason than women's accusations. It brings men to the Court possibly to face feminist prosecutors that take "the offense" personally because of their passionate hatred of men. If one somehow survives the Criminal Court, he is often forced to the Civil Court for punitive damages. The accuser may then be rewarded with a good amount of money for the short time worth of effort of reporting the violence. The process is configured to create ample grounds for evil women to destroy others and/or to dig deep into their personal accounts and possessions. The effortless economic opportunity inspires those with negative energy that do not want to work for living, to break the accused and their families and manufacturing time bombs out of kids denied full parental and/or sibling assistance necessary for their decent upbringing. They are systematically programmed to fall into the production machine of prison oriented labor camp venture.

An accuser does not even have to appear at the trial and can simply stay home then without any consequence for the inflicted damages on the accused and on social resources because "she cannot psychologically face her assailant." Would somebody also be concerned about the traumatic experience of an accused facing his false accuser for the sake of fairness?

In the meantime, real victims are bypassed because the objective reality steals away a big chunk of their much-deserved social resources. "False reports take personnel away from other calls for service, increasing response time for real victims. . . . It also taints the Jury pool in Orange County for true legitimate rape cases," says Sgt. Art Eld of the Orlando Police department in unspecified press conference.[46] In short, the way we approach false accusation denies justice to real victims of rape.

After personally going through this experience, it is not hard for me to conclude that it is only a matter of time for every family to feel the heat when the brutality directly or indirectly hits home at the unfortunate moment and situation. What happened to me could happen to any American.

Many studies have been conducted to approximate the magnitude of false accusation in the US. According to *False Accusation Issues* in Men's Rights Online, Charles P McDowell's research confirms that 60% of rape accusations were false. Purdue University sociologist Eugene J. Kanin's research with two Midwestern state universities concluded in 1988 that the figure was between 50% and 64%. This study states that, "considerable amount of women from the main report were members of the lower socio-economic

---

[46]*Police: False Criminal Reports Must Stop*/WESH.com (June 22, 2010) Retrieved from: http://www.wesh.com/news/23991233/detail .html

131

demographic -- indicating that false accusations could be linked to income and educational status." While DNA based approach asserts that from 10% to 50% rape accusations could be false, a former prosecutor from Colorado, Craig Silverman, puts the figure at 45%.

Similarly, the 1996 Department of Justice report concludes that, "in about 25% of the sexual assault cases referred to the FBI, the primary suspect has been excluded by forensic DNA testing." Clearly, not all victims get the chance of going through DNA testing and this result cannot possibly be expected to represent the objective American dilemma. It is in fact far lower than the average reports provided by other neutral elements. It, however, confirms that at least one in four rape allegations was fabricated. Let us together do a minor calculation with this minimum figure to assess the grossness of the epidemic.

Out of the 262,803,276 American population, a total of 97,470 forcible rapes were reported to law enforcement agencies in 1995, the lowest total since 1989.[47] This is a sharp drop from the 102,555 cases reported in 1990, when the population was 249,464,396.

Considering this figure, one can safely conclude that at least a quarter of the figure, or 24,367.5 of the charges could have been bogus. Assuming a single accusation affects at least about 10 people (relatives, family and friends), approximately 243,675 innocent Americans should have been traumatized that year by the problem. Further assuming that 50% of the sufferers in this approximation are female, feminism should have lost about 121,837.5 short and long-term potential women supporters in 1995.

Contrary to my assumption that this disaster was bound to expand in time because it may be directly proportional to population growth in the country, I was surprised to learn

---

[47] *Crime in the United States*, US Department Of Justice

that the crime dropped to 88,097 in 2009 when the American population stood at 307,006,550. I thought this was important to mention here for the record. The fact remains, nevertheless, that the tragedy worsens considering the effects of fatherless upbringing, shattered hopes and revenge-induced violence.

Feminist leaders may ignore this reality in favor of their fame, power and pockets, but I have it hard understanding why the system chooses to be part of this devastating attack against its own citizens in spite of the dirty money available from the prison industry.

My Position on Sexual Crimes and Gender Equality

Rape is dehumanizing. My mind fails to comprehend the mentality of those that push for sex after they hear or sense the other person saying "no" directly or indirectly. My Justice System on the issue is one-directional. I believe in permanently isolating proven pedophiles and child pornographers at the first offense level of their sickness and I have no problem with painlessly castrating habitual sex offenders, if only because that is the best solution to their uncontrollable psychosexual drives.

My moral and political stand on this subject has a long history since I was introduced to political awareness of gender equality as a teenager. In particular, I might have emotionally benefited from the active participation of Eritrean women in the national struggle for independence. I know the country's liberation would not have materialized without their solid contributions. The list includes my lovely sister Rishan, who gave her life for the cause in the Eritrean struggle. This makes women vital elements of my life that I must respect, appreciate, protect and fully support.

I am also from a large family with seven sisters and an extremely loving mother. I thank my dad for absolutely keeping his hands away from my mom, which I know was instrumental to my personality later on in life. There is no illusion as to how I would have been affected had I once, and only once seen him physically abusing her, although I heard them occasionally arguing like any other people in society. My sensitivity assures me that my character and overall human potential at any stage of life would have shrunk by at least fifty percent if that had taken place, not to mention the prospect of hurting him for vengeance. I have never identified with those who utilize the religious account that Eve tempted Adam to sin as "ethical" excuse to undermine and oppress women including my mom and my sisters for eternity.

I condemn backward cultures that allow insecure men to kill female sexuality by means of female genital mutilation. I ridicule the mentality of atrocious virginity obsessed men who endorse female infibulation because of fear. I repulse the communities that brutally punish women for committing adultery.

I despise violent men and hold them directly responsible for this crisis, which would probably never have gotten to this mark of insanity without their sadistic actions. Abuse is a syndrome and low self-esteem the disease. Abusers of children and women have no self-confidence and suffer from intellectual inferiority complex. They just don't have it upstairs to carry out reasonable communication with women and are too weak to admit their stupidity. Most men who physically attack women are cowards who don't stand their ground in front of other men. They depend on domestic violence to cover up their masculinity related problems.

Anybody that gets a kick from hurting people or animals is disgusting and anyone who tries to stereotype everyone is unfair. By excluding my experience as something related to a few individuals, I have no reason to rebel against all women including those who pulled me out of the trap. Even at this level of my contradiction with gender radicalism, I continue to identify with the cause and I refuse to give up my feminism, for true feminism is a state of awareness and ideological identification that has nothing to do with gender. Every good man after all is a feminist by default.

My strong belief in gender equality is not a favor or a matter of pity, but a conviction at the psychic level of the theme. To me, equality means equality and it had better be impartial to be practical. Putting aside the physical and emotional differences of our nature, this fundamental understanding explains the reason behind my voluntary participation in the common struggle against violence. Most importantly, education and severe punishment should continue to work against offenders and I am willing to continue as part of the effort without expecting something in return except that American feminists accept men as their equals, respect their lives, and admit the existence of mendacious accusers and properly deal with them.

I am not asking for favors from feminism here but respect for human life. I am asking for equality. It is time for women to call the spade a spade.

A Bureau of Justice report indicates that, "women are the perpetrators in 41 per cent of spousal murders," males tend to kill their wives themselves, with knives or guns, and often commit suicide afterwards. In sharp contrast, females tend to use poison or to have their husbands killed by other males, either a professional killer or a boyfriend. The last two methods of killing are classified as "'multiple offender killings,' and are not counted as female-perpetrator killings."[48] The question is if a crime has to be committed directly and openly to be considered a crime. Should a person who masterminds and indirectly commits a crime be vindicated from a related criminal charge? Yet, the question is if feminism will ever practically accept the existence of false accusers if it indeed accepts the existence of criminal women in all other criminological fields of society?

How much more does a person have to suffer before left alone to live the rest of his life? What does it take for society to stop feminism from being above the law to deny released convicts breathing space by harassing them wherever they go after legally paying their dues for what they were accused?

It is time for feminism to stop taking exceptional rights for granted and settle for gender equality in America. I resist treating women better than men in the Criminal Justice System because it is a qualitative departure from equality. It would mean discriminating men based on gender and replacing male dominance by another form of dominance. Likewise, with all empathy, I cannot accept a woman's accusation as more important than a defendant's right to defend his life with unrestricted applications of reason. I simply cannot justify jeopardizing the fate of our children by snatching their fathers and brothers away just because women accuse them. Equality should apply in all activities of life because it is unhealthy for society to arm bad women with a rape machine gun without checking and balancing the target of its bullets.

Frequently, prosecutors obscure cases in the absence of tangible evidence by asking why the so-called victims

---

[48]Lauritsen, John. *Does Feminism Discriminate against Men?*/H NET BOOK REVIEW Published by H-Histsex@h-net.msu.edu (May 2008) Retrieved from: http://paganpressbooks.com/jpl/FARR ELL.HTM

accuse people unless they were truly victimized. It happened in my trial. Aside the counter-question, "why are innocent Americans amassed in prisons?" the most direct answer to that is I do not specifically know why. But, I know that the argument is neither evidence nor relevant to innocence or guilt of an accused and I leave it to psychiatrists to tell us what they think about it. Whether feminists like it or not, women are human beings and human beings inherently lie. Women cannot be Godly or perfect in issues of violence and human beings or imperfect otherwise. In my situation, there were at least some of these possible motivations for my accuser to do what she did: jealousy, revenge (for refusing intimate relationship), political framing, compensation, donations from her community, attention, political fame and of course the fact that she was evil and a liar. To speculate on something is defensible but to play with life by means of unconfirmed speculation is a crime.

At the bottom line, I strongly believe in full investigation and exposure to trial of any person reported to have committed such a crime, as long as he can freely exhaust all means of defense without restrictions to prove his innocence – as much as the limitless freedom prosecutors enjoy proving otherwise, simply because a life is at stake here.

The public should also participate in assisting the accused to get meaningful representation in the Justice System. We should be responsible to cover defense bills in such cases, since it is a social problem the majority cannot afford and the government has failed to help. It is only fair for me to ask my government to allocate a fraction of my taxes to this noble cause at the same magnitude of what I have been providing the prosecution end of the duality for years. This is certainly one of the areas where Americans are not represented through their taxation. I believe there is a need in this country for a Civil Rights movement to this effect, simply because we cannot afford the consequence of the void in terms of human life and family destruction.

Procedurally, it does not make sense to bring an accused in front of a Jury and expect a miracle from a crippled defense system. The exclusion of acquaintances, boyfriends and former spouses in such criminal cases should be condemned by all peace-loving people even in the presence of concrete evidence that supports allegations. If the situation narrows down to hearsay contest, an accused should be allowed to use his accuser's vengeful behaviors and other relevant issues in other relationships without question, because character becomes the only solution to the problem in the absence of substance. This is too basic for ordinary commonsense. Unfortunately, we are caught in cross roads: there may not be a lot we can do with a government that intentionally does wrong as a matter of policy.

Gender Equality in View of Radical Feminism

Coming back to my research, the intense power and ideological struggle between feminist sects especially in the sixties should have exerted sporadic pressure on them. It must have been a complicated season of ideological dominance, attention and popularity at the height of the feminist fad that left activists in general saying anything that came to mind, regardless of its social consequences. Who had gone to the extreme rather than who focused on the problems seems to have been the challenge at the time feminism emerged as a symbol of rebelliousness for young women in America; very much like the hippies experimenting with acid and other tranquilizers in the psychedelic Height-Asbury culture of San Francisco.

The threat of feminism did not stop at men, but family structures were rejected as well; the institution of marriage condemned in favor of prostitution, heterosexual relationships were considered to be against women's sexual interests and trashed in favor of lesbianism (with my honest respect to lesbians), and motherhood and love were denounced as slavery of women by men. It was like a progressive disease that grew into all facets of society.

The chronological order of presence immaterial, neo-feminism is one product of confusing feminism because it is based on the assumption that women are superior to men in everything. A neo-feminist rejects the inbuilt role of women in society because she takes it as something imposed on women by men. She exaggerates the difference between men and women to the point of denying her natural female instinct.

A posted material[49] puts the situation as "Anyone who personally knows a Neofeminist realizes why she is so desperately unhappy and bitter. She is struggling pointlessly to become the very person she loathes so passionately: *A man.*" Further, "While she snivels about "gender discrimination" and "misogyny," a Neofeminist refuses to use the word "woman" because it is derived from the word "man." She uses instead the words "wimmin," "wymyn, or "womyn" [sic, sic, sic]. Some Neofeminists despise men so much that they dehumanize them with such descriptions as "pentapods."

My question is why the ideology does not accept the word "woman" in the reverse condition that the word "man" be considered as the derivative of "woman." Even beyond,

---

[49] *Chapter 129 — Neofeminism: Religion of Despair: American Life League/*Pro-Life Activist's Encyclopedia. Eternal Word Television Network (n.d.) Retrieved from: http://www.ewtn.com/li brary/prolenc/encyc129.htm

don't kids need mothers and fathers? Who will take care of motherhood in the absence of the mother that denies her role of motherhood at equal footing with a man's responsibility to take care of his fatherhood role in society?

Dangerous separatist groups germinated to advance their sexual interest by infusing poison into the minds of susceptible women and systematically reducing them to their sexual experimentations. One of them is the SCUM,[50] which showed up to bolster women's hatred of men. The group not only was disturbed and offended by men's natural existence because it believed they were exclusively responsible for adverse social conditions but also wanted to exterminate them. Here are few citations to that effect.

"A small handful of SCUM can take over the country within a year by systematically fucking up the system, selectively destroying property, and murder." The manifesto further predicted, "SCUM will kill all men who are not in the Men's Auxiliary of SCUM. Men in the Men's Auxiliary are those men who are working diligently to eliminate themselves. . ."[51]

Radical feminist Valerie Solanas, the mastermind of SCUM was an educated writer who had many problems ranging from homelessness to prostitution. Valerie's utopian feminism as articulated in the SCUM manifesto strongly "encouraged male gendercide and the creation of an all-female society." Apart from the troublesome life style she was known to have had, Valerie, who tragically died at the age of 52, "April 26, 1988 in a welfare hotel in the

---

[46] Valerie Solanas IS THE ORIGINAL FOUNDER OF THE SCUM (Society for Cutting up Men)

[51] *Solanas, Valerie. SCUM Manifesto.* (n.d.) Retrieved from: http://www.womynkind.org/scum.htm

Tenderloin district of San Francisco"[52] was said to have been broke and lonely towards the end of her life and did not seem to have materially benefited from her brand of feminism. As far as applying her violent sexist ideology, there are good signs that Valerie tried to but did not seem to have been successful in effectively putting it together to the point of her satisfaction probably because of constant Police surveillance.

The question is whether feminists had at any point in the process reduced or tried to reduce the SCUM manifesto to practice.

Frankly, I have neither come across information or suggestions for killing and murdering dispatched from the central command of feminism, nor could I imagine it to go that far, but the issue is controversial depending on how one defines killing or murder. To me, breathing does not signify living unless it comes in a package with time and freedom because quality of life is a function of moments and space. Anyone that significantly kills a person's lifetime or freedom is therefore a killer of the person in question. In view of this, I consider all prisoners taken away for a long time as dead as those six feet under.

People may find this theory hard to swallow but how about the objective validity of a portion of SCUM's style of feminism in so far as practical experimentation is concerned! I mean when it comes to "fucking up the system" through child-support mechanism (where countless people have their family finances looted and put under penal supervision without breaking the law), dangerous laws, corrupting politicians and destabilizing families. How about "destroying property" in terms of abusing public funds and

---

[52]*About Valerie Solanas-Biography* (n.d.) Retrieved from: http://www.womynkind.org/valbio.htm

private funds (unjustified defense expenses and compensation from the accused)?

There is no question that child support is necessary in general. All divorcing mothers regardless of character are entitled to it in America and I believe this is one of the positive achievements of feminism for the sake of children. However, American style child support sometimes has little to do with fathers walking away from their children. Many fathers feel victimized by the system and I feel their pain from my heart. I don't think, however, that their situation is equally destructive to society as sending people to jail without proper cause because at least part of their input is invested in their children. In so saying, I must confess that I have not researched this area well enough to discuss it with authority and I apologize for my statement if it distresses somebody in a peculiar situation.

Apparently, feminist leaders are not only materially dependent on the number of true and false accusations of sexual violence but also on criminological statistics (number of criminal and innocent convicts per total number of accusations). The higher the ratio, the more justified their appeal for funds and the more stable their income. Therefore, their survival is directly proportional to the human and material destruction of society. After all, the money comes from the "male institution" (the government) and the lives come from the male gender, although society suffers at large when children are left unattended to end up in the streets on their own without education and hope for the future.

The provocative, irreverent, shallow-in-content but strategically deep and precarious teachings came one after another, displaying ferocious intentions against men and their families. Leaving the rest aside for reasons of brevity, the following quotations are examples of how the current law governing violence was to be influenced by feminist lobbies:

"And if the professional rapist is to be separated from the average dominant heterosexual [male], it may be mainly a quantitative difference." -- Susan Griffin "Rape: The All-American Crime"

"I claim that rape exists any time sexual intercourse occurs when it has not been initiated by the woman, out of her own genuine affection and desire." -- Robin Morgan, in 1974 [53]

"All men are rapists and that's all they are." Marilyn French, "The Women's Room"[54]

Then comes a feminist who according to an article[55] said, "I think that what women are conditioned socially to experience as love is a form of annihilation of self . . . Feminism stresses the inability to distinguish the difference between prostitution, marriage and sexual harassment. Compare victim's reports of rape with women's reports of sex. They look a lot alike... In this light the major distinction between intercourse (normal) and rape (abnormal) is that the normal happens so often that one cannot see anything wrong with it."[56]

Could a love-less life be the reason for one of the teachers not to self-annihilate? I do not know. What could have made women who loved heterosexual sex believe that

---

[53]*All Men Are Rapists*/Sex War (n.d.) Retrieved from: http://feministhate.tripod.com/id51.htm

[54]French, Marilyn. *The Women's Room*

[55]The Origins of Gender Roles and Sexual Identity, and the Implications for Deviant Behavior (August 5, 2003) Retrieved from: http://www.rationalmind.net/writing/49sex.html

[56]MacKinnon, Catharine. "Hard-Line Feminists Guilty of Ms.-Representation"/Wall Street Journal (November 7, 1991) page A14

intercourse was rape, and still enjoy the affair assuming they were raped? I have no idea.

I know, nonetheless, that all these messages greatly discouraged women from forming families through heterosexual relationships and strongly encouraged them to drift towards homosexuality. They inspired unethical hatred against men by motivating any woman displeased with a man to relate the tension directly to rape.

Finally, one hits home: "Men who are unjustly accused of rape can sometime[s] gain from the experience."[57]

I do not ascribe to such sadistic assumption even in my emotionally ridiculous state of mind. This is like saying women who had been raped can sometimes gain from the experience. I do not think any man can get away saying something like that about women without being crucified by feminists.

Human beings from time to time say things without thinking but in such issues of high social significance and human suffering, people need to be careful of what they say. They need to check their words if they can't keep quiet. Compassion asserts that men are living things who feel pain of injustice. For me to take a person seriously on the subject of rape, the person needs to take my false accusation induced trauma seriously just because fairness breads fairness and empathy is a two-way concept that requires impartial consistency.

Although she was right, in that I have transformed to a higher degree of awareness at the expense of tremendous pain, the way she approached my suffering defeats her purpose of defending victims of rape. But, I refuse to drop my ethics to that level of coldness in response to what she

---

[57]My Favourite Feminist Quotes/HERETICAL SEX (May 31, 2007) Retrieved from: http://hereticalsex.blogspot.com/2007/05/my-favourite-feminist-quotes.html

chose to do with her heart. Here I am lucky enough to survive it somehow without being the same person any more. My situation was terrible but it could have been worse considering most innocent men languishing in prison have absolutely no lifetime left to learn from their experiences. This doesn't take into account the people that have already been wasted as a result.

In view of the natural fragility of human beings and the time frame of life, the freedom of innocent convicts after serving time usually does not catch up with the effects of the injustice done upon them because they are permanently wounded.

One typical example in this regard is the sad story of a "Texan man Michael Anthony Green who has spent the last 27 years imprisoned for a rape he didn't commit"[58] I do not think Mr. Green appreciated the "education" he gained from the experience. Based on the comments of his attorney, "Green became too emotional and angry while waiting in a holding cell when he was brought in front of visiting state District Judge Mike Wilkinson . . . on the day he was to be freed for a crime he didn't commit, [he] became upset that he was put in handcuffs and leg restraints one final time as he was taken from the county jail to the courthouse. . ." Attorney Wicoff continues saying that "Green (who entered prison as 18 year old and set free as a 44-year old man) "was justified in his anger as his life had been taken away.

Would the comment of the feminist apply to the heartrendingly injured Donald Eugene Gates who served 28 years for the fabricated rape and murder of a young university student? Would it be fair for one to say that he had benefited in terms of education from the horrible experience that stole the best portion of his life? What is he

---

[58]Texas Man Walks Free After Serving 27 Years for Rape He Didn't Commit/Associated Press (July 30, 2010)

going to do with it considering his current age (about 60) and how much catching up he needs to do in society?

I refrain from emotionally reacting to something that hurts in order to satisfy my ego but there are some people who do. I mean people who can compromise their integrity to the extent of refusing to acknowledge the suffering of the poor student [Gates] in revenge to feminist coldness on the pain of innocent victims of deception. What are we trying to get from this confrontation? I challenge feminists to explain this situation from the angle of spirituality, fairness and academic civility.

The character had no problem admitting the existence of false accusers; but instead of tackling the problem by directly dealing with the source, she adds insult to injury by stopping at the victim's advantage level of the distress. Had the focus been on social welfare, the correct approach would have been towards punishing false accusers and redirecting resources towards assisting their victims because the damage is equal to that of true rape victims' except that the legal conspiracy further penalizes them for being offended. Unfortunately, this feminist's desire to punish innocent men for how other criminals live their lives is similar to the thought that kids must be punished for the crimes of their parents.

Evidently, some feminists have the tendency to ignore the similarity of men's sensitivity to pain and that of women's to the point of being enticed to experiment on men's pain intensity as if a chemist would experiment something on chemical compounds or a biologist on living things. To this cause and more, "Men have been silenced, threatened and abused. They have been slighted and dismissed by the law" because of "gender feminism" that aims at "not equality with men, but advantage over them," said Wendy McElroy[59] in one of her activities against bad feminism. In my understanding, she rejects the mythical propensity of women to think that they were "systematically discriminated against." At the bottom line of the problem, she believes in the notion that, "Men aren't taken seriously as victims of domestic violence and sex abuse. Divorce and family Courts are stacked against them. Health research for women's ailments outpaces research for men's illnesses in some areas. . ."

In the same article, Dianna Thompson[60] states that there exists, "bias against fathers in Court" and that "90 percent of custodial parents in divorced couples are women." Further, "Custodial mothers routinely deny fathers access to their children, and the men's only recourse is to pursue additional Court orders that could still be ignored."

Clearly, extremism emits extremism and what we see here is the result of genuine feminist struggle by all inclusive women turning anti-society at the end of the day by the opportunist clique that never cared for the cause of women beyond using it as stepping ground to its own material and power gain to begin with. They continue benefiting their greed knowing that false allegations hurt the cause of real victims. Can you imagine what an average person who went through false accusation can do as a juror in a real rape trial? Can you imagine a man or a woman who lost a father, a husband, a brother or a friend for false accusation of rape can do in the same position?

---

[59]Feminist Wendy McElroy is the founder and editor of IFeminists.com and an activist struggling with other feminists to redefine gender wars. Sexton, Steve. *Changing paradigm; A different sort of feminist fights for men's rights* /Washington Times A2 (July 18, 2003)

[60]Diana Thomson is the spokesperson for the American Coalition for Fathers and Children.

Karen Stephenson says, "Men are not the only victims of women who make false allegations. Women, who are the real victims of rape, are further victimized by those who make false accusations. Words and actions by a false accuser rob the real-life victims of rape of badly needed services. These women abuse police, prosecutors and victim group resources, taking time, money and resources away from those who truly need and deserve help."[61]

The success of feminism in achieving gender equality in America was the deadline to the relationship between real and fake feminists who were motivated to be part of the resistance by personal advantages. This is typical in most universally known struggles for justice because leadership after success is completely different from the time of struggle. There is no power in human nature without the possibility of abusing it at some points of its application. The question is how much power is necessary for leaders of any organization to run it at the executive branch of the structure, and how much power should society have to check and balance its policies. Feminism is power and it has to be scrutinized by women and society in order for the leaders not to change its fundamental focus at will.

Good women stand for justice consistent with what the end goal of feminism was supposed to be. They are not part of the group enjoying the material curse of feminist retreat but that of the disappointed group who struggled expecting to enjoy the spiritual advantages of gender equality. Their activism to regain the lost vision of feminism aims at safeguarding women's equality that every woman enjoys today through the hard fought struggle of yesterday.

---

[61]*False Allegations: Wrongful Accusations of Rape*/Abuse@suite101 (May 14, 2007) Retrieved from: http://www.suite101.com/content /false-allegations-a21219

By all accounts, the scuffle between true and false feminists in the absence of a meticulous approach can hurt an unintended group of society in the background. For example, the propensity of feminists to defend men's rights against affirmative action (a policy imposed by the lucrative sexual-harassment industry) as long as gender feminism continues to ridicule men, may sound good on the cover but it can sadly punish children at the tail of the effect. I have no suggestion as to how to handle this intricate challenge especially without unfavorable conditions to challenge gender feminism legally, but we need to refrain from approaching the matter emotionally and take extra care to avoid harmful social consequences.

As for Wendy McElroy's statement that, "NOW-style feminism is dead because it turned the sexes against each other in the workplace and in academia," I tend to differ a bit from that conclusion. It looks to me like NOW has no problem getting away with contradictions as usual, although I sometimes wonder how long it would survive with the convention. The way things are today, nothing will happen to NOW and it is here to stay, at least for a while. Nor did its style expire because genuine feminism is not assertive enough to change the situation as yet, although there are a significant number of young women against gender feminism in today's America.

Not only is NOW alive today but so is its flirtation with powerful men. Doug Powers writes the following statement: "Jerry Brown[62] announced he has received the endorsement

---

[62]"Brown was sworn in for his third term as governor on January 3, 2011, succeeding Republican Arnold Schwarzenegger. He will be up for re-election in 2014. Brown is working on a budget that would shift many government programs from the state to the local level, a reversal of trends from his first tenure as governor"

of the National Organization for Women, less than 24 hours after the emergence of a recorded message in which Brown can be heard in a conversation with advisors in which someone calls Whitman[63] a 'whore.'"[64]

In this controversy, the article states, "NOW prez Terry O'Neill" clarified her earlier statement as, "We are not saying anyone on the Brown campaign be fired," O'Neill said. "What I should have made clear was that anyone who says the 'W' word from here on should be fired."

This statement of course raises a question whether the word was allowed any time before the election for governor of California was conducted since 2010. Whatever the situation might have been NOW has one more time stopped a woman (besides Hillary Clinton) from taking a powerful position in society in favor of a politician whose circle identifies a female political opponent as a "whore."

What bad feminists are doing today is taking advantage of the notion that repairing a misdirected cause after victory is more difficult than fighting for the cause before victory because the struggle naturally consumes most of the available energy stored in genuine activism. This is the

---

Jerry Brown/Wikipedia (n.d.) Retrieved from: http://en.wikipedia.org/wiki/Jerry_Brown

[63]"Meg Whitman is a pro-choice woman who was ranked among the world's most accomplished women in business." She was running to become the first woman governor in California's history." *Jerry Brown Associate Calling Meg Whitman 'Whore' Has Effect on NOW Endorsement*/Michelle

Malkin (October 9, 2010 09:56 AM) Retrieved_from: http://michellemalkin.com/2010/10/09/jerry-brown-associate/

[64]*Jerry Brown Associate Calling Meg Whitman 'Whore' Has Effect on NOW Endorsement*/Michelle Malkin (October 9, 2010 09:56 AM) Retrieved from: http://michellemalkin.com/2010/10/09/jerry-brown-associate/

common fate of activists in many different scenarios from Cuba to Vietnam, China to North Korea, and Eritrea to Mozambique and more. In my own experience, I do not have the energy to actively monitor some problems associated with the outcome of the Eritrean struggle needless to state that I don't have the time and the interest to participate in Eritrean issues at the same level of intensity as before the Eritrean independence although my attitude can change depending on the situation. The struggle had already taken its toll on me to watch passively what is happening from distance. I can no longer trust any other group that claims to fix the problem without popular mandate either because I do not want to see the current situation happening again in beautiful Eritrea.

Whether we like it or not, the momentum of struggle decays in time and stays dormant for years before it starts to impact society by new generations once is betrayed. That is why opportunists ignore older activists and concentrate on cultivating new followers from new generations.

NOW is so comfortable with this unavoidable ambiance, it has taken society and especially women for granted to the extent that it no longer has to be diplomatic to exercise its hypocrisy, at least until the time arrives for its total down fall. Unfortunately, by then time catches up with everybody and people pass away without getting a break. A reason in point is its position on powerful men's questionable sexual behavior with women. In Clinton's saga for instance, the organization defended him saying that "While President Clinton's record for women's rights is less than perfect, on balance women have had an ally in the White House." Further, "As feminist leaders, we will not stand idly by while a Congress made up of nearly 90 percent men attempts to remove the first president elected by women voters."[65]

This position officially gives the White House clearance from the criminal zone of feminism in "respect of the cause" as long as it is under the Democratic Party. This is just turning 180 degrees from its original principle in one exceptional case for political reasons "advantageous to women." It betrays the question of women for a splash of experience in the process of taking one step backward in order to leap forward twice, still "for the cause of women" in America.

Ironically, NOW is a highly delicate organization responsible for creating havoc in society. It was responsible for extending the meaning of sexual harassment and rape beyond reason into almost all branches of relationship between men and women. It was the front-runner in the infinite definition of trauma and implementation of the inhuman Rape Shield Law, which is accountable for throwing people to prison for just one alleged mistake, proven or not. This is an organization that renders children fatherless and mothers helpless and it still had the courage to declare the presence of an ally in the White House who almost turned the place into a private sexual enterprise!

NOW couldn't have been more fearless than it came about breaching the cause of women in defense of the president, whose multiple accusations pressurized men of power in the congress to consider impeaching him from his post. In other words, the congressional representatives showed more sympathy to the "victims" of sexual harassment than feminism itself. NOW did not stop there

---

[65]Women Leaders Take Action To Stop Impeachment, Warn What's At Stake For Women And Who's on Third to Succeed/Now (September 24, 1998) Retrieved from: http://www.now.org/press/09-98/09-24b98.html

but rather took the matter further by directly attempting to save the man from losing his job because of the allegations. It could not have expressed its revisionism better than the way it did in blatant and direct style of communication without any diplomatic effort to cover up its contradiction.

There is no doubt that NOW took a big risk of losing its credibility on women's issues but got away with it. It self-destructed to the point of extinction as a karmic consequence of its endless sins of injustice in the past without any detrimental impedance. The question was if it could rebound back to its old form or if it was destined to remain out of sync in principle with good feminism. These questions will remain for a long time to come.

The way I look at it, rebounding is unimaginable by the leaders who are benefiting materially and psychologically from the current situation. Why should they change now after they infringe the fine lines of fairness for this goal? I do believe though, that it cannot continue like this forever. Something will have to take place before the crisis backfires on the coming generations of women.

In so coming forward, I fully acknowledge NOW's positive role in general. The success of feminism is a byproduct of cumulative effort by all feminist groups and I do not want to be misunderstood. Whether you think I am biased or deceived about how my unconscious mind is affecting my judgment, I would give President Clinton the benefit of the doubt in my current state of awareness. This position synchronizes with what had been of feminism's at the time of the crisis but emphatically for different reasons. It is in fact partially a product of feminism's inconsistencies and endless definitions of rape. I am literally confused about what exactly it is leave alone to accuse a person without clear-cut evidence with all respect to his accusers.

The Convoluted Meaning of Rape and Women's Burden of Struggle

According to my experience and research, consensual sex is not punishable by law but becomes a crime if reported as rape, because the very nature of sex involves force. For a man to penetrate a woman he must apply pressure and for a woman to accommodate penetration, she must resist. This is simply the scientific law of intercourse. Regrettably, any pressure no matter what level can be interpreted as "rape" and any level of resistance to penetration as "a woman's reaction to rape" depending on the mood of bad feminism.

In a debate-based article,[66] independent Scholar, Warren Farrell states, "the very concept of 'rape' has become so muddled and mystified that college students and administrators are no longer sure what the term means." He then asks, "If the female decides afterwards that she really didn't want to have sex, was she raped?" My answer is yes according to feminism's twisted definition of rape and the government's hunger to waste people by means of prejudice, especially if the woman in question reports it to the Police.

"The area where contemporary feminism has suffered the most self-inflicted damage is rape. What began as a useful sensitization of Police Officers, prosecutors, and judges to the claims of authentic rape victims turned into a hallucinatory overextension of the definition of rape to cover every unpleasant or embarrassing sexual encounter", adds Camille Paglia.[67]

---

[66]*Does Feminism Discriminate against Men?* Reviewed for H-Histsex by John Lauritsen Retrieved from: http://paganpressbooks.com/jpl/FARRELL.HTM

[67]"Camille Anna Paglia (born April 2, 1947) is an US author, teacher, and social critic. A self-described dissident feminist Paglia

To this projection, here are facts on the ground.

"All sex, even consensual sex between a married couple, is an act of violence perpetrated against a woman."[68]

"In a patriarchal society, all heterosexual intercourse is rape because women, as a group, are not strong enough to give meaningful consent."[69]

There is no doubt in my mind that they had a point based on the existence of violent and oppressive marriages and relationships, although it is time for them to stop hallucinating and philosophizing for the sake of image and go to work in parts of the planet where women are helplessly crying for justice.

I can relate to the frustration-driven emotional discharge of feminism in the past. I do justify women's reaction to their oppression for all practical reasons and to some extent, excuse whatever they said in the era of inequality but my tolerance is not open ended. It is rather a time sensitive matter that does not apply after reasonable gender equality is practically crystallized in society.

Analyzing the global history of human struggle for justice helps me to observe the extraordinary feminist uprising neutrally.

(pronounced with a silent "g") has been a Professor at The University of the Arts in Philadelphia, Pennsylvania since 1984. She also writes articles on art, popular culture, feminism, and politics for mainstream newspapers and magazines." *Camille Anna Paglia*/eNotes (n.d.) Ret rieved from: http://www.enotes.com/topic/Camille_Paglia

[68]Catherine MacKinnon according to Feminism and Sex [It has been reported that she denies saying this.]

[69]MacKinnon, Catherine. Feminism and Sex in; Professing Feminism: Cautionary Tales from the Strange World of Women's Studies, p. 129. Retrieved from: http://deltabravo.net/custody/quotes.php

The question of women without a doubt instigated a genuine struggle for equality as that of Afro-Americans' and Third World people's, respectively against slavery and colonialism. Inequality, slavery and colonialism obviously disgraced humankind and created division based on sex, color, and economic exploitation. It was natural for gender oppression to install hatred of men on women as much as slavery, racism and colonialism made colored people of the world resentful of white people; the all-inclusive nature of the correlated negative emotions being regrettable and unfair to good members of society (men, white people, etc.).

Oppressed women manifested resistance in terms of *feminism*, dehumanized Afro-Americans in terms of *Black Power*, and colonized Africans in terms of *Pan-Africanism*. Of course, the analysis does not cover global conditions of the subject matter, specifically what went on in Central and South America and Asia; needless to say the dark history of mankind in the German/Jewish experience and black against black ethnocentric violence in Africa and especially in Rwanda, to say the least. It, however, reflects a subset of the domain to which anyone can universally relate. It goes without saying that extremism is the emotional result of injustice.

Undeniably, women had to fight gender inequality at the second priority level of their struggle for all-inclusive freedom with some of their culturally programmed enemies (men). To this reality, a prominent activist declares that, "The feminist movement is the most important revolution that has ever occurred on earth."[70] I agree, because it was impossible for women to stop activism at the resolution level of a given problem in society, be it colonialism, racism or other forms of injustice. It could have been a complete

---

[70]French, Marilyn. *From Eve to Dawn: A History of Women*/McArthur and Company

journey for men at least sociologically speaking, but only half way in the road for women, the remaining half being the struggle for equality. Women slaves for example had to fight slavery with their men until the end of it before picking up the steam against male chauvinism in their communities. So was the situation of all other women in any other social scenarios. Maintaining this tactical relationship for common cause with their oppressors must have been difficult and exhausting. The feminist outburst, no matter how atrocious, was therefore as legitimate a reaction as those in any other injustice driven human relationships.

In view of the fact that the initial stages of any genuine struggle usually carry significant emotional flavor, I tend to justify the following explosive statement of an angry feminist: "My feelings about men are the result of my experience. I have little sympathy for them. Like a Jew just released from Dachau, I watch the handsome young Nazi soldier fall writhing to the ground with a bullet in his stomach and I look briefly and walk on. I don't even need to shrug. I simply don't care. What he was, as a person, I mean, what his shames and yearnings were, simply don't matter."[71]

I, nevertheless, resent the statement a bit because I wish women had it smooth with men throughout for such a feeling against the entire male gender never to have surfaced. Unfortunately, the damage against them was done by some negative men and the feelings already expressed. The effect of her words on her listeners and its compounded consequence on all of us is hard to discount considering the

---

[71]French, Marilyn *The Women's Room*/Ballantine Books (September 12, 1988)

success of the book, which sold 21 million copies around the world after its exposure to public in 1977.[72]

Feminism's Brutality against Society

All benefits of skepticism and empathy given, the emotional feedback of oppressed people in general appears to have faded away because of change, reason and forgiveness. The oppressed seem to modulate their anger by accepting equality and choosing to coexist peacefully with their former oppressors. Cases in point include Afro-Americans in relation to white Americans, South Africans in relation to Afrikaners, Native Americans and Australian Habergeons with their invaders and Jewish people vis-à-vis the Germans.

What makes feminism different is its refusal to accept pleasant coexistence after achieving victory, its insistence on vengeance by going to the extreme and keeping on biting beyond its fair share. What is terrible is its persistence on the initial categorical attack against men long after significant time in the struggle had already produced tangible results.

At the end of the day, the dominant extremist wing went for oppression reversal. Not only did it not stop even after achieving special status in society, but it also fell short of advancing women's sexual and other natural interests. It continued philosophizing on the simple and direct agenda as if it were NASA space research and arrived at the devastating position into which it gradually developed. The absence of social challenge from the onset of the insanity finally gave it an uncontrolled upper hand to abuse salvation for retribution. Lunatic as it may sound like, the Justice

---

[72] Showalter, Elaine. *Post-feminist Heroine/* The Washington Post (September 29, 2009)

System today lamentably practices the mad woman's social theory like an exact science without the slight consideration of counter issues. As a result, men can no longer defend themselves based on equal footing.

One of the results of this brutality is the humanly inconceivable Rape Shield Law, sometimes referred as "feminist jurisdiction" by some law experts, which came to active existence in the 1970s. As its name implies, it completely shields accusers and totally exposes the accused. A keen observer puts it, as "the double standard of rape-shield law is crippling weapon they use against men to shield a woman's sexual past from being used against her in Court. No law shields a man's sexual past from being used against him in Court. . . . Regardless of the intention of these laws, they violate due process and thus prevent a man from receiving a fair trial."[66]

Whether the excuse behind the law was justified, and still whether its negative effects were incidental or accidental; its application has been disallowing juries from hearing strong evidences relevant to the moral status of accusers. Most Americans are said to agree that a woman's past sexual life should be immaterial in a rape case. I agree too, in clear-cut cases involving unquestionable physical damage and murder but little do they know about the effect of shielding an accuser's history of multiple rape accusations in the past or hiding important information from the Jury on the fate of the accused. No one wants to be in that position. But, as we stand today, assertive feminist lobbies in courts and legislatures have since the 1970s succeeded in redefining rape to be interchangeable with consensual sex.

From James Anderson's conviction of rape in Oregon in 1989 to Charles Steadman's 1993 conviction of rape in Wisconsin, from the falsely convicted Texans recently released through DNA based nullification after serving 27 years (Michael Anthony Green) and 14 years (Ronald Gene Taylor) to William McCaffery's fate in New York prison and far beyond to countless victims of injustice across the country, America is suffering today from the mismatch between the society's capacity to free the victims of false accusation of rape and the system's relatively faster rate of incarcerating innocent victims of the crime.

The Rape Shield Law affects all types of men including the famous and rich. What happened to Marv Albert[73] was a classic example. This man was conditioned to plead guilty to the sexual assault accusation by his then girlfriend after the law disallowed him to use his accuser's habitually hostile and merciless actions against men who broke relationships with her (Albert was about to marry another woman). This was probably based on "remoteness"; the time elapsed since the relationships ended, though I do not think this excuse exists any longer. He was also not allowed to use the testimony of a former boyfriend who claimed that the allegedly improper act (Assault and battery charge) brought for argument at Court was the accuser's acceptable act of sex in view of her style of sex practice with men (her interest in rough sex.)

One of the classically countless cases of discrimination against men in today's sexist America was applied against a Columbia University doctoral candidate Oliver Jovanovic who first met his accuser on the internet, where they engaged in intense sexual discussions within a certain period of time. According to Wikipedia, the free encyclopedia, the accuser had clearly expressed interest in sadomasochistic sexual practices to Jovanovic through e-mails. "In one such message she describes herself as a "pushy bottom" (a submissive person who pushes the

---

[73]A legendary American sportscaster who lost everything he built in life because of Rape Shield Law.

dominant partner to inflict greater pain) and in another as the slave of her sadomasochistic boyfriend."

Then they met by their own free choice to experience their common sexual fantasies in person. After their meeting, "Oliver Jovanovic was accused in NY of sadomasochistic torture of Jamie Rzucek in 1996."[74]

There is one solution to a situation like this where different versions of an event appear in Court should we be talking about justice and that is to treat the versions equally. In this case, however, the opposite was done. The defense lawyers were set to show evidence to the theory that the accuser had indeed expressed the desire to engage in sadomasochistic sex with the accused. As direct as the matter had been, what they had in mind when they told the Jury in the opening statement of the trial was her own e-mails sent to the accused through the Internet. This happened to be the only defense for the accused in view of the accuser's testimony under oath that, "she never gave Jovanovic any indication that she was interested in sadomasochism; a claim his lawyers believe is contradicted by the email record."[75] Anything less should have been unjust.

Unfortunately for Jovanovic, continues the article, "the Jury never got to read the most damaging email messages. Manhattan Supreme Court Justice William Wetzel ruled

---

[74]*People v. Jovanovic*/Wikipedia (n.d.) Retrieved from: http://en.wikipedia.org/wiki/People_v._Jovanovic

[75]*How blind should justice be?*/Equity Feminism (April 14, 2000) Retrieved from: http://www.equityfeminism.com/articles/2000/how-blind-should-justice-be/ "The extraordinarily bizarre trial and conviction of a man accused of raping a woman he met over the Internet may prompt a much needed reevaluation of Rape Shield Laws."

almost 20 percent of the email correspondence between the two inadmissible under New York's Rape Shield laws."[75]

The integrity of the evidence could hardly stay the same without its most important contents to the issue on the platform. I just cannot understand why the Court had to go through this childish pretension of integrity when it could have better served justice by trashing the entire evidence to begin with. I do not blame Justice Wetzel as he only did what he had to do according to the law but my immediate reaction to this joke on human life was a depressing smile.

The defense team in the situation might have been forced to work with what was left in the evidence, which was no more, just out of desperation to prove that there at least was contact between the two people prior to their meeting: that they met by agreement and were not strangers. But, I believe this move was as dangerous as facing the trial without, as if the parties never had any contact prior to their meeting. I do not even know if this was possible in view of the strong tendency the opportunity had given the prosecution team to expose the existence of pre-meeting contact, since the so called evidence would by then perfectly serve its interest of convicting the man on the stand. Because the absence of the most relevant defense element in the disintegrated e-mails would imply that, there was no pre-meeting agreement to the type of sex, by the two individuals who consensually or forcefully performed in the occasion, though their meeting was previously agreed upon.

Even worse was the compromised integrity of the defense, in view of the Jury as a result of promising to present material evidence to the mutual agreement of the sexual act in question (but failing to come up with it because of the Rape Shield Law) that was probably applied at a point after the opening speeches (which the Jury would not know). I cannot see any other possibility for the Jury than considering the defense team deceptive and unreliable, a situation that would negatively polarize its judgment. My verdict as a Juror would most probably be against the defendant only for this reason let alone with the other terrible things that took place in the trial against the poor defendant, which I choose not to discuss here.

Either way, the defendant had no chance of survival. "After a Jury trial during which the woman testified for six days, Jovanovic was convicted and sentenced to 15 years to life for kidnapping, sexual abuse and assault. Shortly before the Jury's verdict, Jovanovic had refused a plea bargain offered by the prosecution. Jovanovic served 20 months in prison during which a fellow prisoner harmed [him] in his neck area."[76] This was a lot better than the 15 years sentence he received (despite the fact that he could have lost his life) before the Appeals Court ruled "that the Rape Shield Law had been improperly applied by the judge in charge of the case" and he was "released in December 1999" after having expended about "$500,000 in legal fees."[77]

The sad story of this man brings an important issue to the table. People who go to prison in general must explain their reasons for arrival and each convict is treated according to the crime he committed either in organized manner or not. To my information from quite a few former prisoners, people accused of rape crimes most likely suffer humiliating punishment from the Prison Justice system within the prisoner-community. The physical attack directed to Jovanovic could have been because of this reality needless to state that he could have faced problems that are

---

[76]*People v. Jovanovic*/Wikipedia, the free encyclopedia (n.d.) Retrieved from: http://en.wikipedia.org/wiki/People_v._Jovanovic
[77]*Excluded evidence: The dark side of rape shield laws*/reason.com (February 2002) Retrieved from: http://reason.com/archives/2002/02/01/excluded-evidence

more serious had he continued to be a prisoner in his unfortunate experience.

It seems like when a given civilization reaches its peak, it tends to recycle its experience, meaning that it changes direction towards its origins, which is basically barbarism. Physics predicts this law of nature on objects reduced to momentum due to vertical motion in the atmospheric pressure that ends up moving down to the opposite direction because of gravity. However, I wonder what would express social degeneration to this level of nonsense by deliberate choice of a government that runs a country with probably the longest history of democracy and a remarkable bill of rights.[78]

To my further surprise, my research says that judges used to allow defense lawyers to cross examine women about their past sexual experiences and question them about their sexual partners. Judges also used to instruct juries, "to take into account the lack of a woman's chastity[79]

---

[78]"The Bill of Rights is the collective name for the first ten amendments to the United States Constitution which limit the power of the U.S. federal government. These limitations serve to protect the natural rights of liberty and property including freedoms of religion, speech, a free press, free assembly, and free association, as well as the right to keep and bear arms. They were introduced by James Madison to the 1st United States Congress in 1789 as a series of legislative articles and came into effect as Constitutional Amendments on December 15, 1791, through the process of ratification by three-fourths of the States." United States Bill of Rights/Wikipedia (n.d.) Retrieved from: http://en.wikipedia.org/wiki/United_States_Bill_of_Rights

[79]"As defined by Wikipedia, the free encyclopedia, Chastity is sexual behavior of a man or a woman acceptable to the ethical norms and guidelines of a culture, civilization, or religion."

when deciding on her credibility."[80] They can no longer do this in America.

Although justice was served in the end, the Appeals Court came a little too late in this case, after permanent damage had been inflicted on Jovanovic materially, physically and psychologically. There was nothing wrong with the development. It was only a corrective step that allowed him to use clear evidence for his defense and to reverse the injustice done against him. Yet, feminists were outraged against the process because they saw it as discrimination against women.

After securing his release, he became "the plaintiff in a lawsuit in federal court. He alleges that a police Officer and an assistant district attorney, while acting in their official capacities, fabricated evidence, gave false testimony, and made damaging extrajudicial statements to the press in an effort to secure a conviction against him."[81]

Apparently, this tragedy is so gross that it has attracted attention from the high caliber academic community throughout the country. Colleges and Universities are worried about the problem and it is influencing the traditional socio-political approach of American scholars negatively. The situation is draining academic resources and brain potential that could have been directed to other socio-political creativities.

Chastity/Wikipedia (n.d.) Retrieved from: http://en.wikipedia.org/w iki/Chastity

[80]*How blind should justice be?*/EquityFeminism (April 14, 2000) Retrieved from: http://www.equityfeminism.com/articles /2000/how-blind-should-justice-be/

[81]*A Case in Point - How Framed Defendants Fight Back - Jovanovic v. City of New York*/LIESTOPPERS (Wednesday, September 06, 2006) Retrieved from: http://liestoppers.blogspot.com/2006/09/ca se-in-point-how-framed-defendants.html

Here is the reason: The problem is not something that only affects people in certain social categories such as homelessness or drug addiction, where scholars remotely research on from their safe grounds. It threatens everybody one way or another because a man's life has legally become vulnerable for random attack by any woman at will. It can happen anytime and anywhere. Men aware of the situation are living with this apprehension and uncertainty in the backdrop. This psychic trauma is breaking down the confidence of men to relate and produce. It is attacking the society at the nucleus level of its composition because the fundamental right of Americans to live freely and safely in their country is at stake. Scholars used to research on the subject matter from academic point of view. Today they also do it from the angle of personal freedom and security.

Columbia University law professor George Fletcher states that, "It is important to defend the interests of women as victims, but not to go so far as to accord women complaining of rape a presumption of honesty and objectivity."[82]

In this criminal law, "reputation and opinion evidence of the victim's past sexual behavior" is not admissible under "KRE 412 a."[83] This proscription means that no witness may testify in a rape case about a victim's morally abhorrent conduct including some of the victim's recorded violations of law. To play with words on the very essence of such crimes, evidence of past sexual behavior may be admitted

---

[82]*WHO SAYS WOMEN NEVER LIE ABOUT RAPE?/* Salon Newsreal (May 10, 1999) Retrieved from: http://www.salon.com/news/1999/03/cov_10news3.html

[83]Kentucky Rules of Evidence: Article IV. *Relevancy and Related Subjects KRE 412 Rape and Similar Cases; Admissibility of Victim's Character and Behavior* (7/01/2003) Retrieved from: http://www.kybar.org/documents/kre/kre_412.pdf

only if the Court finds it relevant: in the condition "that the probative value of such evidence outweighs the danger of unfair prejudice," according to the phrasing of "KRE 412."[84]

I see bias against men here in that the condition does not consider the possibility of said unfair prejudice against the accused because of unlimited application of their history in trials the way the law secures this for women. At the most immediate level of the damage, a defendant has the burden of proving the significance of the evidence in relation to its detrimental effect on the plaintiff's behavior.

How is it possible for an accused to do this? This is not something that can be mathematically proven and *any evidence* is highly important for the life of the accused and impartiality of trials. Isn't fairness impossible without the probability of prejudice, taking into account that it demands absolute exposure of facts on the ground, which could somehow affect the two opposing sides in question? Nobody even knows yet if the evidence in question can save the man from conviction! The law indirectly acknowledges that women are more valuable than men and this paradox practically exchanges life for reputation. The law qualitatively changed the comparative elements of the equation from man vs. woman to man's life vs. woman's image. America is pushing men to the level of humiliation where they must legally prove that theirs lives were as equally valuable as the reputation of their accusers.

Under this law, a perpetrator can be prosecuted for sexual assault without witnesses to the attack or any relevant physical evidence so long as the "victim" says it took place. It appears to be based on the fallacious reasoning that there is absolutely no chance for a woman to

---

[84]Notes to Rule 412/Cornell University Law School (n.d.) Retrieved_from:_http://www.law.cornell.edu/rules/fre/ACRule412.htm

be wrong when it comes to reporting violence. I think this ridiculous position applies only to sexual violence related cases.

The scope of legal terrorism concerning the number of innocent people convicted because of the charge has reached a critical proportion. Because of an alarming degree of distortions and misinterpretations, America today is at war with itself. Behavioral patterns and highly relevant evidences that can protect the accused are no longer allowed.

The suffocating Shield Law was introduced to the Justice System because of political greed and powerful feminist lobbies under the pretext of encouraging victims to come forward without the risk of being exposed; but it highly jeopardizes the accused by disarming their defense. I equate this violent and partial law to apartheid laws in old South Africa.

My confusion is how in the world we arrived at this point! Did we complicate the concept of civilization by philosophizing beyond the necessary?

I do not know the complete answer to my confusion but I wonder if there is any other country on the planet, with the probable exception of Canada and Sweden that does the business of justice the way we do in America. I am not yet sure about the Australian and the rest of European experience in this regard but I did not find them to be as irrational in my limited research so far. I am, however, certain that no Third World country on this planet practices pretentious justice by disintegrating evidence, although most of them practice injustice more aggressively and openly. The e-mails in Oliver Jovanovic's saga would either have been completely accepted or rejected and there would be no nonsense, such as accepting only a portion of evidence in any underdeveloped country that I have so far researched: it is either 100% or none of it, meaning that they either give you justice or deny it to you. They do not have the time and judicial grounds for Rape Shield Law because it is ridiculous.

I do not like to be exposed to both situations (pretentious justice and clear cut injustice) but I happen to be one that prefers to be a victim of full-fledged injustice than phony justice if you can guess what I mean; I would rather be a Slave than a Buffalo Soldier.

Although, I came to this heaven called America because of injustice in Africa, I certainly did not expect this. Of course, I am lucky to be an American for many other aspects of justice and I care about this society very much. I love all Americans equally without bias and I know it is special to be an American. America has blessed me with so many things I do not even know where to start. We Americans self-express without inhibition better than any other people in any other societies. We are innovative, fast, versatile and tolerant of each other. We do respect individual freedom and opinion differences on individual basis and we defy dictation more effectively than any other people in the world. We are beautiful and powerful as well. We have one of the most advanced justice systems in the world. But, I can bet anything that no men in any part of the world have been taken for a ride by feminism the way American men have. We did not only surrender gender supremacy but also lost gender equality.

The Significance of Rape Shield Law to the Concept of Gender Equality in America

By all accounts of logic, the Rape Shield Law is proof to the fact that women have achieved gender equality in America. Let me explain why I think this way. The National Organization for Women (NOW), for example, came in to existence in 1966 with the sole purpose of achieving gender equality. Historically, this organization is one of the feminist groups that fought hardest for the implementation of the Equal Rights Amendment (ERA).[85]

In ERA's own phrasing, "equality of rights under the law shall not be denied or abridged by the United States or any state on account of sex." Although ERA might not have been ratified based on the same source of information, the fact that NOW and other feminist groups fought for its ratification in the past was because women did not have equal rights to men and it was necessary to make themselves equal by law through clear amendments such as this.

The struggle of women for equality finally succeeded because of relentless effort by genuine feminists from both sexes. The Feminist movement continued to hammer out the details and did a good job of securing the most important if not all rights conceivable for women in society.

Feminism could not have stayed in its original form after this success. It naturally had to go through ups and downs, divisions etc. Some of its members had to leave while the fittest survivors of the movement stayed behind to lead under different conditions, which radicalized the concept of rape by amending the law and even by creating new laws.

The Rape Shield Law happened to be the product of feminism's hard push to one side of the pendulum, probably because they thought there was nothing left to do for survival after the success of the ERA: that the door was closed to making a living both materially and psychologically in the name of the struggle for equality.

Upper hand as a subject is not feasible in any society without equal opportunity; for equality is the medium

---

[85]*Feminism*/Wikipedia, the free encyclopedia; (n.d.) Retrieved from; http://en.wikipedia.org/wiki/Feminism

between under dog and upper hand. The oppressed must guarantee equality first before aiming at oppressing others because equality is the prerequisite to oppression. Discriminatory laws in general and the Rape Shield Law in particular could, therefore never have existed without the substantial liberation of women. It would have been procedurally and conditionally impossible to implement without it. This is analogous to saying that black people could not possibly have struggled for their voting rights before the legal end of slavery or Hillary Clinton could not have run for president before her right to vote like any other citizen was legally realized.

During my trial, they investigated my relationships with female employees at work, after they exhausted my history and had my fingerprints nationally examined through their network of computers. On the other hand, they blocked me from using most of Hazen's recorded criminal counts and closest acquaintances that had experienced her offenses at the trial.

I shared the experience with an associate at work and he told me that it had been some time since he started to leave his office door open any time a woman co-worker entered to visit. This is what we Americans have finally ended up to be.

The Infinite Rape Trauma Syndrome and the Complicated Definition of Rape

Rape leaves its victims traumatized forever. No matter how closely we approximate their situation, men who have never been raped, including me, cannot truly experience their pain. It is similar to the difficulty of white people to feel the real sensations of racism no matter how sincere they might be, simply because theory and practice are two different things. Can you imagine what a victim of rape goes through? Someone is penetrating into your body by force and possibly ejaculating inside you, in a true rape situation. If this humiliation is not traumatizing, nothing is.

Considering that people sometimes react to things differently, I assume the traumatic effects of rape should also differ from person to person depending on ethical, physical and psychological factors beyond my focus to explain. Aside the hypothesis of physics that everything in nature was finite with the controversial exception of space, feminism's Rape Trauma Syndrome, leaves reality behind for hallucination. Everything an accuser does may be considered as a logical feedback of a rape victim. If she recollects memory and admits her assailant-identification was a mistake, a rape trauma expert may be used to testify that the denial was consistent with typical behavior of a rape victim. The original story may stand valid based on the argument that victims change their minds for many reasons. This may be true in some circumstances but not in all circumstances.

To my understanding, there is no room to readjust or to correct false accusations in the American Justice System. Any type of feeling can be boundlessly correlated to the trauma because the subject matter is not a definite science that can be precisely proven. It is simply at the mercy of an expert's mouth. In a nutshell, an accuser is irrelevant once the government accepts the case and feminists take control of the show. She (the accuser) cannot reverse her claim no matter what.

Is it practical for a woman to pardon her rapist after she reports the violence to the Police? Anything is possible to a certain degree but I seriously doubt it. Is there any possibility for an accuser to have over-reacted in a momentary bout of anger? Not according to feminists. The list of emotions associated with such crimes covers almost all fundamental human reactions one can imagine.[86]

This approach contradicts the "equality" the movement claims to have been fighting for, and in fact nullifies it. It also undermines women's natural intelligence, their capacity to express true feelings and of course their humanness at large.

Further, prosecutors may have the freedom to multiply a single rape into multiple rape counts. My source of information puts the situation this way: "More disturbing is the prosecutor's ability to turn a single alleged rape into numerous counts because different sexual acts during one encounter can now be considered separate crimes. For example the "falsely convicted" could be sentenced to two years for intercourse, two years for rape with a foreign object (i.e. a finger), and two years for sodomy if the Jury finds the defendant guilty. If the complainant alleges that the accused stopped the rape and then started over, each new act becomes an additional count. Extreme sentences of 18 years or more years have become commonplace as a result of these changes."[87]

I have no problem with this type of proceeding of our Justice System in respect to fair trials but I am more than worried about the safety of people in general in the existing setup.

The deeper I get into the matter the more bothered I become. I do not even know where to stop as far as the extent of injustice in today's America is concerned. I am a fairly well educated person and used to think of myself as a well-informed individual about the social affairs of the

---

[86]Clancy, Atosha. *Rape Trauma Syndrome/*Clinical Med Au (n.d.) Retrieved from: http://216.55.99.51/clinical/psychiatry/rts.html
[87]*RAPE CASES/*falselyaccused.net (n.d.) Retrieved from: http://www.falsely-accused.net/rapecases.html

United States. Unfortunately, I cannot believe how ignorant I have been about many things in this country. I would never have been exposed to the realities of the System and the meticulous workings of feminism without going through the excruciating experience of false accusation. Even with that and the amount of material I have worked on and come across since 1998, I find myself far behind where I should be.

There is no doubt that American moral values, the essence of freedom and equality have been fundamentally compromised. Today we have a country that imprisons innocent people and allows immoral pedophiles like Phillip Ray Greaves[88] to benefit from destructive books in the name of freedom of speech. Paul Elam, in *On Jury Nullification and Rape* teaches that, "With the epidemic of false rape reports, poor and sometimes corrupt police work, prosecutors blind with power and ambition, and an unconscionable but successful feminist campaign to define rape in the most ludicrous terms possible, we have created a monstrous system of abject injustice, with rights of the accused routinely ground to dust in the name of convictions, and to our national disgrace, in the name of sexual politics."[89]

So much damage has been done already without the mental attendance of ordinary Americans, that I cannot suggest anything as to what should be done to resolve the extremely complex problem. Honestly speaking, it may be too late to fix it.

In *Rape Trauma Syndrome*, the author states that "rape is an easy allegation to make but one that is hard to disprove. In fact, the biggest threat of being falsely accused

---

[88]The author of The Pedophile's Guide to Love and Pleasure: a Child-lover's Code of Conduct

[89]*On Jury Nullification and Rape*/antimisandry.org (August 1, 2010) Retrieved from: http://antimisandry.org/?p=1080

of a crime was that of being accused of rape."[87] This reality used to be considered in the past by the Courts and the judges had the freedom to "inform members of the Jury that such allegations were easy to make by the complainant but difficult for the defendant to disprove. Today, this Jury instruction is no longer allowed to be given as a result of changes in the law, changes that also mandate giving a very different set of instructions. . . . The judge now informs the Jury that 1) an allegation of rape does not require any evidence of corroboration; 2) there is no requirement for medical evidence; 3) there is no requirement for DNA evidence; and 4) there is no requirement for a second witness. In short, there is no requirement for obtaining a conviction other than the bare allegation made by a complainant. Even the manner in which the Jury is selected is tainted with this attitude that evidence does not matter. Prosecutors can demand that during the selection process, each perspective juror must agree that he/she would not require corroboration of a crime. If the juror disagrees with this demand, he/she can be excused."[87]

To this theory, former Boston sex-crimes prosecutor Rikki Klieman says that "People can be charged with virtually no evidence...If a female comes in and says she was sexually assaulted, then on her word alone, with nothing else – and I mean nothing else, no investigation – the police will go out and arrest someone."[90] "A defendant who can absolutely prove his innocence . . . can nonetheless still be convicted, based solely on the word of the accuser," and that "In North Carolina, simply "naming the person accused will support a verdict of guilty" because "Crime laboratories are notorious for falsifying results to obtain convictions" say

---

[90]Baskerville, Stephen. *American Gulag – Feminist Laws Persecute Men* (February 5, 2010) Retrieved from: http://www.henrymakow .com/america_-_feminisms_gulag.html

Stuart Taylor and K.C. Johnson in Baskerville et al *Until Proven Innocent*.[90]

In 1998, the California Legislature passed "Evidence Code 1108, which further took away the defendant's right of protection by allowing prosecutors to introduce other accusations in order to prove the rape indeed took place. However, no physical evidence is necessary. No convictions, criminal charges or Police reports are required."[91]

Clearly, feminism has disturbed criminal justice and rendered long standing constitutional protections irrelevant. Crimes have been substantially reconfigured to imitate normal behaviors and new ones invented. In the process, the pre-conjecture of innocence has been eroded, deception glorified and innocent people imprisoned without trial. "The new feminist jurisprudence hammers away at some of the most basic foundations of our criminal law system," Michael Weiss and Cathy Young write in a Cato Institute paper. "Chief among them is the presumption that the accused is innocent until proven guilty," says Stephen Baskerville in *Feminist Gulag: No Prosecution Necessary*.[92]

Are you telling me there is equal justice in America? Do you seriously believe that the law represents American men who pay their taxes with that service in mind? Are we Americans really capable of securing justice elsewhere with such internal disarray where we put "Some seven million Americans, or 3.2 percent under penal supervision,"[92] and incarcerate a larger percentage of our population

---

[91]Turvey, MS, Brent E. *Offender Modus Operandi, Signature, and the Law.* Retrieved from: http://www.corpus-delicti.com/ signature_law.html

[92]Baskerville, Stephen. *Feminist Gulag: No Prosecution Necessary*/New American. (January 7, 2010) Retrieved from: http://www.thenewamerican.com/index.php/culture/family/2705-feminist-gulag-no-prosecution-necessary

surpassing all countries in this regard? If this does not contradict the American claim as the freest nation on the planet, what does? Do we really think other people take us seriously for champions of peace, freedom and democracy?

Everything in society is interrelated starting with the family structure to community and further to nationhood. Family structure is therefore the nucleus of society and when that is endangered, society is in serious trouble. The spiritual culture of American respect for family has been vandalized to the extent of men losing confidence in making it without fear.

A professor, according to In China, the New Villain, posted at the Washington Post's publication Express, 10/29/2010, addresses a class of students in Beijing by first asking, "why do great nations including the USA fail?" Then he answers that, "they all make the same mistakes, turning their back on the principle that made them great." The professor might have been looking at the matter in terms of technology, because at this point China stands ahead of us by inventing the fastest microprocessor ever made; but our lagging behind the country after dominating technology for ages is a reflection of something wrong in our society, which I believe, originates from a family structure.

Sometime in July 2011, I happened to be in a Math class in DC assisting a teacher where all the students were young teenage girls kept in house for various juvenile charges. Two women officers in the class were assigned to monitor the girls who were in custody at the time. In the middle of it, two girls started cursing at each other and the situation worsened to the point where the stronger one picked up a chair and threatened to attack the physically weaker opponent. Fortunately, she changed her mind and rather violently rushed to beat her up, overpowering the two women officers who tried to stop her. In the meantime I found myself positioned between the two girls and instinctually held the aggressive girl to protect her from hurting the weaker girl. She was fit and too strong for me to succeed without being pushed around and getting hurt in the elbow, although not too badly, in the process.

The officers then used the opportunity to unlock the door and take the other girl out of the class at which time I released the aggressor. What happened to me was certainly a lot better than what was going to happen to both of them. The teacher (male), however, stayed in his position without getting involved in the situation. He advised me to report that the girl came to my position and created a scenario where I had to be involved because she did not want to fight. I appreciated his offer to help me out of any problem associated with what I did, but I was surprised by the idea, which must have come from his long experience as a teacher and awareness of how negatively it could develop against me as a man. I then went to the office and informed management about what happened. We all wrote about the incident, complying with the formal office procedure and everything went back to normal. In the meantime, I was treated in the school clinic and I joined other teachers in the main office. Apparently, at least two other teachers told me that I made a mistake getting involved in a situation that was none of my business and advised me never to do it again. They also said that I could be in trouble should the aggressor claim injury or being touched in an indecent body part.

I was saddened by what I heard. I cannot understand this approach because it denies a teacher or any other decent member of society from carrying out the responsibility of protecting kids from dangerous situations when the opportunity is offered. The problem is that I could not see myself being complacent in that particular situation and I would do it again under similar circumstances no matter what the consequence may be; God forbid that from taking place! Unfortunately, this is where we now are morally because of fear.

The article (New Villain) further reveals Secretary of State Hillary Clinton's statement in an interview with historian Michael Beschloss that, "it is not China's fault that we went from having budget surplus to being indebted with a trillion-dollar deficit, those are decisions we made throughout political system. So we have to get our own house in order."[93] This is a cumulative reflection of what is happening in our society. It tells something about where we stand as a family. What we are facing today is the result of misplaced freedom in America. We are more concerned about immoral freedom of expression than human life. People are getting away with criminal behavior in the name of First Amendment right. A case in point is the extent of freedom this country gives pedophiles to openly promote safer ways of committing sexual crimes against children (see *Amazon Pulls Book for Pedophiles* in the Washington Post publication Express, 11/12/2010).

The subject of women and crime has been one of the focal points of feminism since the sixties. In *A Feminist Perspective on Women and Crime*, the author states that "Feminist perspectives, over the past thirty years have not only put some new topics under the criminological cover, they have challenged the theories, concepts, methods and assumptions of most of the people already involved in the study of crime. Criminology has for most feminist writers and researchers been a constraining rather than a constructive and creative influence." There is no limit to feminist agenda as new ideas come from all directions by

---

[93]Pomfret, John. *A fearful view of China*/Washington Post (October 29, 2010) Retrieved from: http://www.washingtonpost.co m/wp-dyn/content/article/2010/10/28/ AR2010102807303.html

feminists in all aspects of society. The article further states that, "... the facts about crime tend to be based on the sex of the offender and not the crime itself. This 'sexism' in criminology is more in keeping with Gelsthorpe's critique of 'accumulated wisdom' about female offenders. She proposes that women are discriminated against in areas such as crime because of their sex and this sexism influences the sentencing, punishment and incarceration of women (1986: 138-149). She accuses many police, welfare institutions and judges among others as assuming 'sweeping generalisations [sic]' about crime as something men are expected to do, because they are men' (Gelsthorpe, 1986: 149). Women are not expected to be criminals and if they are, they may be described as 'mad not bad ' (Lloyd, 1995: xvii)."

It is crazy out there. Yesterday, it was about pushing women into combat and exposing them to heavy physical stress and death in the name of equality where women in the military were encouraged to participate personally in man's dirty games (wars). Today, law enforcement takes the blame for attacking men in the issues of criminology more that women. The extent of misconstrued meaning of equality goes as far as some feminists getting jealous for not being considered equally criminal by the justice system for the same crimes as men and punished equally for them. The feministic concept of equality in this perspective goes as far as feeling discriminated against for being considered less criminal by instinct. In all scenarios where the crying feminists jeopardize the safety of women in the name of equality, none of them has the decency to involve directly as a role model in situations as such and all of them advocate this from a distance in their comfortable homes. They are not that selfless, but they have the guts to throw other women into the fire. They continue creating problem for women in order to benefit from "the unfinished business of feminism" like a dictator pushes his people to war in the name of defending the nation in order to stay in power. At the same time, they are content with discriminatory laws such as the Rape Shield Law. They don't want the law to punish false accusers of rape.

In *Women Who Lie About Rape*,[94] Delores Z Williams discloses that settling claims for cash at civil courts has become a common practice of false accusers of rape because it meets their material objective quicker without having to sit in the witness stand. One classic example in this regard is the case of LA Lakers super star Kobe Bryant, where the prosecution was dropped after the accuser, Katelyn Faber felt uncomfortable facing cross-examination on her promiscuous life style and her mental illness induced suicide attempts, and refused to testify in favor of settling the case at the civil court.

I am not sure where it stands as of today, but disturbing information, according to my lawyer was that feminists might have been lobbying for guaranteed compensation in Civil Courts from men vindicated of rape in Criminal Courts. Men are already at the mercy of women but if this passes, they will legally become their permanent toys, where a telephone call to the Police decides a man's entire future and existence. The accused would be forced to appear at the Civil Court – not to self-defend when that happens (if this ever was the normal procedure) but to discover how much he owes his accuser; the accuser would only have to enforce her uncontested financial reward. A perfect arrangement against men's lives and economic structures if found guilty at Criminal Courts and an unconditional compensation at Civil Courts otherwise; making America not only the home of the highest number of prisoners but also the most dangerous place for men to live. This is far from equality but

---

[94]Retrieved from: http://www.nowpublic.com/women_who_lie_abo
ut_rape

a feminist lynching and determination to drain whatever is left for men in the system.

My fear has become a reality today as the most vicious attack on man is being launched by Radical feminism in America.

Radical feminist Jessica Valenti states that, "U.S. law is so ill-equipped to actually protect women in realistic scenarios is a national embarrassment – not to mention a huge hurdle in obtaining justice for sexual assault victims. Swedish rape laws don't ban "sex by surprise" (a term used by Assange's lawyer as a crass joke), but they do go much further than U.S. laws do, and we should look to them as a potential model for our own legislation"[95] She declares that "Swedish rape laws are a "potential model for our own legislation." What she is talking about is that we should do what, "some activists and legal experts in Sweden [are doing] to change the law there so that the burden of proof is on the accused; the alleged rapist would have to show that he got consent, instead of the victim having to prove that she didn't give it."[95] Further, "feminist author Linda Brookover Bourque argued for a shift in the burden of proof in rape cases to the defense, which would entail that the defense establish with a preponderance of evidence, that it was most likely that a woman alleging rape against her gave clear assent to engage in sex. (Page 178)"[96]

This collective punishment is of course the result of decades of feminist lobbying, exaggeration, deception,

---

[95]Price, W. F. *Why Do Totalitarian Feminists Get Free Publicity?*/The Spearhead (December 14, 2010) Retrieved from: http://www.the-spearhead.com/2010/12/14/why-do-totalitarian-feminists-get-free-publicity/

[96]Hembling, John. *Breaking Bad: The Male as Designated Criminal* (December 20, 2010) Retrieved from: http://avoiceformen.com/2010/12/20/breaking-bad-the-male-as-designated-criminal/

political corruption and greed. Radical feminism has ignited a full-fledged war against the American family structure through this tendency and the groundwork for its accomplishment seems to be already established behind closed doors. We have only to wait until the law is officially reversed and codified in our justice system, meaning that Radical feminism has privatized rape law to the point of drafting it alone. John Hembling calls it the "legal principle of guilt by accusation" and describes it as ". . . the ultimate trump card of feminist utopia, or as I once called it, the lightning-bolt-finger of feminism."[96]

The poison is already infecting society at the higher education level of the hate game. Susan Caringella, "a sociology professor at Western Michigan University," says in her 2008 book Addressing Rape Reform in Law and Practice that, "It is high time to give victims a fair shake, to dismantle the zealous over-protections for men accused of this crime, which have been buoyed up by the myths about false accusations, ulterior motives, and so on, commonly embraced when rape charges are levied."[96]

What they are saying is that false accusations are myth rather than reality: they simply do not exist. They are actually saying that men accused of rape are overprotected but of course no evidence is presented to support this, because there is none. They are saying that any man who ever had sex with a woman since creation is guilty of rape; therefore, there is no need for due process once accused of committing it. These angry women are out of touch with the concept of equality and they know it, but they are determined to destroy society one way or another under the cover of activism. They want to make the planet a prison of the male gender, period!

People! If you are far behind on this topic, you had better try to catch up. Many things have changed in our society. A woman will soon have the right to send a man to prison based on her withdrawal from consent. Analysts say that this is now practiced by law in Sweden. Let me give you a typical scenario for this: Let us say a couple agrees to have an affair and the woman say no "once" and the man continues with the sex. Now, he has legally become a rapist. "Some states, like New York, have rape laws on the books which include "no means no" provisions for intercourse" says an astute observer. [97] You do not want to be a person with hearing problems in this situation because once you miss the *no* you may never have the chance to stop again unless your partner repeats it. Yet, you are still a criminal *after* you stopped because no means no.

Radical feminism has taken sex to the point of quantum physics where a man can be criminalized for having a penis and a woman's word taken as the truth because of possessing a vagina. Furthermore, the penis must respond in nanoseconds like an electron. What is no or stop anyway? Don't we use them often in our explanations and communications though they don't mean anything? How many times should it be said to be taken seriously by a man engaged in sex assuming the consent still exists? When does it apply in formerly agreed upon consensual sex that may suddenly become forced by a woman's sheer utterance of no or stop; or at what moment should the agreement be considered invalid? My question is how much time should be permitted for the man to withdraw his penis completely out of the vagina?

If the penis was already inside the vagina at the time the agreement is breached, would a man be convicted of rape for partially having it there for few seconds in the process of withdrawing? If the first penetration was agreed upon and

---

[97]*Some thoughts on "sex by surprise"*/Feministe (12/6/2010) Retrieved from: http://www.feministe.us/blog/archives/2010/12/0 6/some-thoughts-on-sex-by-surprise/

the third penetration, for example, declared by law as rape consistent to the issue, should justice consider criminalizing the first penetration on the basis of being the foundation for the third penetration?

Should we plug a clock into the vagina or attach it to the penis during intercourse to monitor the relevant times to this dilemma? How do we manage this situation without taking the risk of inserting the clock into the vagina and setting up the circumstantial grounds for its accusation as rape? Should the clock stay outside or inside the vagina? And what conditions should protect one from being accused of rape?

Those who are the victims of deceptions are the raped. The victims are the innocent men. Prejudice is a problem though when gender resolves the difference as to how we judge men and women's "guilt and criminality." From a legal perspective says an analyst, "such legislation would do an end run around one of our most cherished rights -- the right not to testify against oneself. At present, a prosecutor is not permitted even to suggest that the Jury draw an adverse inference from the defendant's refusal to testify. Under this plan, the defendant would have no choice but to testify because it would be his burden to prove he didn't rape the accuser . . . Article 11 of the Universal Declaration of Human Rights which was adopted in 1948 by the United Nations General Assembly by unanimity, describes the principle of presumption of innocence as follows: Everyone charged with a penal offence has the right to be presumed innocent until proven guilty according to law in a public trial at which he/or she has had all the guarantees necessary for his defense."[96] Further, "It is impossible of course for a man to prove consent throughout the entire sexual intercourse short of setting up an all-angles-covered porn recording team in his bedroom, possibly in conjunction with a brain scanner, a telepathist and a psychic. And, if you take feminist concepts of rape into account, even that isn't enough, because they think women should be able to withdraw consent retroactively."[95]

I feel a little uncomfortable throwing out unconfirmed pieces of information that may not have matured yet for easy access by the public. This is not feminist bashing at all, but sharing what I have heard with whoever comes across this work. Realities start as speculations most of the time and I do not disqualify what I hear as baseless any more, especially in important subject matters as such. It is my responsibility to warn people to be careful about another feminist surprise because any organized group that finds justice in the Rape Shield Law can go any distance to abuse society without giving it a second thought, and most likely behind the scene.

I once met a man in a café through an associate and we were randomly talking about anything that spontaneously came up for discussion. Apparently, they met in the Dominican Republic where they occasionally travel to have fun with women without being worried about their safety. The man was a Sheriff in an undisclosed county and told us that a husband is responsible by law to provide child support for his wife's child from another man so long as the marriage was active at the time the child was born. I regret not asking him to tell me the States that apply this procedure during my one time accidental meeting with him, but I went on researching the matter through the Internet and I found the following stories.

According to an article, a New Jersey man and woman who were married and then divorced had a child in the family that grew to the age of seven under the support of the parents. Provoked by the mother's agitating disclosure of important information, the father undertook DNA testing on the child, only to be surprised that, "there was 0% chance he was the biological father. When the results were brought to the attention of the Court, the Court ruled that it was not in the best interest of the child for the paternity issue to be pursued, as the man was the only father the child ever knew. The parents were prohibited from discussing the paternity issue with their daughter and the man was ordered to continue paying child support. The judge's ruling was recently upheld by the appellate Court."[98]

I feel sorry for what happened to the man who lived ignorant of his biological role in the child's parenthood until the time of his awareness. I think it would have been better if the judge had modified the situation for the sake of fairness though I cannot readily suggest anything to that effect. However, I believe the Court ruling in this case was justified in view of the child for the child's situation is more important to society than the differences of the couple in the matter.

In another article, a wife "is urging legislators to change a law so men can use genetic testing to avoid paying child support for children they didn't father."[99] This move was based on the tendency of Kansas State "to garnish her husband's paycheck and keep the family's tax refund to support a child that is not his biological son."

"Under Kansas law, the husband is the "presumed father" of any children his wife has during the marriage. A judge decided that it didn't make a difference that Sprowson wasn't the biological father of the child."[99]

---

[98]Kisselburgh, Robert. *DNA proves man not biological father--but child support must continue*: Child support ordered upheld for man not biological father, Posted On: January 25, 2008

[99]Elder, Gerri. *Wife Urges Change in Child Support Law*:/Total Divorce (n.d.) Retrieved from: http://www.totaldivorce.com/news/articles/legislation/kansas-chil-support-bill-targets-non-biological-fathers.aspx

I leave this with mixed feelings but I have a problem with the revelation that "In 1995, Sprowson's first wife became pregnant by another man, and the couple divorced shortly after the child was born. DNA testing proved that Sprowson was not the father of the baby. Sprowson never has had a relationship with the child, who is now 13, but he was ordered to pay child support."[99] The reason I have a problem here is that there was no relationship between Sgt. Sprowson and the child that could psychologically affect the child in the absence of the judgment. The material effect of the judgment on the child would be obviously regrettable had it went in favor of Sgt. Sprowson, but I still believe that the law was cruel to him, to his family and to all other men in his situation at large. What I think happened here was that the government unfairly shifted its burden of supporting the kid to Sgt. Sprowson.

Dante's characterization of force and fraud as the two forms of malice aiming at injustice makes sense because taking advantage of people by lying and threatening someone's life by false accusation are intentional attack against the victims.

Without complicating the straightforward issue, violence against women is a social problem that affects all people. We make boys and girls together and all parents are concerned about their children. Women could not have fought the problem alone and succeeded. The reason violent men do not practice their conduct in the open is to avoid physical confrontation with good men. In other words, good men traditionally protect women from bad men. The behavior of violent individuals from both sexes does not represent all men and women; and the best choice for us as people was and still is to make the world a better place to live irrespective of race, color and gender. That social role is not assigned only to feminism but rather to society as a whole.

There is no question that bad feminism's unconditional promotion of liars has compromised the dignity of real victims of rape by conditioning people not to believe them; but I also worry about the possibility of revenge-induced violence against women as a result. I am seriously bothered by the notion that we will all go down together in the absence of serious resistance, especially from women within the movement's political structure. I modestly remind women that feminism was sociological and political obligation to terminate sexism in all its facets and humbly beg them to accept this responsibility and save humankind in general and real victims of violence in particular from the destructive feminist intrusion into the Justice System. I beg them to uphold fairness so that we can move forward as a family by dealing with violent men and false accusers at the same level of reason.

The Entrapment of Radical Feminism between Its Own Jurisdiction and Respect for Powerful Men

One of the problems I had writing this book was my inability to stop after addressing momentous issues governing sex violence in America. The more I thought had I finished the project, the quicker relevant issues that I could not ignore surfaced requesting urgent inclusion in the manuscript. In this regard, my experience was to the point of praying for nothing new to happen for at least until the book was published.

Unfortunately, the consequence of radical feminism does not give society a break and attacks it faster than God's tendency to accommodate my prayers. This time, it happened to be the saga of Dominique Strauss-Kahn, who unexpectedly found his future shattered by a rape allegation from a woman with whom he had a sexual encounter in his hotel room in New York City in May 2011.

Who is Dominique Strauss-Kahn?

According to the article in the Washingtonian[100] *Strauss Kahn* has a PhD in economics, had been a professor of economics at the prestigious Sciences Po—as the Paris Institute for Political Studies, a visiting professor at Stanford, France's finance minister in the late 1990s, and a IMF chief since November 1, 2007 where he administered 2,900 people from 187 countries at a budget worth $340 billion. The man is considered one of the most influential [sic] politicians in the world with a work load requiring 150 days of traveling a year across the globe and had a defined mission of; "[Fostering] global growth and economic stability, [providing] policy advice and financing to countries in economic difficulties, and [reducing] poverty in the world." One of his greatest professional achievements appears to have been in the areas of balancing the traditionally unfair IMF conditions of giving loans to developing nations, which the nations considered as "a bully servant of the US Treasury that gives with one hand and strangles with the other." Towards his goal, the politician was capable of "[boosting] the role of emerging economies" whereby "China became the third-most powerful country on the board, after the United States and Japan in November 2010." With all these experiences in his resume, Strauss-Kahn was ready to lead France by democratically challenging President Sarkozy after winning the Socialist primary for the May 2012 presidential election. It was at the

---

[100]*Dominique Strauss-Kahn: What Does the IMF Chief's Arrest Mean?*/Washingtonian (May 16, 2011) Retrieved from: http://www.washingtonian.com/articles/people/19460.html

time "the polls [were predicting] that Strauss-Kahn would have knocked [the election] off with a 61-to-39-percent win" that everything suddenly collapsed around him and his political future in France.

Who is the accuser?

His accuser was an African immigrant who was working as a maid in a Manhattan Sofitel Hotel.

There is no doubt that Strauss-Kahn has paid heavy price as a result of radical feminism's capacity not only to dominate the American justice system but also to reverse the country's long standing belief in the presumption of innocence (*an accused is innocent until proven guilty*). He was jailed, traumatized and lost his job ($500,000 a year with income tax exemption). Too broken to be the leader of France, he suffered house arrest under armed guard surveillance with electronic tag attached to his body. Needless to say, he is no longer the same person from the angle of psychic stability. There does seem to be evidence of a sexual encounter. The question is if he deserved the humiliation he suffered assuming he actually did what he was accused of, and my answer is *yes;* but only after being proven guilty.

As to how the issue has developed so far, the following information has been available for us to use.

FOX news, published July 02, 2011 under the title *Crime & Courts: Hotel Maid Accusing Strauss-Kahn of Rape Reportedly Worked as Prostitute*[101] reads "The Manhattan District Attorney's Office revealed that the 32-year-old woman had committed a host of minor frauds to better her life in the U.S. since arriving in the country seven years ago,

---

[101]Retrieved from: http://www.foxnews.com/us/2011/07/02/hotel
-maid-accusing-strauss-kahn-rape-reportedly-worked-as-prostitute

including lying on immigration paperwork, cheating on her taxes, and misstating her income so she could live in an apartment reserved for the poor" further, "[she] has allegedly worked as a prostitute....[and that she] would have sex with male guests at the hotel for money." She was also said to have, ". . . misrepresented what she did immediately after the alleged attack by Strauss-Kahn -- instead of fleeing his luxury suite to a hallway and waiting for a supervisor, she went to clean another room and then returned to clean Strauss-Kahn's suite before reporting the encounter."

The article *Dominique Strauss-Kahn walks free after maid rape case crumbles* revealed that, "substantial credibility issues" had been discovered about the maid, following a "comprehensive and thorough investigation of all aspects of this case, including the background of the complainant and her various statements about the incident." Apparently, the accuser (Guinean single mother) had admitted to lying on her application for asylum in the US in 2004, lied about previously being raped and lied on her income tax returns."[102]

In *Stunning Turn, Strauss-Kahn Is Freed from House Arrest amid Doubts about Sexual-Assault Case*, MICHAEL ROTHFELD and CHAD BRAY disclosed that, "Prosecutors said in a court filing that the maid had lied about her whereabouts immediately after the alleged attack, about the circumstances under which she sought asylum in the U.S.,

---

[102]*Dominique Strauss-Kahn walks free after maid rape case*/The Telegraph (July 17, 2011) Retrieved from: http://www.telegraph.co .uk/finance/dominique-strauss-kahn/8611957/ Dominique-Strauss-Kahn-walks-free-after-maid-rape-case-crumbles.html

and on her tax filings in recent years."[103] Further, "the maid admitted in subsequent interviews with prosecutors that she had fabricated that account, along with another she had given them about being the victim of a gang rape in her native country." "During the interviews where she initially said she had been gang raped, 'the victim cried and appeared to be markedly distraught,' prosecutors said in the letter they filed on Friday. Later, she told them that she had memorized the rape account as part of her asylum application, they said. She still maintains she was raped in Guinea, on a different occasion, the filing said." The prosecutors also said that the maid initially told investigators, and later the grand jury, that she fled Mr. Strauss-Kahn's hotel suite and "reported the alleged incident to her supervisor after she observed Mr. Strauss-Kahn get on an elevator," but that "she has since admitted that she cleaned a nearby room and returned to clean Mr. Strauss-Kahn's suite before reporting the incident, said in the letter."

It was further disclosed that, "she admitted to declaring a friend's child as her own to increase her tax refund and to misrepresent her income in order to maintain her current housing, prosecutors said in the letter." In one of the most dramatic events of the accusation according to the source of information, "Prosecutors also have obtained a tape of a conversation the woman had a day after the alleged attack with an inmate incarcerated on drug charges in Arizona, people familiar with the matter said. In the conversation, which occurred in her native language but was translated by the prosecutors' office earlier this week, she described the

---

[103]*Judge Releases Ex-IMF Chief/*The Wall Street Journal World News (July 2, 2011) Retrieved from: http://online.wsj.com/article/ SB10001424052702304584004576419673636254478.html

alleged attack and also said she expected to make money from it, one of the people said."

According to Philip Sherwell of the Sydney Morning Herald,[104] "The initial portrayal of the 32-year-old Guinean-born hotel maid who accused Dominique Strauss-Kahn of sexual assault as a pious devout Muslim has again been torn apart with claims that male guests at New York's Sofitel hotel paid her for sex." "The first indication that the woman had links to African criminals in America came less than a week after his arrest on May 14." Further, "Prosecutors and investigators were told of a recorded conversation between the subject of a drugs inquiry and another man, who said that the woman in the Strauss-Kahn affair was his companion. In subsequent weeks, they made a series of alarming discoveries about her relationship with an accused drug dealer, her finances and her asylum status. There were also concerns raised about her account of what happened immediately after the alleged incident."

To summarize, the accuser has been characterized as a liar, sex worker, one who has contact with a drug criminal and one having had money as motivation for her accusation. With all these attributes encapsulating the accuser's character, our system had the temerity to destroy the man without trial just because she claimed he abused her sexually.

The question is how people feel about the highly publicized mess.

---

[104]*Maid in Strauss-Kahn case accused of selling sex to hotel guests*/The Sydney Morning Herald, New York (*July 4, 2011*) Retrieved from: http://www.smh.com.au/world/maid-in-strausskahn-case-accused-of-selling-sex-to-hotel-guests-20110703-1gx85.html

The following observations were made in *Comments on American Thinker:*[105]

Schmutzli comments on 06/25/2011 that, "In today's world, the accusation alone against any man (especially one of achievement) -- true or not -- will ruin his life, his career, and the lives of all those associated with him. The anonymous female accusation in America is a modern-day curse on men," and asks, "Would any man who had fabricated a story endangering the freedom of numerous female students be able to walk away free of any charges? Never mind answering this question because in today's America it appears that only women can endanger the freedom of men by a mere unsubstantiated accusation."

GeorgiaBoy61 comments on 06/26/2011 by first thanking the forum ". . . for exposing another of the dirty little secrets of the link between radical feminism and thoroughly corrupt government" and then continues to say "The institutionalized destruction of males (boys, young men, husbands and fathers) in the interest of radical feminism and corrupt lawmakers, attorneys and judges is more responsible for the decline of the culture than any care to admit. But that too is a characteristic of socialism, the bogeyman. The Duke Lacrosse case is one of the greatest travesties of justice in American history, and still no apology from the faculty at Duke. Had those men not been from families able to afford top-notch legal representation, they would likely be in prison today."

Shopna comments on 06/26/2011, "Although I am myself, a woman, it hurts from the point of JUSTICE . . . women are treated as equal to men but it seems this is

---

[105]*Dominique Strauss-Kahn Vs. The American Anti-Male Justice System*/American Thinker (June 25, 2011) Retrieved from: http://www.americanthinker.com/2011/06/dominique_strauss-kahn_vs_the_american_anti-male_justice_system.html

actually not the case --- WOMEN ARE WAY SUPERIOR THAN MEN . . . and [have] the ability to finish the career, reputation, lifetime, of not just any man but one who is POWERFUL AND FAMOUS . . . . I am sad to see famous, brilliant, successful men are fallen down in no time by the thrash of the magic knife the women possess in some countries . . . . and are not only equipped to do so, but also are protected so that no one can get them. WHY? "

frenchfrog comments on 06/26/20: "As a woman, I agree that the superiority women are treated over men in the justice system is very unfair. The attack of the media against DSK was absolutely disgusting. His trial hasn't even started yet. And I agree 100% with Mrs. Guigou about the presumption of innocence being more respected in France than here."

Tom in Michigan suggests, "It is just as bad in the business world. All woman has to do is accuse a man of virtually anything, even raising his voice and, he will be punished and likely terminated. They just don't want to deal with the possibility of a law suit. I personally and quietly avoid the women with whom I work, only interacting when I must. If the conversation even turns to any sort of "women's issue," I find an excuse to leave the room. Every office has at least one "victim" looking for a grievance. When our resident feminist starts on her high horse; I leave the room rather than risk being drawn into the conversation."

The situation obviously agitated many observers and the fear of women has permeated the psyche of American men but the following comment regardless of its grammatical integrity touched me most because it expresses how frustrating it was for peaceful women who have experienced the tragic consequence of radical feminism on their own safety and integrity.

Shopna lamented, "This is sad you know because such women are spoiling the reputation of all women --- just like the terrorists spoiling the Muslims' reputation. I feel doubly [embarrassed] now; first for being a Muslim, secondly, for being a WOMAN!!!!! dam! wish I was a bird or something if I had to be born as a female!!!!!!!!!!!!! (with due respect to GOD). Thank God I have all sons no daughter to endanger men's life with the power of the biological difference. One thing I don't understand: in our country (3rd world) the women cannot do everything men does and therefore some of them has this grudge against men secretly --- but why women in such countries where they can do anything men does including looking like them? THIS I WILL NEVER UNDERSTAND."

There is no doubt that the situation is of concern to every fair minded human being on the planet except the destructive feminists who have so far failed to fairly address the issue of sexual violence in America. None of the powerful feminist organizations has come forward either to show sympathy to Strauss Kahn's downfall or to condemn the character of his accuser. They simply do not care about the safety of men and women as long as they remain materially comfortable because of the problem.

In the usual one-dimensional approach of powerful feminists to sexual violence issues, Terry O'Neill, the president of NOW takes the following position on the Strauss-Kahn crisis.[106] After mentioning two other relevant examples of sexually assaulted women, she said, "And now, Dominique Strauss-Kahn, the head of the International Monetary Fund (IMF) and a strong contender to become the next president of France, has been charged with sexually assaulting and attempting to rape a woman who was

---

[106]*Violence Against Women Is a Serious Problem: IMF Chief Must Go*/Huffpost Politics (Posted: 05/18/11 02:51 PM ET) Retrieved from: http://www.huffingtonpost.com/terry-oneill/violence-against-women-se_b_863585.html

working as a housekeeper in the New York hotel where he was staying. These three stories have more in common than timing; they serve as stunning examples of our society's tendency to downplay the seriousness of the crime and re-victimize the woman."

She further said that, ". . . programs to address violence against women continue to be woefully underfunded, sending the message that this crisis has yet to be prioritized in proportion to its impact on the community [and that] we must call rape what it is -- not a randy man carried away in the heat of the moment, but a disturbed man who seeks to control women through violence." She then concluded her statements saying that, "Mr. Strauss-Kahn should resign or be removed immediately from his position as managing director of the IMF."

While I believe society should highly consider the plea of every victim (true or false) and serve justice accordingly, I found Terry O'Neill's input to the effect that we should prioritize the issue in proportion to its impact on the community a sexist joke on American people who are suffering from the completely biased feminist approach to the problem. The statement does not consider feminism's negative impact on society by inclusively supporting negative women in the issue of violence. I believe society cannot afford to fund feminism beyond its share of funding while completely ignoring the concrete grounds to start funding the cause of men falsely accused of rape parallel to the cause of true victims of the crime. What feminism has to do to solve the problem and secure the unanimous support of society is to address the issue of rape neutrally. It is feminism that must recognize rape for what it is rather than complicating it to the point of denying Americans the right to enjoy sex without fear. Ms. O'Neill needs to admit that a false accuser who is motivated to control men through psychic violence is equally as disturbed as a rapist.

Further, I found her proposal that Mr. Strauss-Kahn should one way or another step down from his position before he was proven guilty as a one sided brutality against men. I challenge her to deliver her opinion about the character of his accuser as well. Her complete silence about the accuser's character suggests that Ms. O'Neill believes that the accuser must be allowed to get away with her inconsistencies and lies by default of her gender. If this is not part of the problem what is?

In the progression, I could not ignore discussing the duplicitous nature of radical feminists on this account, based on the void of the Rape Shield Law, which failed to protect the accuser in this case? How on earth did the defense attorneys and the prosecution team manage (in violation of the Rape Shield Law) to expose the history of the accuser without effective feminist outrage?

An information source titled *Strauss-Kahn accuser sues N.Y. newspaper*[107] stated that "The top investigator said prosecutors will agree to drop the charges" because "We all know this case is not sustainable," and that "The credibility of the hotel housekeeper who accused Strauss-Kahn of sexually assaulting her in May is so bad now, we know we cannot sustain a case with her." The person who gave the comment further said, "She is not to be believed in anything that comes out of her mouth -- which is a shame, because now we may never know what happened in that hotel room."

How did the prosecution team take this position and get away without serious challenge from radical feminism considering the norm of our prosecution process that does not vindicate an accused even when a rape accusation is

---

[107]Upi.com - US News (July 5, 2011) Retrieved from: http://www.upi.com/Top_News/US/2011/07/05/Strauss-Kahn-accuser-sues-NY-newspaper/UPI-20931309849200/

reversed by the accuser? Could there have been a hidden conspiracy involving feminist leaders to pressure the prosecution team into abandoning the accuser? I am asking this because nothing like this could have taken place had the accused been an ordinary person.

My next question speaks to how the so-called trauma experts that feminists traditionally use to cover up the inconsistencies and lies of accusers disappeared from the scene and failed to rescue the accuser from the output of her own lies. Shouldn't she have been traumatized to the extent of lying (not about her immigration process and tax matters) about what she said she did immediately after the "crime" took place in the hotel? Weren't the accuser's lies triggered by the traumatic experience of rape as experienced by most ordinary human beings?

To my understanding, the development once again displays the fact that rape cases are strictly business to powerful radical feminists who bend to powerful men no matter what they do to women. Dominique Strauss-Kahn would have been history by now had he been an ordinary man. The Rape Shield Law would have applied to him from the onset of the incident with no possibility for the defense team to violate it with full cooperation of at least the prosecution team, if not in full view of the public, including the freedom of journalists to write anything that sells. Any attempt to this effect would have agitated feminists to invaded New York streets to stop it from happening. To the contrary, the prosecution team, which most probably operates with direct involvement of powerful feminists, has been helping Strauss Kahn by exposing his accuser's dirt without any problem. Traditionally though, we would not have known the history of his accuser and the trauma experts would have been ever present to justify the accuser's inconsistencies as having been the result of psychological damage inflicted upon her by the crime.

Apparently, the case was dropped completely from prosecution instead of radical feminists prosecuting it themselves by using their own lawyers as they normally do in ordinary rape cases.

By all accounts, the way the situation was handled clearly demonstrates that radical feminism protects powerful men more than the victims of rape. Their outcry for justice against the man to my thinking was nothing more than pretension and NOW's statement only a toothless cover-up of its own contradiction.

At the end of the day, Strauss Kahn's case offers Americans another opportunity to reassess their court system's integrity in the issue of rape. It gives them a chance to question the discrepancy of radical feminism in relation to men of power and to seriously start pressuring politicians into drafting laws that punish false accusers of rape (although I am not saying the accusation was false) so that the problem does not continue to plague us any longer. If the destruction of one of the strongest politicians on earth who earned his status through decades of hard work by the word of a woman so tainted with multiple ethical issues and the unhealthy silence of feminism on the accuser's character does not wake people up to repair the problem, I do not think anything will.

FROM FEMINIST TO RAPIST

FEMINISTS ON FEMINISM

The Informal Acknowledgement of Gender Equality by Notorious Feminists

Eventually, rationality replaced sheer emotions and the negative effects of the movement on women it was supposed to protect slowly came into the open by transformed activists. They started to see the shadow of bias inside the light of unity and came to realize how destructive the movement had been to women in some ways.

Kay Eberling[108] happened to be one of the distinguished women who grieved the negative effects of the movement after relentlessly serving the cause for years. The veteran feminist sounded disappointed to me about the casualties inflicted to humanity and especially to children because of the ideology's rejection of the natural differences between the sexes and injuriously confronting men to manipulate a vulnerable audience.

When it comes to gender politics, prejudice has been the pain of humankind in every society. Billions in most parts of the world are still facing it in its most conventional form, millions are hurting elsewhere from its relatively moderate forms of violence and here we are in beautiful America

---

[108]Kay Eberling was a dedicated feminist who gave her second thoughts of the movement in "The Failure of Feminism", Newsweek Magazine, (November 19, 1990)

falling victims of the most sophisticated version of prejudice. But, bias in its bidirectional makeup is simply running out of steam to be used as effective means of promoting the interest of gender in civil society. The divisive excuses of those who call themselves vanguards of equilibrium are slowly colliding with the concept of balanced feminism, as some women have come forward to say enough is enough to human destruction in the name of their cause.

"[N]o assault has been more ferocious than feminism's forty-year war against women'; says an activist.[109] She characterizes the catch (my interpretation) as ". . . delusions and hypocrisy behind a movement that threatens our families, our economy, and our security." As hard as it is to deny the achievements of feminism in view of the truth so is it to rebuff that "violence" has become means of survival, fame and sadism to some extremists.

The book "Who stole feminism?" appears to highlight author Christina Hoff Sommers' discomfort with "the outright lies perpetrated by establishment feminism."[110] It addresses the movement's habitual invention of stories and distortion of statistical data in order to meet its goal, whatever the goal may be. It is about the misrepresentation of genuine feminism by today's sold out feminists. The interest of today's feminism is against the interest of women in general, the reason such writers choose to expose what has been going on behind the curtain of struggle for women's dignity. The author collapses today's feminism into two categories: the anti-feminist or anti-women and anti-society philosophy called *Gender Feminism* that only

---

[109]Schlafly, Phyllis. *Feminist Fantasies*/Spence Publishing Company (February 2003)

[110]Hoff-Sommers, Christina. Who Stole Feminism?: How Women Have Betrayed Women/ Simon & Schuster (May 1, 1995)

benefits the Radical feminist leaders and the *pro-feminism* or pro-women and pro-society philosophy that addresses the most fundamental issues of women.

In my journey of learning from people's experiences on this topic, I came across something enticing in a popular newspaper[111] that I hoped might have been the beginning of breakthrough to the crisis at hand. It was about the Radical feminist Gloria Steinem,[112] who contributed to the birth of the "MS Foundation for Women" in 1972 with other dedicated feminists to "build women's collective power to ignite change across the United States." The distinguished symbol of the "ultimate single girl" had openly voiced opinions against marriage throughout the struggle. Her infamous expression, "a woman needs a man like a fish needs a bicycle" dismissed the institution altogether. "Legally speaking, it was designed for a person and a half" was how she referred to marriage when she described it as "mating in captivity" that women should unconditionally reject.[113] Finally, she got married at the age of sixty-six and few other feminists seem to have embraced the new approach.

---

[111]Frey, Jennifer. *Feminism's Unblushing Bride*/The Washington Post (September 7, 2000)

[112]"Gloria Marie Steinem (born March 25, 1934) is an American feminist, journalist, and social and political activist who became nationally recognized as a leader of, and media spokeswoman for, the Women's Liberation Movement in the late 1960s and 1970s" *Gloria Steinem*/Wikipedia (n.d.) Retrieved from: http://en.wikipedia.org/wiki/Gloria_Steinem

[113]Broughton, Philip Delves. *Marriage at 66 for radical feminist Gloria Steinem*/The Telegraph (September 7, 2000) Retrieved from: http://www.telegraph.co.uk/news/worldnews/northamerica/usa/1354464/Marriage-at-66-for-radical-feminist-Gloria-Steinem.html

I accepted the situation with mixed emotions. If the pacifist choice were a product of wisdom, informal admission to fully achieved equality and spiritual transformation, it would be fantastic. Otherwise (conforming for personal advantage), the problem will linger on with the same intensity.

Considering the fact that feminists opposed marriage in the past for political reasons, the new development implied that the political problems were now out of the way and that feminists can chose to marry if they wish.

I took this new development seriously considering that feminists were against marriage in principle because of political reasons. Although not enough information was available in the news, I thought breaking the political barrier and advocating marriage were signs of acknowledging the existence of solutions to the political problems that conventionally separated men and women in the past. I wondered if the statement implied the end of the struggle by virtue of its political goal legally attained at least here in the US. This of course with clear understanding that violence will continue to exist until the end of time as something intrinsic to human nature. Nevertheless, thinking of the situation as something that could provide verbal and practical opportunities of nationwide reconciliation between the sexes by itself was optimistic to me.

The next step would then be how to undo the damage wreaked by the activists themselves and how to repair feminism as a whole in this period of contemplation. Still the question was how to reverse the partial laws and what to do about their innocent victims.

In my opinion, the issue boiled down to what exactly the role of feminism was going to be if it had to exist as an active socio-political force in society. The challenge ahead was how to replace the hypersensitivity and disgust with reality based actions that could benefit humankind and especially women's conditions in general.

As it always turns out to be, oppressors do not give up oppression willingly and feminists did what they had to do to liberate *themselves* from oppression. It had to be done by any means necessary including encouraging women to remain single for life, and many women loyally followed them and remained single. I do not think the new brides owe them an apology, for they were in the same boat themselves; but I still could not help thinking about the reaction of their followers on their taking a different stance in the opposite direction of the spectrum (approving heterosexual marriage).

In due time, I have patiently waited for the metamorphosed activists to apply the wisdom gained from experience in cleaning up the mess here at home to direct the focal point of the movement towards international issues of women and children where the work had not even started. I have been looking forward to their effort in pulling the sinking ship they ill-navigated back up to the surface by showing compassion to our convicts of injustice and teaming up with other humanist groups like the Innocence Project[114] for their freedom. Unfortunately, an action to that end is absent yet to my knowledge.

---

[114]According to *www.Innocentproject.org/about/mission-statement.php*, The Innocence Project was founded in 1992 by Barry C. Scheck and Peter J. Neufeld at the Benjamin N. Cardozo School of Law at Yeshiva University to assist prisoners who could be proven innocent through DNA testing. To date, 245 people in the United States have been exonerated by DNA testing, including 17 who served time on death row. These people served an average of 13 years in prison before exoneration and release.

In addition, according to *On Jury Nullification and Rape,* By Paul Elam, Sunday, August 1, 2010, "In a review of the 251 cases in which they

My Subjective Position on the Fate of Feminism and Beyond

Let me go back in time and express my feeling from the bottom of my heart. The birth of feminism was good news to all oppressed people of the world. As a tough challenger to any form of oppression, women made the struggle of humankind for freedom psychedelic. It was wonderful to witness men and women side by side dismantling oppression a piece at a time in the long and rough journey of the struggle. The all-inclusive resistance of humankind for freedom without feminism was like hoping to make a "tasty" dish without spices. It simply would not have worked. By being conditioned to face oppression twice as much, our mothers and sisters were in the front line as the material and psychological leaders of all forms of struggle for justice anywhere on the planet. They created us, men through the process of long and torturous physical burden and raised us with unconditional love and care. They were our role models of endurance to multiple challenges in society. They were our teachers of peaceful coexistence through forgiveness. They were our comfort zones through softness and compassion. Men went to them to feel the luxury of their touches and hugs when they got tired and felt hopeless of their quest for freedom.

The effect of feminism in society was, therefore not only limited to forces of all-inclusive resistance but also to the art of philosophy itself. Political philosophy without feminism was like having the sixties without the hippies or a band

---

have succeeded in freeing innocent men, nearly all of them were for sex crimes, and their average length of incarceration was 17 years. Most of those were freed only because they were lucky enough to have DNA evidence that could be evaluated. Many others are not so fortunate."

without a drummer. It was indeed like the Woodstock musical fest without the musicians in the event. It felt good to identify with the ideology and history was made.

Plainly, a family is composed of individuals and society, composed of families. Society without a healthy family structure is thus, like a body with sick organs. Likewise, a spiritual woman is the nucleus of a family structure and thus the balancing force of society. She is compassion, emotion, forgiveness, love, life, patience and perseverance in a package. All the blessing came as a unified energy through feminism, which blended well into the universal struggle to kill the concept of domination in all its forms once and for all.

We finally made it together for a new beginning where humankind was about to start living based on equality forever. We could not achieve the bliss at the end of the tunnel though, as life proved itself to be in opposition to the plan.

To consider the irrefutable, there is no illusion to the reality that the issue of women in society was clear from the beginning of its actuality. The mission was not to change the nature of a man but to monitor his behavior. It was not about treating women better than men, but about having them respected. It was not to hallucinate about the meaning of rape or trauma but to face them directly for what they were. It was certainly not about tit for tat, but to narrow down the misunderstanding by accepting our natural differences.

The outstanding demands of the movement strictly revolved around equal educational and financial rights, employment opportunities, equal role in public politics, voting rights and sexual freedom.

Looking at where society stands at the moment, women have made quantum leap in education: 8.5 million women and 6.7 million men were enrolled in American colleges and the number of female graduate attendance increased by 57% between 1999 and 2000 out-spacing that of men's by 17%.[115] Further, 'the enrollment rate of girls (71.6%) continued to exceed that of boys (61.4%) in 2004"[116] and the momentum remains positively intact as of the end of the decade. Besides there were "approximately sixty active women's colleges in the U.S"[117] in the eighties according to my source of information.

Financially speaking, women are doing relatively better than men are, to the point of replacing them as the economic backbone of American families. We have professionals at all levels of society enjoying equal employment opportunities. Statistically, men lose their jobs faster than women and women have better job security than men in Today's America.

Women today are effectively participating in politics. The political roles of Condoleezza Rice, Geraldine Ferraro, Hillary Rodham Clinton, Sara Palin and Susan Rice speak in favor of this postulate. They have secured their voting rights and sexual freedom ranging from homosexuality to pornography.

There is of course a wide economic gap between men and women just as the situation is for any other minority group in relation to mainstream Americans. The gap is the result of years of inequality that is currently shrinking at a reasonable rate to its eventual disappearance in time. The

---

[115]Sexton, Steve. *Changing Paradigm*, Washington Times (July 18, 2003)

[116]Reitz, Victoria *More kids going to college* (June 2, 2005) Retrieved from: http://www.allbusiness.com/transportation/aerosp ace-product-parts/1049575-1.html

[117]*Women's colleges in the United States*/Wikipedia (n.d.) Retrieved from: http://en.wikipedia.org/wiki/Women's_colleges_in_t he_United_States

effort has already been accelerated by President Obama's signature on a law that guarantees equal pay for men and women in all work environments in the country.

In a straightforward manner, the outstanding demands of the movement have all been achieved in America. This objective reality implies that the role of feminism has long been notoriously exhausted because of the concrete equality of women to men, similar to the role of anti-slavery activism to the end of slavery in the US. There is no real reason for feminism to remain important except to assist real victims of violence and perhaps to monitor the continuity of women's comprehensive achievement in this country from an academic perspective. The founding mothers of Feminism did not create the movement for eternity but only until it achieved the objectives.

Alas, in any known struggle of humankind tragic social conditions take place after victory. Those who are earnestly involved in a cause close their chapter of resistance and move to other pending challenges of society; but those with vested personal interests cling to dead issues, complicating the result. It is indeed after victory that the real motives of active socio-political players come to the surface.

The glamorous results of conquest are only attainable from a distance, never from proximity. Victory is a straightforward issue in conventional competitions but a double standard phenomenon in socio-political dimensions. Victory comes with disappointment when sabotaged by opportunist leaders associated with the struggle. Expectations and promises magnetize people to give anything for victory but once in it, they face duplicity if they are unlucky enough to be still alive. It is like dreaming while sleeping and confronting reality when awake except that society pays an incalculable price for victory. The fear, paranoia and insecurity of saboteurs emanate from the fact that victory inevitably takes away personal gain, because the closer one gets to the breakthrough of any social problem the less the relevance of the actors in its solution. It significantly diminishes their income, power, fame, attention and/or other advantages to a point that the situation tempts them to resent the hard gotten results in order to protect what was to be lost.

What happened to Feminism was what happened to other struggles of humankind. It was too selfless to get there but too selfish to return from the bottom line. It drastically failed to complete the job. It could not avoid entrapment by delusion of permanence, material, power and greed. Its revisionism proves to me that there is no such thing as complete victory for humankind. It is impossible without ego and gluttony on one side and humility and disappointment on the other. It is sad that we tend to forget that we will die to the point of breaching our purpose of existence.

Christina Hoff-Sommers well articulates this in *"The War Against Boys."* The book to my interpretation is based on the decision of feminism to have a change in principle after victory. According to a critic,[118] it challenges unfounded feminist rhetoric such as what is claimed in Susan Faludi's *Backlash: The Undeclared War against Women*. It discusses extremely important issues such as, "The notion that feminists love to see men and society as literally attacking and assaulting women and girls, and much in the way of their bogus statistics is supposed to support this view." This explosive deliberation exposes the root cause of its self-contradiction. It targets Katherine Hanson, director of the publicly funded Women's Educational Equity Act Publishing Center as instance in

---

[118]A critic by Christina Hoff Sommers, Simon & Schuster, The War Against Boys, How Misguided Feminism is Harming Our Young Men (2000)

point for misinforming the public that, "every year nearly four million women are beaten to death."

Christina thinks that this practice was typical feminist modus operandi to stay important endlessly, and statistically challenges the statement as a far fledged inflation of the truth. She substantiates her position by claiming that, "the total female deaths per year are no more than one million, while female homicide deaths are actually about 3,600 -- cf. pp.48-49."[118]

The number of women victimized by domestic violence every year as provided by Christina's account is still a disturbing problem, intolerable by any healthy society, because one death is one more too many. Nonetheless, the fact remains that Katherine Hanson may have exaggerated the number by a little more than 1111% may be for the sake of her own personal advantage.

Through the book, Christina attacks the damage done by feminists in the area of "self-esteem and educational disadvantages of girls, which gave rise to a decade of feminist rhetoric and activism to promote the cause of girls in schools."

Obviously, like all other points of view in society, feminism will appear on and off as the philosophical fashion of the season for generations to come. In this regard, Christina has put forth a tremendous effort disclosing the existence of women that use deception as a stepping-stone to recruit the younger generation of women into their fanatical viewpoint, through which they continue to materially exploit society. They know the devastating interference hurts everybody in the long run, as it affects regulations at the government level of the criminological game, but they do not care. To this provocation, Christina delivers substance by yet claiming, "The federal "Educational Equity Act" itself was a consequence of this tendency, as the "Violence Against Women Act" was the result of the overheated rhetoric and overblown statistics about women's physical safety."

In her book *A Fearful Freedom: Women's Flight from Equality*, Wendy Kaminer confines the situation to two forms of feminism: "egalitarian" and "protectionist." The first upholds equality between women and men conforming to genuine feminism and the second focuses on legal protections for women through partial employment laws to female workers and biased divorce laws that sometimes infringe men's rights.

There is no way to go upwards after reaching the pinnacle of anything, only down ward. The airtight closure of the cause should certainly have pushed bad feminists to a desperate situation of scavenging for immediate reasons for survival. They could not do what they chose to do without introducing new agendas to outlast the consequences of success. They had to distort the fundamental scope of their principles to continue benefiting from dead issues, for creativity becomes important at that point of heartless detachment from humanity. After all, feminist leaders are from the middle and upper class of society, they are educated and had all the material resources and political connections they needed to promote their status.

"The feminist agenda is inconsistent with independence for women. In short, it is an agenda that replaces dependence on men with dependence on government," says Carrie L. Lukas, the "Director of Policy at the Independent Women's Forum."[119] It sounds like she thinks that feminism after years of obstinate struggle had secured gender equality in America by transforming the "legal structures" that stood in the way of women. She gives some good

---

[119]Lukas, Carrie L. *Dependency Divas: How the Feminist Big Government Agenda Betrays Women* (January 30, 2004) Retrieved from: http://www.iwf.org/publications/show/18681.html

examples on the matter in an article in the Washington Times (2/20/2004) but balances her opinion by stating that, "Today, however, many feminist groups seem reluctant to acknowledge the great gains women have made and have turned their backs on their own one-time goal: equality under the law" and that, "Many feminist groups are instead asking the government once again to treat women as second-class citizens."[119] She backs this allegation by pointing out that, "NOW's 'economic justice' proposal aims at "government provided healthcare, steeply progressive economic and tax policies, regulations to ensure 'pay equity' for women, no private investment in Social Security, and mandatory family supports such as employer-provided childcare and paid family and medical leave."[119]

As a particular creativity exhausts its life cycle, another is bound to appear to keep the momentum of greed rolling. Any creativity, however, eventually fades away because of its natural limitations. It is like Michael Jackson's case after *Thriller*, the Eagles experience after *Hotel California* and *New Kid in Town* and that of The Fleet Wood Mac's after *Rumors*. An artist in this situation can choose to enjoy life adjusting to the change or to miserably live in the past missing the spot light. Whatever the choice may be the outcome does not go beyond impacting personal life. The result is different, however, when big names like feminism decide to play with socio-political issues: society carries the heavy burden of their games. Survival by means of excessively rewarding a small portion of society at the expense of the rest can last in view of the few opportunists taking advantage of it because life is short but it ends up creating resentment later on for generations because society moves on forward.

My point is this: about 88,097 sexual crimes had been reported in 2009 in America and a quarter of such numbers (25%) is statistically known to be one of the lowest false accusation rates in the country. In view of this, about 22,024 accusations (88,097 x 0.25) must have been false that year. These criminals account only for about 0.007% of us assuming one accuser-per-accusation relationship and considering that the population stood at 307,006,550 that year. Now, assuming that an accusation affects about 10 people who are associated with the accused, it is logical to say about 220,240 people or 0.072% of the society should have suffered that year as a result. The consequence of false accusation on society, therefore exponentially exceeds the number of false accusers based on this simple calculation. The effect is also additive or progressive in pattern considering the damage done each year to our society. Chances are every one of us will face it one day if it continues at its current rate of expansion because the effect may surpass our rate of population growth eventually catching up with every American at some point in the future.

What feminist leaders did that year can then be summarized in the following three speculations:

- The first is sacrificing the entire population (307,006,550) in the end for the few criminals (22,024) who chose to lie for personal reasons.
- Secondly, sacrificing the cause of women in gender equality through a few criminals for personal material and power advantage, and
- Thirdly, endangering the healthy coexistence between men and women by pushing men to the limit and igniting a war between them to be settled one way or another in the future.

The result is sacrificing the trust of all the people affected by the dilemma because of victimized women in society. The rate of this mistrust (which is exponential in nature) should have been at about 220,240 people per year in 2009 alone.

Taking these figures (population and people affected by the problem each year) as constant, it would take about 1394 years (307,006,550/220240) for American society to nullify the case of victimized women completely. Of course, this assumption does not consider all the factors that influence the situation, but gives an idea as to where Radical feminism is navigating the cause of victims of rape in the long run.

It seems from the above citation as if there is still hope for an activist too frightened of victory to aim at a creative retreat, should the yesterday's person of mission degenerate into today's pain of society. However, this too has to stop at what I prefer to call the creativity stagnation point, where those who cannot leave society alone entertain impractical ideas out of more fear.

The Jews were made the object of contempt in Hitler's Germany to justify the killing of innocent people in the millions and the Tutsis did the same in the Hutu's ethnic genocide in Rwanda. It is as if the CIA is responsible for every failure of a nation or applying the Kashmir theory[120] as excuse for the wicked revolutionaries of the past to hold power for life. In the case of the rich women in the top hierarchy of feminism, the inborn existence of violent men became the new tool of remaining a social parasite forever because it is at least controversially usable to give the impression that all men were not only culturally but also naturally programmed to be rapists.

Feminism did not have to be afraid of its own success. It did not have to be that desperate for survival. It could have stayed important by helping Third World women, whose

---

[120]The territorial claim of Kashmir by the Indian and Pakistani governments and their refusal to settle the difference has been the main cause of regional competition for nuclear superiority, power abuse and people's suffering for decades.

217

situation is humanly deplorable, without compromising its integrity and/or comfort zone.

The Situation of Women in Some Third World Societies and Western Feminism's Reaction to It

Some dynasties, like Hammurabi's (First Dynasty king of the city-state of Babylon, in 1792 BC) might have offered a few progressive codes of gender law such as punishing both (husband and wife) to death by drowning or burning for unfaithfulness. This I think is better than the partial barbarism enforced against women for the same offense in the Blackfeet tribe of Native Americans, to the ancient Egyptian and the entire Far Eastern societies of yesterday and few societies of today. Yet, women's sexuality was legally sacrificed to ensure the legitimacy of the family structure, a husband/father had the legal right to control a family's wealth and a man had the right to enslave his wife if she initiated to break up the marriage. All these were a serious violation of women's rights.

"Earlier this month . . . [a]n Afghan woman appeared on the cover of Time magazine, her nose cut off because she fled an abusive marriage. The other was the pregnant widow in Baghdis province accused of adultery. . . . The local Taliban commander ordered 200 lashes and then shot the woman to death. A Taliban spokesman denied responsibility in both cases but said that the woman should have been stoned to death instead."[121]

---

[121]Lawrence, Quil. *Brutality Against Women Stirs Fear In Afghanistan*/NPR (August 20, 2010) Retrieved from: http://www.npr.org/templates/story/story.php?storyId=129306237

This kind of cruel punishment takes place often in the Far Eastern societies. In Pakistan: *Woman loses her nose over alleged affair*, (April 6, 2009) Kal El reports, "A husband cut [his] wife's nose on allegations of having illicit relations with another man here in Kashmor."

In *Afghanistan Crossroads*, (March 18, 2010) the author exposes the saga of 19-year-old Bibi Aisha whose nose and ears were cut off according to Taliban justice for "shaming her husband's family."

There is a rampage going on in some Third World societies against women. "Over 32,000 murders, 19,000 rapes, 7,500 dowry deaths and 36,500 molestation cases against women were reported in India in 2006,"[122] according to *Crime Against Women in India*.

In *Taking on Violence Against Women in Africa*, Mary Kimani teaches that the World Health Organization (WHO), estimates about "50 per cent of women in Tanzania and 71 per cent of women in Ethiopia's rural areas reported beatings or other forms of violence by husbands or other intimate partners" in 2005. About "130 million girls have undergone the procedure [genital cutting] globally and 2 million are at risk each year, despite international agreements banning the practice." Further, "A local organization in Zaria, Nigeria, found that 16 per cent of patients with sexually transmitted diseases (STDs) were girls under the age of five, a sign of sexual assault. In the single year 1990, the Genito-Urinary Centre in Harare, Zimbabwe, treated more than 900 girls under 12 for STDs."[123]

---

[122]*Crimes Against Women in Indian*/Azad India Foundation (n.d.) Retrieved from: http://azadindia.org/social-issues/crime-against-women-in-india.html

[123]Retrieved from: http://www.un.org/ecosocdev/geninfo/afrec/vol 21no2/212-violence-aganist-women.html

Man has been and is still experimenting on female genetalia as if he has a personal problem with the vagina. The vagina has been used as the worst target of his sexual problems. The stronger his resentment about his sexual difficulties the more determined he became to disfigure its beauty. He has literally exhausted his creativity of physically destroying the vagina so far by applying four forms of genital assault; one wonders what he will do next in this regard. He first started by practicing Circumcision or Sunna, which involves removal of the hood of the clitoris by cutting while the body of the clitoris remains untouched. He developed his insanity to Excision or Clitoridectomy, which is the removal of the whole clitoris and part or all of the labia minora. He then came up with what is called an Intermediate circumcision, which includes the cutting and removal of the whole clitoris, all of the labia minora and part of the labia majora. He ended up practicing infibulation or Pharaonic circumcision, which involves the "complete removal of the labia minora and clitoris, as well as most, or all, of the labia majora. The resulting edges are then stitched together, covering the urethra, excluding a small opening for passage of urine and menstrual blood"[124] All forms of FGM (Female Genital Mutilation) are practiced on girls usually between the ages of five and fifteen in many countries around the world, but extensively in Africa.

In addition, breast mutilation may still take place on infant girls in the Amazon, while rape has been used as a weapon of war in many underdeveloped societies. This took place widely in Darfur for example and excessive sexual violence against women is normal in the Democratic Republic of Congo (DRC) where "Women are gang-raped, often in front of their families and communities. In

---

[124]Roth, Eric Abella. *Culture, biology, and anthropological demography*/The Press Syndicate of the University of Cambridge p.37

numerous cases, male relatives are forced at gun point to rape their own daughters, mothers or sisters,"[125] says Yakin Erturk to Reuters in GENEVA, Switzerland.

Four desperate sisters in Syria were convinced to marry their rapists (government militiamen) by choice as the best alternative "to reclaim their honor" and "[to avoid probable capital punishment from their families or to not ever being forced staying single]."[126]

The savage stoning of women is still practiced in the mullahs' governance of Iran. Hundreds of women of different age groups have suffered the brutality throughout Iran in the name of Islam despite the Quran's and Prophet Mohammad's disapproval of such behavior.

This problem is going full speed ahead throughout the world. According to Dehai.org (an Eritrean web site operating from the US) disclosure on Thursday, November 19, 2009, "A 20-year-old Somalian divorcee has been stoned to death for committing what a judge has said was adultery." The execution took place as recently as November 17, 2009 by Court order of "Sheikh Ibrahim Abdirahman," a judge authorized to take care of justice by a fundamentalist group called "al-Shabab." His verdict condemned her to be "buried up to her waist before the stoning took place" in front of the public and in the face of US and French troops next door in Djibouti.

It is impossible for me to think about what happened without diverting my attention elsewhere as soon as it comes to my mind, let alone to have the courage of watching the barbarism in person as some people did.

---

[125]U.N.: *Brutality against women in Congo 'beyond rape'*/Reuters (July 30, 2007) Retrieved from: http://www.cnn.com/2007/WORL D/africa/07/30/congo.rape.reut/

[126]Al Jous, Khirbet. *Acts of Healing in Syria*/Washington Express, (June 21, 2011)

The issue is very serious and needs the full attention of people regardless of gender. We have a lot of work to do out there and we cannot get anywhere divided on the issue of gender equality. We just cannot ethically face mortality ignoring the plight of Third World women for the advantage of the immoral few standing in the way of our unity to defend humanity. Although the United Nations Development Fund for Women (UNIFEM)[127] and the Committee on the Elimination of Discrimination against Women (CEDAW)[128]

---

[127]"The United Nations Development Fund for Women, commonly known as UNIFEM was established in December 1976 originally as the Voluntary Fund for the United Nations Decade for Women in the International Women's Year. Since 1976 it has supported women's empowerment and gender equality through its programme offices and links with women's organizations in the major regions of the world. Its work on gender responsive budgets began in 1996 in Southern Africa and has expanded to include East Africa, Southeast Asia, South Asia, Central America and the Andean region. It has worked to increase awareness throughout the UN system of gender responsive budgets as a tool to strengthen economic governance in all countries." *United Nations Development Fund for Women*/ Wikipedia (n.d.)

Retrieved from: http://en.wikipedia.org/wiki/United_Nations_Devel opment_Fund_for_Women

[128]"CEDAW was officially established. In 1992, the committee affirmed that violence against women was a "violation of their internationally recognized human rights" and "a form of discrimination" that "nullified their right to freedom, security and life." The effort of women in this regard has successfully worked for implementation of international treaties such as the 1979 United Nations Convention on the Elimination of All Forms of Discrimination against Women. This convention pressurizes governments to transform biased practices and laws in their societies."

existed for a while, their collective achievement does not look very impressive compared to how long they have been around. One of the reasons for this in my opinion is lack of attention from hard core American Feminism, which is probably the richest and strongest feminist structure in the world. It is responsible for diverting resources from the cause of international women through gender feminism. I do believe that an organization so powerful to change the law in America can do something better to address the issues of international women through the UN. One of the things it needs to do is change its approach of false accusation in this country and attack the problem with full concentration elsewhere.

I also believe that American Feminism by now could have better influenced the world by becoming a legitimate organization for all women and by having Ambassadors all over the world for the cause had it continued on the path of genuine feminism. All the resources wasted since the seventies to implement discriminatory laws in America could have been invested in lobbying the UN to address the issue more effectively. The UN after all is heavily financed by American taxpayers and feminism is very good at manipulating American politicians in the government. Our politicians could have been better pressured to polarize the world against crimes of violence internationally through the UN. Unfortunately, feminism failed terribly here for personal reasons.

Case in point:

"The struggle of Iranian women that erupted into visibility in 2009 should have been a clarion call for feminists and feminist organizations worldwide to stand in solidarity with women in Iran from June 2009 forward. From the start, it has been a woman's revolution. However, Western feminists, and especially American feminist organizations, largely refrained from becoming active in support of the struggle of Iranian women. Even when the Islamic Republic was given a seat on the UN's Commission on the Status of Women at the end of April 2010, giving it a voice in determining global policy recommendations on gender equality and empowerment for women in all countries, no feminist organizations spoke up to condemn the selection of the misogynist regime.

In the aftermath of the Islamic Republic's ascension to the UN Commission on the Status of Women, Mission Free Iran renewed its outreach to feminist organizations, sending repeated requests to the National Organization of Women, Feminist Majority, and Code Pink, via email, phone call, Twitter and Facebook, asking them to take a position on the Islamic Republic vis-à-vis its abject violence against women, and its absurd legitimation by the UN Commission on the Status of Women. None of our overtures to these organizations received any response."[129]

To ignore the plight of women in Iran who are victims of "bad hijab," a traditional norm that allows men to harass women everywhere for showing an ankle and to fine them for using nail polish and lipstick is unfortunate. Iran is a country that stoned to death Sakineh Ashtiani, Maryam Ghorbanzadeh, Azar Bagheri, and more than ten other women since the mullahs came to power. This is a country where the government legally considers a woman half as good as a man and that permits child molestation in the name of marriage (a man can legally get married to a 9-year-old girl). What is worse is that American feminist organizations did not have the time to communicate back to

---

[129]Sotoudeh, Nasrin. *American Feminist Organizations Begin to Demonstrate Support for Iranian Women*/facebook (posted by missionfreeiran, November 16, 2010) Retrieved from: http://www.facebook.com/note.php?note_id=175011209191539&id =157026050976786

those who directly approached them for help knowing that the Iranian government arrests female human rights lawyers, and renders women entirely voiceless.

As for American feminism's pattern of misbehavior elsewhere, the article says White American feminists engage in widespread racist hate speech.[130] It states that, "Over the last few years there has been a disturbing trend of white American and Western European women engaging in widespread racist hate speech against non-white (or non-Arian-white) women from Latin America, Asia, and Eastern Europe. White feminist women openly degrade foreign women by calling them 'whores,' 'subservient,' 'submissive,' 'China dolls,' etc.; all because foreign women 'dare' to date and marry American and Western European men." Further, "White feminist women hate foreign women because they are viewed as 'not western enough' and therefore not suitable to date and marry American and Western European men' and that 'White feminist way of thinking is profoundly bigoted, racist, white-elitist, and insulting to all foreign women...'" It further states that this brand of feminism assumes that foreign women do not know how to live their lives, and western women have to tell them how to do it." and closes the message stating that "Adolf Hitler in the 1930s wanted all Arian men to only marry and have children with Aryan women. One wonders if modern feminist women embraced Arian supremacy as their new ideology."

This allegation of course does not apply to all white feminists and I take it as subjective opinion, but I believe the

---

[130]*White American feminists engage in widespread racist hate speech*/Godlike Productions (8/26/2008) Retrieved from: http://www.godlikeproductions.com/forum1/message594032/pg1

inaction of the big feminist organization to the cause of international women implies Western feminism's racist and ethnocentric tendency to a reasonable extent.

People can meticulously address racism and ethnocentrism in disguise. According to Courtney E. Martin,[131] Jessica Valenti in The Washington Post writes, "American women's tendency to look far across the oceans to get their pity fix while ignoring the sexism that still pervades our very own communities, classrooms, and workplaces." She flatly denies the objective reality that women were legally equal to men in America and says that Americans were suffering from "the mass delusion that women in America have achieved equality." Valenti argues that the tendency of American women to help international women was nothing but "feel-good illusion" and advises them to stop it by asking ". . . what about the women who still struggle for safety and economic opportunity in our own backyards? What about the woman who just did your nails who doesn't have health insurance? What about the SAT-prep course you just splurged on for your own daughter while your caregiver's daughter struggles to afford the price of taking the test at all? What about maternal mortality, not in Chad but in California?"

This is probably motivated by hidden agendas, in my opinion, because American Feminist Organizations are being accused of neglecting the cause of international women after achieving victory in America. There is simply no tangible evidence for her remarks to this effect, which seemingly targets the third wave of young American feminists who are challenging bad feminism's departure

---

[131]Martin, Courtney E. *A Challenge to American Women: The American PROSPECT* (March 8, 2010) Retrieved from: http://prospect.org/cs/articles?article=a_challenge_to_american_wo men

from the cause. They are trying to get the principle straight needless to state that the current maternal mortality rate in Chad is equally important to genuine feminism as the maternal mortality rate in California and elsewhere.

She further states, "You can bet that university women's centers, feminist philanthropists, and nonprofit organizations all over the United States are brimming with outrage today. They are marching against sex trafficking in Eastern Europe, donating to women-led microenterprise efforts in India and Bangladesh, sending their bake-sale money to help build Eve Ensler's "City of Joy" in Congo." This is clear-cut prejudice in my understanding.

The "struggle for safety and economic opportunity in our own backyards" is not the problem of women only but of American men as well. The problem with "the woman who just did your nails who doesn't have health insurance" has nothing to do with equality, for lack of health insurance is rampant in countless situations of working men in America. Even worse, we have homeless men and women here who don't have jobs and struggle every day for the basic necessities of life, needless to state that many American boys and girls cannot afford the price of SAT (Scholastic Aptitude Test) as a matter of poverty.

What is implied here is the psychological transformation of America's feminism through the years into a different level of makeup. The comfort level of its leaders has obscured the very cause that brought them to power thereby degenerating them both in substance and spirituality at the local and international stages of humanity. Sexism has turned their mind from the essence of equality to the point of totally disregarding the condition of men in our society and of women elsewhere.

On the flip side, Jessica Valenti in *The fake feminism of Sara Palin*, Washington Post, (May 30, 2010) criticizes Sara Palin for claiming to be a feminist by "[invoking] the words "feminism" and "feminist" no less than a dozen times [and calling] for a "pro-woman sisterhood" and [addressing] the "sisters" in the audience" in a speech. She also bluffed Palin's "regular references to gun rights" and her sounding like "Gloria Steinem."[132] The question is if she is a genuine feminist herself, considering at least the whereabouts of her concept of sisterhood towards Third World women and her illusion about the common problems of Americans. Further, can one be classified as feminist solely for being pro-choice and against gun laws? I do not think so. In any case, Jessica Valenti concluded her article by being sarcastic about 'Phyllis Schlafly feminism'.

It seems like Radical feminism is trapped between true feminists of the likes of Phyllis Schlafly, third wave feminists and conservative feminists like Sara Palin. It has become the victim of its own divisive and sexist propaganda and is desperately fighting for survival. It is having a hard time collecting women under its central command, which is a good sign of the beginning of the end of Radical feminism in America.

Clearly, the existence of false accusations can no longer be discounted without taking the risk of hurting the cause of women at large. This is not a football game where a team intends to win by any means necessary. We need to close this chapter with tangible unity. The least feminism can do is to differentiate the good from the bad in both genders. Minus this, the result will be diverting resources away from the helpless that are facing the fatality of gender supremacy without any attention from Black, White, Liberal or Radical feminism.

Feminism cannot use the situation of Third World women as an excuse to punish men through false

---

[132]Retrieved from: http://www.washingtonpost.com/wp-dyn/content/article/2010/05/28/AR2010052802263.html

accusations and remain inactive at the same time. It needs to deliver tangible results where it is due. It should carry its responsibility of defending freedom rather than hurting innocent men here in the US. What else can good men do beyond helping society to make laws that protect women from violent men? What can good men do to remain feminists and have the mercy of feminism without changing their gender?

What happened to the poor girl in Somalia and other victims of violence should have been in the movement's written materials and speeches globally. There should have been protests everywhere to expose the situations and to trigger universal actions against the problem just as the Egyptians and Tunisians handled their political business against their heartless dictators.

Let me now challenge the movement on this ground: Where are NOW and other feminist groups in this crisis and in, for example, the poor Somalian girl's predicament? How did they address the tragedy (if they ever did) to be seriously taken as vanguards of women's quest for freedom?

Either way, I do not believe enough effort was taken to change the situation and my common sense legitimizes the following reasons for why inaction has become the order of the day for American upper class feminists.

At the face value of the matter, they are unwilling to make a living by working hard considering the amount of dedication required to challenge chauvinistic cultures and religions internationally. In the unconscious backdrop though, this reluctance seems to originate from a factor that I cannot afford ignoring. They call it prejudice, a congenital human sickness that can only be remedied by honest internal drive. Upper class feminism could not have overlooked the situation of women elsewhere without being racist.

Consistent with the fundamental difference between black feminism and mainstream feminism in the past, colored women of Gloria Jean Watkins' caliber might have this in mind when they separated themselves from the conventional white middle class feminism of yesterday based on "the issues that divided women."[133] The voices of post-colonial feminists against Western feminism's ethnocentric tendency of dealing with the common problem might also have had elements of truth in view of this hypothesis.

This provokes a question to black feminists of today. What is the essence of your excuse of detachment from the conventional movement beyond verbal pretension? If racism vindicates today's upper class white feminists from focusing on the suffering of international women, what type of ethnocentrism vindicates yours?

The silence of feminism on its prior responsibility and its choice of attacking men here based on their gender compromises principles, causes, spirituality and rationality at large because trying to normalize violent men is as challenging as turning an evil woman around, a subject matter beyond extrinsic involvement that can only be rectified by individually driven psychic transformation. The choice is simply theirs but to criminalize the entire gender inclusively based on the existence of such men is to declare unconditional war against *all* men, women and children.

Good people have always been part of the resistance to liberate women from the shambles of chauvinism and are still driven to continue the sacrosanct mission globally.

---

[133]This was the situation of colored women around the world, which was aggravated by European Colonialism. It was about the situation of women under white man's rule in view of white middle class based feminism, which seemed to have been inexistent at the time of the ideological confrontation.

President Bush' approval of "Laci and Connor's Law"[134] to protect unborn children from domestic violence is clearly the byproduct of combined effort and an example of how we could together tighten the noose around cold criminals. President Obama's official approval of the law on equal pay for equal work is likewise another blow to sexism. The continuation of such achievements is, however, stringently up to good feminists.

All said, no evil stays potent forever and the fate of bad feminism cannot be different. Its abuse of society should stop and it should be soon. American men and women should be aware of what is going on and actively participate to protect themselves and their children from bad feminism. The good news is the birth of a new scientific support system in brain fingerprinting[135] that has the potential to answer the status of a crime in parallel with DNA technology. But, it is up to every good feminist to pressure

---

[134]Note: HR 1997 was placed on the U.S. Senate calendar on March 25, 2004, passed by a roll call vote of 61-38, and signed into law by Pres. Bush on April 1, 2004

[135]"Brain Fingerprinting is a controversial forensic science technique that uses electroencephalography (EEG) to determine whether specific information is stored in a subject's brain. It does this by measuring electrical brainwave responses to words, phrases, or pictures that are presented on a computer screen (Farwell & Smith 2001). Brain fingerprinting was invented by Lawrence Farwell. The theory is that the brain processes known, relevant information differently from the way it processes unknown or irrelevant information (Farwell & Donchin 1991). The brain's processing of known information, such as the details of a crime stored in the brain, is revealed by a specific pattern in the EEG (electroencephalograph) (Farwell & Smith 2001, Farwell 1994). "*Brain fingerprinting*/Wikipedia (n.d.) Retrieved from: http://en.wikipedia.org/wiki/Brain_fingerprinting

the government into making the tools mandatory in all violence-related cases if we intend to survive as a family.

The Need to Reject American Style Feminism in the Third World

Things are certainly changing in favor of women in some Third World countries. With all the problems associated with global liberation struggles, the condition of women has shown significant improvement through the years. Direct involvement of women in the struggle to improve human conditions in Cuba, Nicaragua, Eritrea, Ethiopia, Rwanda, Uganda, and South Africa has shown significant result in transforming the condition of women in society.

The Eritrean government for example, banned female genital mutilation (FGM) in 2007. Two ministerial posts are filled today by veteran women of the struggle for independence: Askalu Menkerios (Minister of Labor and Human Welfare) and Fozia Hashim (Minister of Justice). Children are not bitten by elders as they used to be and boys and girls have equal opportunity to join the Army and to attend school. More work is necessary, however, because chauvinism is rooted in the Eritrean society.

In Rwanda, women account for 56 percent (45 out of 80) of the Parliament, first in the world in which women hold a majority. This achievement is the result of challenging patriarchal laws that prevented women from inheriting land. The legislature has passed bills to end domestic violence and child abuse, at minimum.

Education of women has been the priority in Guinea since the early 1990s. The government did a great job in building latrines, assisting pregnant students, distributing free textbooks and increasing the number of female teachers. "By 2000, the country had more than doubled the number of girls in school and increased boys' attendance by 80 per cent"[136]

The trend is positive in all African countries except Somalia, which is considered the second worse (to Afghanistan) country for women in the world.

In Latin America and the Caribbean, the situation of women is improving. Since 1990, at least Argentina, Chile, Costa Rica, Guyana, Nicaragua, Panama, and Brazil have had elected women presidents. In this regard, they stay way ahead of the United States. So is the trend in some countries in Asia. Women in Islamic societies still have a long way to go, though there are good signs that change is unavoidable.

One thing that has become apparent so far is that there is a big mentality gap between what Western feminists and Third World feminists think about Third World women as much as there is a gap between how the two feminist sects look at feminism as a collective subject matter. Western feminists could not help undermining the cause of Third World women by the simple historical fact that the white man dominated the world for centuries. He could not have done it all by himself without the support of women, meaning that white women were also involved in racially and economically dehumanizing people of color internationally. Whether they were dragged into it or not is immaterial; they were there with him throughout the inclusive dominance over all other races on the planet. Further, the white race directly or indirectly has been the technological leader of the world for centuries.

It was, therefore, natural for white women to have been psychologically inclined in favor of indifference towards the rest. In empathic expression, white women were the

---

[136]Mutume, Gumisai. *African women battle for equality*/Africa Renewal (n.d.) Retrieved from: http://www.un.org/ecosocdev/geni nfo/afrec/vol19no2/192_pg06.htm

circumstantial victims of colonialism in terms of inculcated racial and academic supremacy over all other women in the world. Therefore, the tendency of Western feminism to lead and dictate is an inherent result of the white experience in society that it cannot help adopting. This proclivity is unstoppable and irreversible even by genuine personal effort for it is the psychic consequence of cumulative prejudice.

Superiority complex ". . . refers to an overly high opinion of oneself. In psychology, it refers to the unrealistic and exaggerated belief that one is better than others. In contrast, inferiority complex sufferers mimic this as a way to compensate for unconscious feelings of low self-esteem or inadequacy."[137]

To my understanding, the contrast did not apply in the past because the white man, in a way, earned that mentality by means of practical experience. It may not apply today, however, because of many other factors that defy the theory; but this development took place sometime after the damage was already done to the white psychological makeup. No matter how clever one may be in depressing the tendency, chances are it will come out at different occasions because it is permanently instilled in the unconscious mind if not in the conscious mind of all white people.

Apparently, Western feminism has, in many ways demonstrated the "Rush Limbaugh/Mark Levin syndrome" (a fixation in my opinion that does not flinch from assuming the white race is the best if not the only qualified race of leadership) over Third World feminism on many different occasions.

Instance in point is what happened in the 1993 World Conference on Human Rights in Vienna, where women of all

---

[137]*Superiority complex*/Wikipedia (n.d.) Retrieved from: http://en.wikipedia.org/wiki/Superiority_complex

backgrounds arrived to discuss their human rights issues. The wide gap that separates "Third World" women from "First World" women came out in the open for everyone to see. According to Azizah al-Hibri,[138] a law professor and scholar of Muslim women's rights "Third World women were surprised to see that this task had been performed on their behalf by First World women, who used their organizational skills to take control of the conference and determine its agenda." They "noted that they could not very well worry about other matters when their children were dying from thirst, hunger or war . . . The shock was so profound that, immediately upon leaving Vienna, Third World women began internal discussions to define a course of action that would avert a future repeat of this undemocratic/patriarchal situation." This behavior was earlier detected in "the 1981 United Nations Mid-Decade for Women conference in Copenhagen, [where] the gulf was already apparent. At the Forum, the concurrent unofficial conference held in conjunction with the official UN conference, the gulf became so wide that a series of Third World women's meetings were held impromptu on site. As a result, at least one plenary session designed to express the views of Third World women was added."

A few things frustrated the Third World women in the conference according to the author. Firstly, First World women behaved in such a way that they represented all women in the conference without mandate. Secondly, they selected a Third World woman as the spokesperson of the group independent of its consent and created an environment where the person performed strictly from First World point of view. This was nothing more than

---

[138]al-Hibri, Azizah. *Who Defines Women's Rights? A Third World Woman's Response* (n.d.) Retrieved from: http://www.wcl.american. edu/hrbrief/v2i1/alhibr21.htm

participation without inclusion, where Third World feminists joined the conferences and Western feminists decided their needs and spoke for them without any prior discussion.

The situation was so bad that Third World women protested against the International Conference on Population and Development (ICPD) recently held in Cairo "for not being responsive to their concerns."

The writer puts the consensus of Third World women in general, as "The impact of American feminism on Third World women has been positive. Unfortunately, however, the positive effects have been diminished by some vocal First World women activists who appear to dominate international [sic] fora. The problem lies with the approach these activists take. They refuse to treat Third World women as equals, even as they claim[s] to fight for their human rights." [138]

Analogous to the perception that men were better than women by cultural and traditional orientation, the postulate that Western women feel intellectually and culturally more developed than the rest of the world through human experience of dictation is a phenomenon beyond their capacity to change. To this effect, the article intelligently addresses the psychological fixation of white women where the veil used by white colonial women in Algeria is used as excuse "for rejecting the Algerian woman's culture and denigrating her" and for making her feel that she "[was] 'superior to' these veiled women. . . "[139] The veil may not be as significant to the question of women's equality as some

---

[139]Lazreg, Marnia (an Algerian-born feminist) *The Eloquence of Silence* (Routledge 1994)

people think; not at least to Naghibi,[140] who states "Reza Shah Pahlavi (the first of Iran's two emperors) banned veiling [1936] as part of an attempt to 'modernize' Iran. Women who resisted the ban had their veils ripped from their bodies. Naghibi suggests that the 1936 ban was, in many ways, quite similar to the ban on unveiling that would be imposed in 1983. Both pieces of legislation, at their roots, attempted to use women's bodies to promote a particular form of nationalism, whether westernized or anti-imperialist. 'Beneath these two polarized representations,' she writes, 'lies a desire to possess and to control the figure behind the veil by unveiling or re-veiling her.'"[141]

Naghibi further attacks Western feminism for being a victim of delusion by further stating, ". . . the visibility of Muslim women—whether veiled or unveiled—has caused a great deal of anxiety for Western feminists, who have largely ignored the indigenous presence of Muslim women's activism. During the Constitutional Revolution (1905-1911), for example, Iranian women participated in protests, acted as couriers and even took up arms. Naghibi argues that such actions threaten feminists' perceptions of themselves "as liberated and modern in contrast to imprisoned and backwards Persian women, and . . . as leaders of the international women's movement."[141]

---

[140]Nima Naghibi is an Associate Professor of English at Ryerson University. She is the author of *Rethinking Global Sisterhood: Western feminism and Iran* (Minnesota Press, 2007)

[141]Wiegand, Erin. Unveiling Muslim Feminism, Culture : Muslim women's bodies are too frequently used to symbolize the state of Islam in Iran, and the degree to which it associates itself with the West/In These Times (September 7, 2007) Retrieved from: http://www.inthesetimes.com/article/3310/unveiling_muslim_feminism/

Apparently, Western feminists could not have properly identified with the needs of Third World women without being exposed to their experience or consulting their feminists. In Copenhagen, they misidentified their highest priority as related to "the veil and clitoridectomy (female genital mutilation)" and in Cairo, as related to "contraception and abortion." A good effort, but the Third World women disagreed because they thought "Peace and development" were their priorities, only to receive a head nod and nothing to change. Their sense of hope was certainly shattered by the improper actions of Western feminists who ended up "forcing the issue of abortion on every one from [their own] perspective." They addressed issues like the need to reduce producing babies in the Third World in order to safeguard universal resources "[when in fact the white societies were responsible for abusing most of the resources on earth.]"

One classical example to this misunderstanding took place in recent past between Palestinian feminists and Western feminists. Adel Samara touched on this issue stating that the first had a problem with the very orientation of the other. She teaches that "western feminists did not deal with the class issue, because they themselves are not Marxists and some are actually opposed to Marxism. Their point of reference, therefore, was not class analysis since they are either liberal or radical feminists. That is why, they failed to deal with the class weakness in the Palestinian feminist discourse and struggle, and hence the focus of their critique was the weakness of Palestinian feminism."[142] Western feminists simply failed to notice that the

---

[142]Samara, Adel. *Adel Samara - What if Palestinian Feminism was Class Oriented?*/Uprooted Palestinians (Friday, July 24, 2009) Retrieved from: http://uprootedpalestinians.blogspot.com/2009/07/adel-samara-what-if-palestinian.html

"Palestinian women were and still are the real component of the Palestinian resistance movement, so class weakness in analysis, struggle and discourse is shared."

Western feminists were obviously focusing on future Palestinian women being in the kitchen after independent Palestinian State is realized. This is true says Samara but it is "nothing new and therefore, does not constitute a new contribution. It is rather a repeat, in a colonial manner of a well-known fact, of other experiences that Palestinians are familiar with... The irony came from the ground crystallized in the fact that Palestinian resistance, the "secular" current, reached a point of deadlock, it failed to liberate Palestine or even the Occupied Territories of 1967, but even internalized the defeat and accepted the conditions and terms of their triad enemy." I bring this to your attention because it clearly tells me that the priority of the Palestinian people is forming an independent state. Anything else is then secondary. This fundamental contradiction was misguided because the westerners approached the issue from the angle of their situation (citizens of sovereign countries).

By all accounts, the denial of the Palestinian right to self-determination automatically deters the development of a Palestinian constitution or any other legal institutions that ought to take the question of Palestinian women to the next level. It seems to me, that the immediate priority of the Palestinian and the Afghani women for that matter should be the safety of their children and their brothers that are being wasted in conflicts: the first, through fighting to form an independent state and the second through lack of peace and a stable government. Among other issues, the expulsion of 750,000 Palestinian refugees in the creation of the Israeli state in 1948 and their unchanged situation to date further directs women's priority away in favor of the Palestinian question.

Furthermore, the two sides of feminism lack common understanding on prostitution. Radical feminism encouraged it as means of liberation from male domination and its followers did it by choice. Third World feminism understands prostitutes as voluntary sex workers. It is a necessity in the Third World, however, that women involuntarily engage in for survival. The question is how Western feminism can possibly produce positive results in the situation of victimized sex workers in the Third World! How can they help family structures elsewhere when they fight to destroy it at home?

Then comes pornography (supported by some Western feminists), which is defended by the constitution of America as freedom of speech but impossible to implement in most Third World cultures. It simply will not work. Knowledge to this effect is freely provided by many Third World feminists for anyone interested to learn.

Apparently, Western feminism is not only incapable of resolving the issues of Third World women for many important reasons but it also seems that its definition of "Third Word" contradicts with reality on the ground. In Third World and Third World Women, Gayatri Chakravorty Spivak[143] explains that the term "Third World" originated as a result of the new environment created after the Second World War by "the initial attempt in the Bandung

---

[143]"Gayatri Chakravorty Spivak (born February 24, 1942) is an Indian literary critic, theorist, and self-described "practical Marxist-feminist-deconstructionist." [1] She is best known for the article "Can the Subaltern Speak?", considered a founding text of post colonialism, and for her translation of Jacques Derrida's Of Grammatology. Spivak teaches at Columbia University, where she was tenured as University Professor in March 2007." *Gayatri Chakravorty Spivak*/Wikipedia (n.d.) Retrieved from: http://en.wiki pedia.org/wiki/Gayatri_Chakravorty_Spivak

Conference (1955) to establish a third way -- neither with the Eastern nor within the Western bloc."[144] She then says, "it was not accompanied by a commensurate intellectual effort" and only encompassed the situation of resistance reflected by the overall norms of social order in the Third World societies of the time.

Kumkum Sangari argues that "Third World [is] a term that both signifies and blurs the functioning of an economic, political, and imaginary geography able to unite vast and vastly differentiated areas of the world into a single 'underdeveloped' terrain" and criticizes the west for "indiscriminately lump[ing] together vastly different places."[145]

Chandra Talpade Mohanty defines the Third World, as "the nation-states of Latin America, the Caribbean, Sub-Saharan Africa, South and South-east Asia, China, South Africa, and Oceania constitute the parameters of the non-European third world. In addition, black, Latino, Asian, and indigenous peoples in the U.S., Europe, Australia, some of whom have historic links with the geographically defined third worlds, also define themselves as third world peoples.'" She argues that, "what seems to constitute 'women of color' or 'third world women'" was therefore the commonality in "women's oppositional political relation to sexist, racist, and imperialistic structures" rather than their "color or ethnic identification." She then friendly criticizes Western feminists for taking the "third world woman as a

---

[144]Graves, Nicola. *Third World and Third World Women*/Emory University (Spring 1996) Retrieved from: http://english.emory.edu/Bahri/ThirdWorld.html

[145]Sangari, Kumkum. "The Politics of the Possible" *The Nature and Context of Minority Discourse*, Eds. Abdul Jan Mohamed and David Lloyd, New York: Oxford UP, (1990) Retrieved from: http://english.emory.edu/Bahri/ThirdWorld.html

singular monolithic subject" and a product of "discursive colonization" and also for the contradiction in trying to explain the "third world difference" from yet the same angle of "discursive colonization."[146]

An interesting part of this exchange of ideas between feminists of different backgrounds is how naïvely Western feminists can miss the point concerning the "Third World women" theory by asking the question "'why do we have to be concerned with the question of Third World women? After all, it is only one issue among many others." This sounds like Marie Antoinette's "let them eat cake" to the starving people during the French revolution. Trinh T. Minh's sarcastic answer to this shallow question was, "delete the phrase Third World and the sentence immediately unveils its value-loaded clichés."[147]

In view of this, what feminism reflects to Western women was artificial feminism within "the context of (neo-colonialist) anthropology" to Third World women. After stating that the "term Third World applied in two ways: to refer to 'underdeveloped'/overexploited geopolitical entities" Cheryl Johnson-Odim says that there is no single ideology that defines feminism although the general consensus in the Third World supports the notion that the movement "emerg[ed] from white, middle-class western women [that]

---

[146]Mohanty, Chandra Talpade. "Introduction" and "Under Western Eyes" *Third World Women and the Politics of Feminism*, Eds. Mohanty, Russo, Torres, Bloomington and Indianapolis: Indiana UP, (1991) Retrieved from: http://english.emory.edu/Bahri /ThirdWorld.html

[147]Trinh, Minh-ha. "Difference: 'A Special Third World Woman Issue." /Discourse 8 (Fall-Winter 86-87): 10-37. Retrieved from: http://english.emory.edu/Bahri/ThirdWorld.html

narrowly confine themselves to the struggle against gender discrimination." [148]

Likewise, tangible differences existed between Western feminism and Black feminism from the onset of the struggle for equality. So has been the situation between Western and African and Post-Colonial feminism. The tendency of Western feminists to consider themselves as the most educated women who deserve to lead the movement clashes with their ignorance about the Third world women in general and Third World feminism in particular. This conflict is well expressed by Elizabeth Warnock Fernea[149] where she disclosed her surprise about how much she did not know before going to the Middle East about the mentality and situation of Moslem women. Fernea went with her husband to southern Iraq having in mind "to enlighten Middle Eastern women" but came back to the States enlightened by them instead to the point of "re-evaluat[ing] [her] view of the world of women." Yet, her peers in the US did not accept her new understanding of the Moslem society and continued to live with their fixation that "Muslim women were living in ignorance and oppression." It so appears from her experience that Western women exemplify Moslem women's conditions as the "worst case

---

[148]Johnson-Odim, Cheryl. "Common Themes, Different Contexts: Third World Women and Feminism." *Third World Women and the Politics of Feminism*/Eds. Mohanty, Russo, Torres. Bloomington and Indianapolis: Indiana University Press (1991) Retrieved from: http://english.emory.edu/Bahri/ThirdWorld.html

[149]"Islamic Feminism Finds a Different Voice: The Muslim women's movement is discovering its roots in Islam, not in imitating Western feminists." *Islamic Feminism*/International Congress on Islamic Feminism (n.d.) Retrieved from: http://feminismeislamic.org/2cong res/participants/

scenario" contrary to how a Moslem woman is accepted by society as the center of a family structure.

The point is that it is wrong to view Moslem women so stereotypically because their societies are as diverse as any other society in the world, depending on economic class distinction, socio-political position and background of origin. They do not revolve around a central axis that uniformly defines them. They interpret and apply the Quranic verses differently similarly to what Christians do with the Bible. The way the Sunnis and Shia Moslems differ on women's inheritance of parental wealth is a reality that supports the narrative. Further, the Islamic dress code is regulated differently in the Moslem world such that women are obliged to respect it in places such as Afghanistan and Saudi Arabia but not in Lebanon, Egypt, Morocco and Tunisia. It is common to see couples walking together and romancing in Egypt for example, and most women wear a headscarf by choice.

Not only was the Islamic world misunderstood but also some Moslems believe the west is in some ways more backward. One argument to this effect states that Islam allows sex to be enjoyed within the limits of marriage while Christianity suppresses it as a value of flesh rather than the spirit.

The bottom line is, women in general have similar concerns of inequality but while western women do it their way, based on the institutionalized separation of the state and the church, Moslem women do it according to their culture without separating the state and religion. This difference has not been settled as yet. A French Feminist Juliette Minces in *The House of Obedience: Women in Arab Society* for instance blames "Islam and some religious manifestations of Muslim women for their so-called 'oppression and backwardness'"[150] needless to state that Islamic societies have a better record than most Third World countries in literacy rate and women's participation in education.

Half of the students in the Egyptian and Moroccan school systems are women and the literacy rate in both countries is higher than 50%. In Kuwait, women won the right to vote in 2005 while custodial mothers today have parental authority in Algeria. Although, women are still underrepresented in politics, the justice system and the private sector, the fact remains that significant change has been registered by Middle Eastern societies for women.[151] Today's new Middle Eastern woman is everywhere in society from education, business, the media, banks, industries to all forms of health facilities. Siham Abdul Rizouki's (the former Assistant Undersecretary of the oil ministry of Kuwait) appointment to the country's board of OPEC supports this postulate.

In short, women in Islamic societies do not seem to have a problem with religion at all. The tendency of women scholars, therefore, leans towards the notion that women's liberation was achievable under Islam. They believe they need legally established equal pay for equal work, abortion rights, maternity privileges, etc. Homegrown feminism to this direction is active today in the Islamic societies. Apart from the most radical Atheist and Secular feminists, Muslim feminists argue that women's imagination of Islam in the Islamic societies was dominated by men's interpretation of Islam rather than by the realistic version of the religion as

---

[150]*An Essay Review by Maha Al-Aranki*/Students' Own Corner (n.d.) Retrieved from: http://unlearningtonotspeak.com/?p=389

[151]Joffe-Walt, Benjamin. *Womens rights improve across the Middle East*/The Media Line (03/07/2010 10:26) Retrieved from: http://www.jpost.com/MiddleEast/Article.aspx?id=170391

written in the Quran. Further, they suggest that women can pick Quranic verses suitable to their cause and ignore the versions that reflect the current society of Islam. In view of this, they suggest that women's freedom can be realized in Moslem societies given "a liberal and feminist review of the [Koran]."

With all these accounts, misunderstanding still exists between feminists from different parts of the world. Rita Liljestrom, a Swedish sociologist, puts the difference between Christianity and Islam as ". . . the Christian Church attacks sexuality in itself. Sexuality is reduced to something "profane and sinful," sexuality signifies the division of human beings into body and soul. Civilization represents the soul's victory over the body, spirit over the flesh, and diligence over lust. Islam takes a different approach. It never repudiates sexuality as such. In fact, sex is a taste of paradise. But Islam attacks women instead."[152] This proposition adversely collides with the view of Islamic feminism, which believes that women's liberation comes from their substantial involvement in the existing fundamentalist and religious movement. One of the most notorious conformist feminists in this sect is Nesta Ramazani, an Iranian scholar who said that, "women's gathering in religious mourning, their presence in Friday prayers, and their participation in revolution and war eventually will lead to their emancipation."[152]

Some analysts point the finger at ethnocentrism as the root problem of this compulsive superiority fixation. Western feminists seem to hold onto their guns in spite of the educated confrontation from outstanding feminist philosophers from different schools of thought and cultural

---

[152]*"Islamic feminism": compromise or challenge to feminism?*/Iran Bulletin (n.d.) Retrieved from: http://www.iran-bulletin.org/political_islam/islamfeminismedited2.html

experiences that seem to clearly identify their problems in today's Third World societies.

If practice was to be considered as a measure of perception, all religions in my opinion acknowledge women's sexual potency. They directly or indirectly accept women as sexually superior to men. Man sees advantage in controlling her sexual power by either masking her beauty or mutilating her vagina. In this regard, most beliefs are the same except that the Moslems do it in manners that are more explicit. Why would men do this then without sexual hung-up? This being controversial, some analysts say that western culture perceives sexual inequality in terms of biological difference between men and women while Islam probably perceives it from the angle of a woman's supremacy.

One way or another, Third World feminist groups do not seem to be interested in destroying their family structures but only in building gender equality around them. Moslem women are trying to tell Western women not to judge their conditions by what is happening to women (such as honor crimes for adultery and disfiguring a woman's face) in extremist societies because the practices are based on social norms rather than on religious instructions of Islam. They are telling them to stop judging their status by their prejudiced conceptions. They do not appreciate comments such as Juliette Minces' view of Euro-centrism as being the only democratic model for women just because they disagree and they have no intention of being westernized, for there is nothing wrong with their society. They are saying that they value their Islamic culture as much as western women value their democracy and that "They will recruit supportive First World feminists to help them in their efforts, but they will specify the kind of support needed, and they will lead their own battles. They will not seek to achieve their liberation by denigrating their religion or culture or by forcing upon their communities inappropriate priorities and demands."[138] This resistance shows that Third World women see no advantage in scavenging for loopholes in the nature of men to attack them with but rather see men as their brothers and fathers who need help to be free from their ignorance.

The Power of Women in Today's Order of the World

There are quite a few powerful women in politics but Hillary Clinton by objective compromise is the most powerful woman of them all. Not only is she feminist by default of her gender but she also has always been one by choice of ideology. The question is how sincere she is in practicing it with consistency.

Apparently, her approach to President Clinton's sexual misbehavior was the ultimate litmus test to her feminism.

An article articulates that "The women's movement stands by Hillary Clinton as a symbol of the right to choose – a career, a home, a marriage. But what has she really chosen? . . . How do we reconcile Hillary the strong-willed feminist leader with Hillary the mistreated wife?" Sara Ehrman answers that, "She's a woman who has made choices [. . .] And her choices are her own" [153]

In Marc Morano's *Sen. Clinton Allegedly Intimidated Husband's Sexual Accuser*, Monday, July 07, 2008, it was said that "[ ] the alleged sexual improprieties of former president Bill Clinton also charges that current U.S. Sen. Hillary Clinton played a major role in threatening and intimidating her

---

[153]Mundy, Liza. *The Hillary Dilemma*/The Washington Post Magazine (Sunday, March 21, 1999) Retrieved from: http://www.washingtonpost.com/wp-srv/politics/campaigns/keyraces2000/stories/hillary032199.htm

husband's accusers."[154] While Candice E. Jackson[155] told Cybercast News that, "Hillary's involvement [in the scandal] is just as devastating and just as important in all this." She accuses her for having been "[] in the inner circle taking a lead in giving these women zero credibility, in attacking them in the public and through the press and in participating in all of these scare tactics, like hiring private investigators to threaten them and follow them." She further states that "[Hillary Clinton] is either as misogynistic as her husband or she is simply willing to conspire to mistreat women if that's what it takes to preserve their political careers. . . ." Attorney Jackson continued, ". . . accus[ing] the Clinton circle in the white house for discrediting, bribing, auditing, threatening and intimidate his accusers and that the extent they did it was suppressed by the mainstream press at the time."[154]

Jackson believes that "the Clintons have really gotten away with a political reputation of being defenders of women's rights and women's issues" and expressed resentment about "the state of feminism in this country" in that no one seems to care "whether women are brutally mistreated as long as politicians support abortion rights."[154]

Hillary was certainly in a very difficult situation and given the extent of the dilemma she surprisingly found herself in, she handled the situation cleverly in my opinion. Reality says that she had a husband to defend consistent with the promise of her marriage. She is only human after all!

There is no question, however, that American feminists were at war against each other on how the matter was supposed to be handled. The situation in fact crossed US

---

[154]Retrieved from: http://www.cnsnews.com/node/30125

[155]Author of Their Lives: The Women Targeted by the Clinton Machine

boundaries over into the international arena of women and one wonders if Hillary's feminism was affected in any way in view of other feminist groups outside the US. To this effect, Neera Sohoni[156] states that, "In the Third World, where [Hillary] has traveled widely, Hillary Clinton has become something of an icon of feminism. This makes her "stand by your man" response to allegations that her husband has cheated on her particularly distressing."[157] She further states, "She is the first lady of a nation that is supposed to lead the world's women in their "liberation" -- a woman long seen as a feminist and as the epitome of the modern day "professional" woman. Yet in response to charges that her husband has cheated on her, she has made a public display of loyalty to him, even joining in his denials. . . . This choice is reason to question seriously Hillary Clinton's credentials as leader for a reformed world for women, especially for me, as an Indian woman living in a still overwhelmingly traditional society." She further expresses her resentment: "The possibility that the whole century of feminist rethinking of gender roles is a mistake or a fantasy is disturbing. The fact that this realization follows from observing America's First Couple is even more distressing. It is not so much the collapse of a Camelot as the devaluation of woman's status within marriage that the newest Clinton affair spotlights." She relates the situation to the notion that a mother advises her daughter vis-à-vis her abusive spouse "Go back to him, my dear. That is your home. He is [yours]" and declares that, "It is painful but necessary to discard Hillary as a feminist. She fails feminism because she placed herself last or least or less than her other incarnations -- as

---

[156]Sohoni is a freelance author and writer living in Bombay.

[157]*Hillary Clinton is a Traitor*/Salon News Real (03-04-98) Retrieved from: http://www.salon.com/news/1998/03/04news.ht ml

wife, as First Lady, as U.S. citizen coming eagerly to the defense of an 'endangered' presidency."

It seems like Hillary did not pass the test similar to how the giant feminist organization fumbled on the issue of Women vs. President Clinton. What may excuse her from the extent of their foul play in my opinion is that the issue was strictly personal.

Yet, Hillary was accused of fumbling again on the question of violence. "More than 100 New York feminist leaders released a joint statement Sunday afternoon criticizing Hillary Clinton and supporting Obama for president . . . Clinton's support for the war in Iraq was the leading reason she lost the support of the group, which calls itself 'New York Feminists for Peace and Barack Obama!'" says Jon Weiner.[158] Add to this her support of Obama's war strategy in Afghanistan; one simply wonders if Hillary Clinton can be taken as an icon of peace, necessary for the condition of women internationally. In essence, though, this projection reflects the theory that big feminist groups in the US have the tendency to discriminate *against* women and to support their men opponents when it comes to the same political position on war.

With all this going on, no one can deny Hillary Clinton's efforts to help women around the globe. The record shows that she had shown concern about China's unacceptable predisposition to gender inequality as replicated by the high abortion rate in the country.

In "the most extensive African trip ever undertaken by a U.S. first lady, Hillary Rodham Clinton visited six African

---

[158]Wiener, *Feminist Leaders Oppose Hillary, Endorse Obama*/The Huffington Post. (February 3, 2008) Retrieved from: http://www.huffingtonpost.com/jon-wiener/feminist-leaders-oppose-h_b_84715.html

countries"[159] in 1997 and addressed her opinion on the continent's social, economic and political situation. She took a trip to the infamous Robben Island with President Nelson Mandela, visited Soweto, and joined former Archbishop Desmond Tutu, Chairman of South Africa's Truth and Reconciliation Commission "in planting a tree in remembrance of the victims of apartheid crimes." She made touching speeches in South Africa and latter in Uganda; she further visited Zimbabwe, Tanzania and Africa's newest country, Eritrea. She made the Goree Island her first stop in Senegal and familiarized herself with "The Door of No Return" through which slaves left Africa for good during the Slave trade.

In her recent visit to South Africa, Hillary spent more time with women to learn about their situation than with the politicians of the country.

In 2009, Ms. Clinton visited the Democratic Republic of the Congo, contacted numerous rape victims and substantially influenced the UN Security council to pass an effective resolution on the issue. As a result, a special representative, Margaret Wallström was appointed to maximize the effort of following the criminals in this respect.

However, people see Hillary's feminism in light of the contradictions displayed above, her current position in international political arena demands recognition for her potential to impress the world one way or another.

Why is this so?

This is so because a major development has taken place at the UN in 2011 that has the capacity to transform

---

[159]Hillary Clinton's triumphant trip to Africa; historic voyage marks the most extensive visit by a U.S. first lady/Ebony (July 1997) Retrieved from: http://findarticles.com/p/articles/mi_m1077/is_n9_v52/ai_19566001/

international status of women more than ever before. This is a great chance to close the gender gap internationally within this century, assuming all appropriate steps are taken, in view of unified feminism in favor of the universal human condition. I formally congratulate humankind in general and women in particular for this achievement.

To touch base with reality, the population of women in this world stands at approximately between 49-50% and half of the world's resources legitimately belong to them. But they could only look at their fair share from a distance for a long time because men have stood in the way since the beginning of society.

Ever since its inception, and especially over the past few decades, the UN has made a remarkable difference in promoting gender equality. A case in point is the Beijing Declaration and Platform for Action and the Convention on the Elimination of All Forms of Discrimination against Women. The official agreement reached in China acknowledges the extreme importance of utilizing half the potential of humankind into productivity through gender equality. The notion that humankind simply can no longer ignore the question of gender equality and cannot afford to miss its enormous socio-economic ramifications was well addressed in Beijing.

Fantastic job! This effort fuels positive changes observed for women in some parts of the world, but women are still suffering from violence, prejudice, high mortality rate, etc. It may be in the future but the UN cannot confidently claim that it was pro women in the past simply because it had other priorities to take care of. Funding was diverted to other causes such as diversified NGO's, wars, religious and border conflicts.

Encouraged by the sight of hope and frustrated at times by the barbarism of men against women in some parts of the world, women lived desperately knocking the door of the UN ever since its inception in October 24, 1945 for a chance to be heard. They however, went back with few concessions that never guaranteed their independence from the bondage of society. Their perseverance and bitter struggle finally paid off and the most dramatic event in the history of the UN took place when the United Nations General Assembly in NY unanimously voted on 2 July 2010 to establish a new power for women to answer the call of billions of suffering women in this world. This power is known as UN Women and its focal point is to accelerate universal gender equality and to energize women in all aspects of society. This new office will empower the existing units (such as UNICEF, UNDP, and UNFPA) operating within the UN system for different agendas of women.

The question is what the agency's priorities may be, how it would influence society in the long run and who was assigned to run it by the UN Secretary General, Ban Ki-moon. The effect of this new development is yet to be seen but experts point out that UN Women will focus on two important tasks: supporting inter-governmental bodies in designing policies and global standards on the status of women and assisting Member States to implement these standards by providing appropriate technical and financial support to those countries in initiative. It will also monitor the UN system for its own commitments on gender issues. However, the old president of Chile, Michelle Bachlet has been appointed for the job.

Bachlet was born in Santiago, Chile on Sept 29, 1951 from an Air Force General (father) and archaeologist (mother). Her father served Salvador Allende's leftist regime until he was overthrown controversially by CIA instigated coup in 1973 where General Pinochet assumed power as a result. He was then arrested in 1973 and tortured for several months before dying in custody in 1974. Bachelet, a 23-year-old medical student and political activist at the University of Chile at the time, was kidnapped with her mother, arrested and tortured in the notorious Villa Grimaldi detention center.[160] She was then exiled in Australia and she went to East Germany to study at the Humboldt University of Berlin. In 1979, she returned to Chile and completed her education in medical science while working as a clandestine human rights activist.

Bachelet appears to have had a few relationships with distinguished Chilean revolutionaries in her youth. One of them happened to be "Jaime López, [who] cracked under repeated torture and gave Pinochet's men the names of other guerrillas fighting the dictator, and later became one of the notorious "disappeared" -- the hundreds of people drugged and dropped alive from helicopters into the Pacific Ocean so their bodies would never be found."[161] She "also had a two-year affair with the communist leader of an armed guerrilla group, who tried to assassinate Pinochet in 1986." According to the article, the father of her third child Anibal Hernán Henriquez Marich was a supporter of the Pinochet regime.

---

[160]"Villa Grimaldi was a complex of buildings used for the interrogation and torture of political prisoners by DINA, the Chilean secret police, during the government of Augusto Pinochet. The complex was located in Peñalolén, in the outskirts of Santiago, and was in operation from mid-1974 to mid-1978. About 5,000 detainees were brought to Villa Grimaldi during this time, at least 240 of whom were "disappeared" or killed by DINA" Villa Grimaldi/Wikipedia (n.d.) Retrieved from: http://en.wikipedia.org/wiki/Villa_Grimaldi

[161]Kennedy, Dana. *Michelle Bachelet Is Chile's Steely Survivor*/Huffington Post (posted Mar 2, 2010) Retrieved from: http://www.aolnews.com/2010/03/02/pres-michelle-bachelet-is-chiles-steely-survivor/

Bachelet, as a pediatric surgeon served the Chilean society by treating countless victims of torture. After Pinochet was overthrown from power in 1990, she intensified her political activism while working in the ministry for health and studying military science at the country's National Academy of Strategy. She was then elected to the central committee of the Socialist Party (Partido Socialista) and served, as the health minister of Chile after Ricardo Lagos became the country's first socialist president since Salvador Allende in 1973. Bachelet then became the first woman to lead the Defense Ministry in 2002.

In pursuing her political career, she ran for president representing the Coalition of Parties for Democracy after 2005 under the campaign banner of at least four important social issues: improving the conditions of the poor, reforming the pension system, defending and upgrading the rights of women, and constitutionally acknowledging the rights of the native Mapuche people. She succeeded in defeating Sebastián Piñera by scoring 53 percent of the vote, became the first elected woman president of Chile in Jan 15, 2006 and ran the country from 2006-1010.

Michael Bachelet at one point in her presidency had the humility to return ". . . to the place where she was imprisoned and tortured more than 30 years ago under military rule, paying homage to those who didn't survive." She toured the memorial park built amid the ruins of the detention centre, [....] stopping at a wall bearing the names of the 229 prisoners who were kidnapped and killed." She also ". . . went inside a replica of the small tower where detainees were often sent before being murdered"[162]

---

[162]Farias, Manuel. *Chile's Bachelet visits site of her own torture,* (Sun October 15, 2006) Retrieved from: http://www.democraticun

President Bachelet was said to have been emotional at the time of her visit where she said "... that people like me who survived this experience are the lucky ones. Thousands of Chileans, including my father didn't survive the pressure and the torture. It is them who we remember today." This reminded me of the fallen activists in the Ethiopian and Eritrean revolutions back in the seventies when the brutal Mengistu took power after Emperor Haile Selassie in Ethiopia.

It speaks of the amazing personality and the rich achievement of the 59-year-old highflying politician! "The legacy left by the government of Bachelet -- who was herself arrested, tortured and exiled by the 1973-1990 dictatorship of General Augusto Pinochet -- includes both concrete and highly symbolic achievements", analysts say.

What is good about all this is that Bachelet is not only a person from upper class background that accomplished so much in life but also was a political victim of dictatorship who personally paid in terms of emotion, time, freedom and torture. She has directly tasted the fate of political refugees. She had the gut to risk her life returning to her country under the Pinochet regime and help his victims of torture. She also helped the poor native people of Chile as their president. The resultant effect of these experiences should certainly make her a qualified leader at the political stage, a dedicated freedom fighter and a compassionate figure in the sociological and spiritual stages of humanity.

Besides, Bachlet is a divorced mother of three who inherently understands the value of life and family structure with or without a husband. This should give her the advantage of easily relating to the problems of single mothers. The question is how her experience in this regard

derground.com/discuss/duboard.php?az=view_all&address=102x25 63136 could have molded her feminism. To this effect, an observer states that, "As a feminist, Michele Bachelet raised all three of her children on her own, and believes in a non-male style of leadership, where a woman doesn't have to become "made of steel" and behave like a man in order to effectively get the job done. To her, this means considering both sides of a problem but remaining tough. She is not politically soft, they say, "yet she brings [] compassion and maternal sense of the world to the job."[163]

The foundation of her feminism pro-life/choice aside should then be built on practical experience of Third World women, not on endlessly philosophizing on the subject matter from the comfortable zone of Radical feminism. It all boils down to balance, which has been practically demonstrated in her administration. (She kept her presidential campaign promise by forming a Cabinet of 10 male and 10 female ministers few weeks into her presidency). Further, she scored the following important achievements:

She made sure men who refuse to pay alimony were seriously punished in Chile. She enforced the establishment of hundreds of nurseries and violence related shelters for women and children, created gender balanced work force, allowed women participation in the naval academy for the first time in the history of the country and provided free contraceptive pills to girls older than 14. She also pushed for Equal Pay for Equal Work bill and few other economic transformations through the good foundation for the future of Chile.

In this opportunity, Bachelet is expected to merge four separate braches: the UN Development Fund for Women (UNIFEM) active since December 1976, the Division for the

---

[163] *Chile's New Leader: Michelle Bachelet*/Go-Chile.info (n.d.) Retrieved from: http://www.go-chile.info/chile-michelle-bachelet.php

Advancement of Women (DAW) active since 1946, the International Research and Training Institute for the Advancement of Women (INSTRAW) active since 1976, and the Office of the Special Adviser on Gender Issues and Advancement of Women (OSAGI) active since 1977. Dependable sources disclose that the agency will have a minimum budget of $500 million dollars, which is twice the budget of all four organizations combined.

Reality Check

Considering two feminists (Hillary and Bachelet) surfacing at the top hierarchy of society, one wonders what the ultimate result of their leadership will be. To approximate this, we need to look closely at the differences between the two women of power.

Bachelet and Hillary are from distinct schools of feminism. The first is a Third Word feminist and the second, a Western feminist. Cultural and traditional differences aside, Bachelet is a feminist who had a typical Third World woman's experience in the ambiance of a dictatorship while Hillary is a theoretical feminist with typical first world women's experience in a democratic environment. Their common ideological denominator is gender equality and the way they came to power, democratically. Hillary has no direct experience of dictatorship while Bachelet has direct experience of democracy. The "dictatorship" content gives Bachelet the political upper hand in this contrast in terms of what could be learned from a dictatorship.

I assume that Hillary has never been jailed, tortured or exiled. Her scope of feminism should then be limited to theoretical knowledge of these factors. Bachelet, however, has suffered them all. Her scope of feminism should then be based on practical exposure to these factors. The "exposure" content gives Bachelet the compassionate upper hand in this contrast in terms of what could be learned from being a victim of jail, torture and exile.

I stand ready to be corrected but Hillary does not seem to have had intimate relationships with leftist revolutionaries. Her scope of feminism should then be limited to the influence of broad-minded politicians from safe grounds of the game. Bachelet on the other hand had had relationships as such. She has suffered the consequence of an executed revolutionary lover, to say the least. Her scope of feminism should then include the influence of one or more revolutionary associates from fatal grounds of the game. This factor gives Bachelet the humanity and humility upper hand in this contrast in terms of what could be learned from being an emotional victim of injustice.

Both of them are differently progressive to their respective societies: Hillary in view of capitalist liberalism and Bachelet in view of Leftist liberalism. Hillary is therefore a freedom fighter for women from the angle of the bourgeoisie while Bachelet is one from the angle of the oppressed.

Hillary's heavy involvement in American politics makes her pro American by default but her status as the third most powerful person in the United States government without a question crystallizes that presumption into making her a dedicated defender of the American imperial position in the global political stadium. Hillary's progressivism must then conform to the conventional American political psychology, which believes in compromising from the upper hand position or challenging governments anywhere in the world. Although she has openly criticized former administrations for wrong political involvement elsewhere, Hillary must have substantially supported the CIA throughout her political career. Simply speaking, her current political position directly attaches her to an all-inclusive American political agenda.

Bachelet came from the opposite political direction. Her leftist tendency at least in the past was anti-American Imperialism including its CIA. CIA's involvement in the overthrow of Salvador Allende's regime may be controversial but it is clear that US did not like his leftist ideology. At the time, her father was serving his administration as a General and young Bachelet's political orientation was shaping towards the left. It is clear that the US happily accepted Allende's overthrow by Pinochet who was responsible for the death of her father and the pain she went through with her mother and comrades. This makes her the direct victim of Hillary's political orientation at least by convention if not by direct impact. Her intense involvement in Chilean politics should be expected to make her pro resistance to Imperial domination by commonsensical default, but her status as left oriented President of Chile suggests that she could have been a dedicated defender of the international leftist movement at large.

Apparently, the two powerful women inherently have antagonistic political outlooks. Hillary may then try to prioritize the interest of the US while Bachelet may stick with her resistive pro Third World position in future UN Women's political confrontation.

Few factors make their contact mandatory. The first is that both are women and UN Women is an agency for international women that cannot prevent any successful woman's participation without a tangible excuse. Secondly, they are feminists and feminism is expected to participate actively in the agency in all its forms. The other important factor to this situation is that the United States contributes at least 22% of the U.N.'s regular budget. Given that Hillary was one of the most influential politicians in the birth of the UN Women agency on top of this, chances are she will have a big say in its activities. Besides, Hillary is a very aggressive politician that will do anything to influence any political structure. She has shown this character very well during her campaign against Obama. This means Bachelet may not be able to work independently of Hillary. Hillary may indeed have about 20% voice (in accordance with America's percentage of contribution to the UN) in the UN overall and in UN Women's activities in particular, whether Bachelet likes it or not. The question is how this input may come about and if there will be any room for further power struggle should they approach the challenge on the ground differently (which is apparent).

In the meantime, Hillary has already aggressively started to do what she has to do in this respect internationally, in advance of the UN Women.

According to Madeleine Bunting, Hillary is currently establishing a foreign policy based on feminist philosophy. She is currently installing her international vision of women through the US government.[164] In so doing, she finds it important for American politicians to understand that the strategic success of US security depends on all-inclusive "empowerment, participation and protection of women and girls." To this cause, national policy has been introduced to the "Quadrennial Diplomacy and Development Review, which aims at redefining US foreign policy around civilian power." This will necessitate heavy involvement of women and girls in all American diplomacy with all governments of the world and in all conflict resolution procedures that America puts its hands on. Civil power in this context implies to "all America's civilian agencies" while the direct impact of the policy is assumed to "prevent and resolve

---

[164]*Clinton is proving that a feminist foreign policy is possible – and works*/guardian.co.uk (Sunday 16 January 2011) Retrieved from: http://www.guardian.co.uk/commentisfree/cifamerica/2011/jan/16/hillary-clinton-feminist-foreign-policy

conflicts, help countries lift themselves out of poverty into prosperous, stable, and democratic state, and build global coalitions to address global problems." According to Hillary, "rights of women and girls are now core to US foreign policy."

For a country that conventionally depended on military force to resolve conflicts, this development may sound terrific at face value. One simply wonders where this is heading considering that the voice of women has become equally important in safeguarding American global interests, a notion that implies the American government only represented men. Is this true? I do not think so; neither do I believe that women are more voiceless than men in America but I do believe this will create problems for men if not for all Americans in the end.

You have to give credit to Hillary's intelligence and ambition to reduce her political philosophy to practice no matter what you feel about her, unless you have a problem accepting the truth. I think she is one of the most influential politicians who ever existed in history and the first feminist to shake the political foundation of America, yet with significant potential to change the world through the new US foreign policy and UN Women agency. For those caught unawares, what she has accomplished is literally synchronizing the new feminist foreign policy of America in the face of powerful men in the government with the actuality of the US Women's agency for whatever she plans to deliver internationally. What a precise calculation of a brilliant feminist of modern times!

There is no doubt that she has done a number on American men in the process, at least in my understanding. The question is whether the reason her vision was smoothly accepted by American politicians was that they saw it as a new way of dominating the world. I question this arrangement because all this in retrospect is like the same old US Imperialistic vision in different makeup. It seems as if it will dominate the world economically and politically by means of Western feminism, while the usual military might stays constant. In the process, feminism will now be directly involved in American foreign policy just as it did in its justice system. In other words, Western feminism has become more powerful to the point of having a say in every decision the US will make internationally. Hillary and her Western feminism are saying that this has to be done because "[sexual violence] is an even more destructive weapon than landmines or cluster bombs on communities because its effects are so long term."[165] Taking into account that the majority of the male gender wants no more than a peaceful coexistence with women; that fewer men hurt women physically and yet with tangible results shown globally on gender equality; this rhetoric sounds consistent with radical feminism's pattern of biting off more than its share in different forms at different stages of development.

Plainly, it is about excluding men from the equation by means of collective punishment. Hillary's formula once again renders men irrelevant in society in that feminists will represent them in the international platform. I think American men are further taken for a ride without anything to gain in return. The formula further fails to recognize the opinions of Third World women that want to be represented by their own brand of feminism. This policy will be reflected in their societies, as their governments will be pressured to accept it as a bargaining chip for political and economic survival with "Superpower" America.

---

[165]*Secretary of State Hillary Clinton's Feminist Foreign Policy*/Freedom's Challenge - A PRIVATE BLOG DEVOTED TO FOREIGN POLICY & THE SECRETARY OF STATE (June 14, 2011) Retrieved from: http://secretaryclinton.wordpress.com/2011/06/14/secretary-of-state-hillary-clintons-feminist-foreign-policy/

Locally, men will be systematically forced to support Radical feminist agenda through their money in the name of American foreign policy while legally still being treated unequally to women in their country. Society is giving away something important to the cause of Radical feminism without any steps taken to reverse the existing discriminatory laws in the American Justice System. What we see here is complete domination of women over men in America (locally and globally), yet without men's consciousness of the dynamics. I do not think this will work internationally because Third World men and women may never accept the Western feminist ideology; but I believe American men are further pushed to the cliff by their own choice (accepting domination without resistance). Before they know it, laws will be drafted and ratified for them to wake up one day and say, "My God! Where have we been?"

The future of American men is simply heading in to the liberation struggle by Masclulinist Revolution. This is probably the time for Masclulinists to have a practical grip of how revolutionaries like Che Guevara did their business back in the days. There is no doubt that the biggest heat will be taken by American men because keen observers believe that all this "gets nowhere in the Middle East and Afghanistan" needless to say Third World men are not crazy enough to buy this after seeing what Radical feminism has done to American men and beyond. In fact, I am one of the believers that Western feminism will further endanger the lives of women around the world. Third World men may react because they are not psychologically set to accept something like this. If there is no inclusion, better it be exclusion, the mentality at its best says to my understanding, from that background.

Hillary and the radical feminists around know very well from their experience, that once something becomes Law, there is no chance for society to easily back out from under when it is no longer beneficial to society. Unfortunately, why not bite American men one more time while they are still napping on matters concerning their freedom!

The article[164] says, "Clinton has insisted peace cannot come at the cost of women's rights." The question is if it should come at the expense of men's! Should the Third World men pay what Western men are paying for women's equality in terms of their inequality? What is sad here is feminism's simulation to resolve international issues of women at yet the devastating expense of American men. To this ideologue, Stephen Walt, a professor of international relations at Harvard states that "the US can't even sort out its own problems of sexual inequality, so it is "overly optimistic" to think it can have much impact in Yemen, Congo or India."[164]

Apparently, this is the beginning of Radical feminism's development to Feminist Imperialism because it was through its foreign policy that American capitalism reduced its Imperialistic flavor elsewhere in the world. The projection to put the world back under the economic and political control of the United States and international men under the control of Western feminism has already started full-speed ahead through the mouthpiece of Hillary Clinton. In other words, Western feminism is trying to force the world into submission at the time that its trust in the west is drastically compromised by US political activities internationally. A few rich American men and women may benefit from this as they have ever since America earned its Super Power status, but what good is this to the average man and woman in America? "From the start Clinton left no one in any doubt where she stood: women's rights are 'the signature issue' of this administration's foreign policy," she said. She mentioned women 450 times in speeches in the first five months in office. "Transformation of the role of women is the last great impediment to universal progress," she declared, ". . . and began to develop what is her standard line: women's issues are integral to the achievement of every goal of US foreign policy." This sounds to me like a classic feminist philosophy that used to come out of any ambitious radical in the sixties like "Whatever they may be in public life, whatever their relations with men, in their relations with women, all men are rapists and that's all they are. They rape us with their eyes, their laws, their codes."[53] Mind you; one woman's feministic view is confidently launched globally without a meaningful sign of resistance from either men of power, American men, members of the public or authentic feminism!

This contemplation has in fact been reduced to practice already where the US foreign policy on the Libyan crisis through violence was said to be heavily influenced by powerful women in the government. Robert Dreyfuss states that "Hillary Clinton, Susan Rice, and Samantha Power pushed Obama into accepting the demands of neoconservatives and enter the civil war in Libya," says Robert Dreyfuss. ". . . Obama's women wanted war against Libya. We'd like to think that women in power would somehow be less pro-war, but in the Obama administration, it appears that the bellicosity is worst among Hillary Clinton, Susan Rice, and Samantha Power. All three are liberal interventionists, and all three seem to believe that when the United States exercises military force it has some profound, moral, life-saving character to it."[166]

Further, "The New York Times, citing insiders, reports that Obama shifted to intervention in Libya only under pressure from the trio: 'The change became possible, though, only after Mrs. Clinton joined Samantha Power, a

---

[166]*Obama's Women of War*/American Everyman (March 21, 2011) Retrieved from: http://willyloman.wordpress.com/2011/03/21/obamas-women-of-war/

senior aide at the National Security Council, and Susan Rice, Mr. Obama's ambassador to the United Nations, who had been pressing the case for military action, according to senior administration officials speaking only on condition of anonymity.'" And "The Washington Post reports that yet another administration woman, Gayle Smith, joined Ben Rhodes and the troika of other women to push for war: 'Obama's decision to participate in military operations marks a victory for a faction of liberal interventionists within the administration, including Rice, Rhodes and National Security Council senior directors Samantha Power and Gayle Smith.'"

Hillary cleverly took advantage of the American people's insecurity with terrorism and attached feminism to US security by saying that ". . . the empowerment, participation and protection of women and girls is vital to the long-term security." In Hillary Clinton's sexist view, the so-called Civilian Power that is supposed to run US foreign policy strictly comprises "women and girls," as if men have nothing to do with it. Western feminism is telling American men that they are good for nothing: to stay away from the foreign policy of America and yet, everything is going its way. Nothing can be clearer as to how feminism has sterilized American men to the point of taking them for granted at will. This is well exemplified by the state department's briefing that, "We are integrating women and girls into everything we do . . . in all our diplomacy with other governments . . . in our work on conflict and crisis." In reality, the strongest resistance in America against Western feminism comes from the third wave feminists. But, this resistance will probably be neutralized by tantalizing economic opportunities (that soon will be manipulated by a very few dominant women). However, the long term consequence that will most likely be similar to the failed Hosni Mubarak's childish attempt of pacifying the Egyptian uprising by nominating a vice president for the first time in his over 30 years of dictatorship. In the first case, the American society will suffer; and in the second case, the Egyptian people would suffer under a harsher Mubarak had they fallen for his mockery.

Caution demands the need for people to pay attention to who may be the so-called women that represent Americans internationally. My guess is as good as yours is, but I believe there will be friction between American feminists in the process. It appears to me as if the subtle power struggle, jealousy, and other personally driven tension within American feminists will be reflected eventually, both locally and globally.

Let me put this briefly to avoid misunderstanding! Whether people understand and accept it or not, there has been a problem between Hillary Clinton and NOW and possibly other big feminist groups as well, at least since the last presidential campaign in America. NOW And other feminists endorsed Obama over her. This came as a surprise of course, because they literally stopped a woman from becoming the President of the United States for the first time in history. How Hillary will take advantage of the current situation (feminist foreign policy) to deal with the grudge depends on two important points in my judgment. She can work with feminists who stood in the way for strategic reasons, if she has a plan to run for the presidency and in fact can make it good for them in exchange for their support in the future. Otherwise, she can make their lives difficult by substantially excluding them and working with other feminists instead.

Hillary states that she "went to Beijing to the UN Conference on Women in September of 1995, and spoke out against a long series of abuses that were human rights violations of women's rights and among those, of course, was trafficking."[167] This is good of course because trafficking adversely affects society and I think she did a terrific job considering the steps taken as a follow up. She also said that in 1996 she, "went with [her] husband to Thailand for a state visit [and then] to the north where [she] met with NGOs [nongovernmental organizations], trying to help young girls who had been sold by their families into prostitution, trafficked into the brothels, mostly in Bangkok?" However, I can't help wondering about what the reaction of the local feminists there could have been considering Mr. Clinton's past sexual harassment accusations.

One way or another, time will tell how we will all be affected by this revolution. Patience will show if Hillary's brand of feminism will blend well with Bachelet's. But there is no doubt that she was one of the most dominant politicians to the foundation of the UN Women and nomination of Michele Bachelet, who ended up becoming the favorite candidate of the UN Secretary General out of 26 other applicants for the post, most likely because of Hillary's influence. Hillary may then put maximum pressure on the agency to have it go her way.

Hillary is said to have said the following when Bachelet's appointment became official:

"[ ] we are very fortunate to have with us today the UN Under Secretary General Michelle Bachelet, the first head of UN Women. I am delighted by her appointment and very grateful for her commitment and the excellent presentation that she has already delivered. I also want to recognize Special Representative of the Secretary General Wallström,

---

[167]*Dying to Leave Interview with Senator Hillary Rodham Clinton*/PBS (September 25, 2003) Retrieved from: http://www.pbs.org/wnet/wideangle/episodes/dying-to-leave/interview-with-senator-hillary-rodham-clinton/1253/

who is working very hard and needs the support of all of us to implement Resolution 1888 concerning sexual and gender violence. These women are both dedicated advocates for women's rights and participation. And I also want to thank Under Secretary General Le Roy, whose Department of Peacekeeping Operations has taken groundbreaking steps to implement Resolution 1325. Thank you for increasing protection measures for vulnerable women and children and for integrating gender advisors into all missions."[168]

I would like to take this opportunity to express that I am impressed by Hillary Clinton and Michael Bachelet and I wish them the best in navigating the question of women fairly. I believe this is a new beginning and a wonderful chance for men and women to resolve their differences peacefully through the leadership of these two intelligent women irrespective of the mistakes made in the past.

My Appeal to Women

Women need to be careful not to waste this prospect for harmony, because it is the best momentum destiny has offered humankind. They cannot afford to let it slip away for it may never come back, and because it can end up being their worst nightmare. It is easy to transform trust to mistrust but it is almost impossible to repair mistrust into trust. Radical feminism's rise was a function of trust and its downfall, a function of mistrust. Today, it is struggling for survival, barely hanging on, looking at its imminent death in the near distance. The harder they come the harder they fall

---

[168]stacyx. *SOS Hillary Clinton at the UN: Women, Peace and Security* (October 26, 2010) Retrieved from: http://secretaryclinton.wordpress.com/2010/10/26/sos-hillary-clinton-at-the-un-women-peace-and-security/

is what happened to it. It did so much for women but it killed itself. I do not think it can recover from the consequence of its mistakes. It must be replaced by creative and humanist daughters of humankind who respect human life regardless of gender.

The UN Women's situation is, nonetheless, different from that of Radical feminism's because it is destined to deal with the all-inclusive question of women internationally. At this momentous point in time, it will face the planet in its completely diversified sociological form, where society is at the highest awareness of western mentality through years of direct psychological contact. The agency is about to confront humankind at a historical time where everything (economically and politically) is exhausted between the West and the rest of the world. It is going to deal with the ideological differences between Western feminism and Third World feminism. As a product of rich experience, Michelle Bachelet is here today to lead women with dignity! God bless her approach!

Universal trust is vested here in the question of society that only deserves treatment without bias. There will be mistakes and obstacles here and there as in any other challenge in life; but I hope sister Bachelet has checked in fully aware that a serious mistake in this forum can cause irreparable damage to women, especially in Third World countries.

Clearly, feminism has produced touchable results all over the world and the big power provided by the UN to women should help the cause of women immensely. On the other hand, a lucrative opportunity to destroy International feminism had been created for the selfish, opportunistic and inhuman Radical feminists, not because of Western women's conditions, which without a doubt are today gender equalized, but rather because of the objective conditions of the Third World women. This legitimizes

Third World feminists to command their struggle at the leadership level of the UN Women agency. You simply do not want to confront Third World leaders and societies with the cultural, economic and socio-political mind set of Western feminism unless you are naïve: It simply will not work and it should not.

Whether Western feminism will continue taking advantage of violence to benefit personally is its business but giving it another chance to mess up society becomes the business of Third World feminists and all of us. In so saying, Third World feminism cannot stop the destructive role of Western feminism in Western societies but it can stop it from playing the same destructive role in Third World societies. One thing is apparent: Radical feminism will take the last chance of survival by doing the best in its capacity to involve itself in international women's business, either through Hillary's foreign policy or by corrupting opportunist Third World feminists. It will pretend to be a friend to the highest point of its creativity and will even go as far as sabotaging the entire concept of gender equality should things fail to go its way. This feminist sect will stand in the way of Michelle Bachelet under the guise of many different excuses; but "Michelle Bachelet is not afraid to do what she wants in spite of social criticism, because she is her own person. Her personal life, had she been a US politician, would have sunk her political career years ago."[163] This gives me the buoyancy that the world is now in good hands and the confidence that Michelle Bachelet has everything she needs to defend her cause intellectually and culturally. Remember that there is a lot of money and power (enough to cause Western feminists to salivate) allocated at the UN for the cause. Please do not let them manipulate the situation at the expense of your people. . . Just be careful.

Western Feminism's Involvement in UN WOMEN Agency Should Be Conditional

Simply put, as desperate as it is, Western feminism will neither accept irrelevance nor be willing to work under other command, not only because it is not used to doing it but also because it is not psychologically conditioned to be directed by women of color. On top of its arrogance over all other sects of feminism, there are concrete facts that reflect its attitude towards the suffering of women in the underdeveloped countries. This should open the eyes of women as to what to expect from it. No matter how long it takes and how hard it may be to be left alone, Third World feminists should never flinch from protecting themselves and their people, because something planted in the west cannot be harvested in the east.

What I am saying is that any feminist organization interested in serving the cause of international women should pass a substance screening process based on positive contribution to the cause in the past. Being pro-choice on abortion alone should never be a criterion for good feministic identification. Any issues of ethnocentrism and racism within the past practice of Western feminism should be brought up for debate by any woman in the experience. Evidence related to organizational integrity should be seriously considered and actions taken accordingly.

I am talking about things such as allegations that "Western feminists, and especially American feminist organizations, largely refrained from becoming active in support of the struggle of Iranian women."[129]

This should raise questions like; why did they ignore Iranian women's cry for help in 2009 and all the way to July 2010, the time Sakineh Mohammadi Ashtiani's (sentenced to death by stoning execution for committing adultery) case attracted international attention to the point of unified denunciation against the regime in Iran? Equality Now could have been the first feminist organization to raise a voice against the injustice on the poor woman but why did they wait until after a few men of political power started to protest against it? Was Western feminism's first attempt to confront the Islamic Republic of Iran concerning abuse of women in October 18, 2010 a desperate act of pretension or an honest concern about the situation on the ground?

According to the chronicle, Feminist Majority, "finally [took] action on behalf of both Nasrine and Sakineh (Iranian lawyers) although this feminist group "had only supported Islamist activists like Shirin Ebadi and the 100 Million Signatures campaign, both of which support the continuation of the gender-apartheidist Islamic Republic and are therefore, fundamentally anti-woman in nature."[129]

This raises the question, could this be because these western feminists support oppressive regimes in order to legitimize their importance in the question of women worldwide? Was this about survival by exacerbating the problem consistent to what prominent feminists of the likes of Christina Hoff-Sommers were repeatedly saying for years? (That is that Radical feminists want to see women mistreated by men in order to take personal advantage of it).

One way or another, Iranian feminists assert that ". . . the National Organization of Women remains silent on the struggle of Iranian women, and worse, that Code Pink[169] has long been an active supporter of Mahmoud Ahmadinejad

---

[169]"CODEPINK is a women-initiated grassroots peace and social justice movement working to end the wars in Iraq and Afghanistan, stop new wars, and redirect our resources into healthcare, education, green jobs and other life-affirming activities." *What is CODEPINK?* (n.d.) Retrieved from: http://www.codepinkalert.org/article.php?list=type&type=3

and the Islamic Republic, most recently during Ahmadinejad's visit to New York City to capitalize on the United Nations."[129] What happened at the end of all this was that the Mission Free Iran exclusively thanked American feminist organizations such as the Equality Now, Radical Women, and Feminist Majority for their solidarity. It also invited them to participate in the effort of women for a UN resolution to criminalize stoning internationally. The National organization of Women (NOW) was, however, neither appreciated nor invited to the extremely important event (for women) that took place in December 11, 2010.

How inconsiderate must NOW have been to drop to this point of antagonism with the poor women in Iran? Should this allegation be true, it should cause the permanent elimination of NOW and the so called CodePink from international gender politics unless UN Women wants to be a hypocrite by including them in this opportunity.

Here is my message for Third World women: You know what Colonialism did to you and how Imperialism is affecting you today. You should also be sensitive to what Feminist-Imperialism can do to your societies should you give it the chance. Your resistance so far is noble but you need to learn more about the destructive role of Radical feminism in society concerning the fate of men and real victims of rape in America and teach the knowledge to your followers. Don't wait until it is too late to figure out the mess in Radical feminism as it took a long time for the world to understand the American system. You should give your support to Bachelet with this clear understanding in the backdrop.

Involving men who have a solid understanding of the issues from all countries is important to the success of UN Women. A favorable environment must be created for producing men who are more progressive in the Third World by male feminists that can recruit boys in favor of the cause faster than women can, because of their capacity to relate to them naturally. The best circumstances in all sociological areas should then be addressed based on common interest and in an open forum to give people the chance to exchange ideas freely from the psychological angle of both genders. Men need to see male role models in order to accept gender equality and to be involved in the revolution.

The preamble of unity must be based on the honest struggle for gender equality behind the slogan "Equality for Equality." We should start the mission by condemning unfair laws and using the experience as an example of how terrible the consequences of gender feminism can be. Enough discriminatory laws and direct human experiences are available that humankind can use to exemplify the cause and effect of extremism in society. Among others, the Rape Shield Law is a monkey on the back of American Feminism with which it cannot communicate with others without ridiculing itself, on the question of gender equality, justice and all-inclusive freedom. Not only is there no forward motion together as it is but also that Radical feminism should be taken as a case study for unjust feminism.

The exchange of ideas between men and women members of the agency should be configured such that honest effort for mutual benefit becomes UN Women's professional mode of operation. Further, enough resources should be allocated for research and development. Third World feminists should be open to relating to the experiences of revolutionary women from Rwanda, Eritrea, Ethiopia, Cuba, Vietnam, etc. They should have enough funding for mobility and education where they can teach each other about their specific cultures and traditional values. Exchanging feminists to work in different societies can strengthen their unity and confidence in the concept of sisterhood irrespective of race and religion. The agency should allow women of different societies to create the best environment for them to implement the issue of gender equality.

The agency should solidly organize international women to take diversified political positions in their countries by directly dealing with their governments. Standard quota systems can be developed for all Third World countries based on different criteria of the populace to accentuate stronger female participation in society.

The strategy for success should be drafted based on peaceful relationship between the sexes and problem resolution should be built in terms of respect and communication rather than on creating war between them. Further, the term *equality* should be well defined by a joint effort of both sexes rather than exclusively by women because the issue is gender blind in essence. A common understanding must be reached between men and women as to what rape and sexual violence mean and laws amended by equal participation according to experience of society in this regard rather than by abusing resources and lobbying politicians for sexist results.

Home based strategies must be laid down as to how to approach the issue and change the condition of women according to what can be accomplished in non-democratic environments without the destructive influence of Western feminists, by allowing them to resolve their issues according to the objective order and priority of their societies. The fact that both men and women are equal sufferers of oppressive regimes must be clearly understood and accepted. Unnecessary feminist fantasies and outrageous philosophies should be discouraged from the get go, with clear understanding that common economic factors contribute to the terrible conditions of Third World women. We cannot improve the conditions of women unless we improve the conditions of men as well in the areas of education, economy and political representation.

UN Women should strive for fairness to free Western men, especially American men, from the burden of sexism by gallantly confronting Radical feminism on biased laws. It should challenge them to take a clear position on innocent men who are convicted of rape through false accusations. It should be willing to help those who unjustly spent a portion of their lives in prison for crimes they did not commit. This can be done by working with groups like the Innocence Project and scientists to develop new scientific support systems that can be applied in rape cases. The agency should further show respect to the cause by discouraging false accusers from hurting innocent men. It should openly group them with sex offenders, for there is no forward movement without accepting them as part of the problem in the struggle for gender equality. The unhealthy quietness of Radical feminism in this regard should be openly challenged for the mission to make a difference in women's conditions internationally. Hillary's feminist foreign policy is for example fruitless unless it honestly tries to clean up the problems of Radical feminism in America first. Trying to improve other people's situation before improving yours is like an alcoholic trying to teach alcoholics to stop drinking. It simply does not make sense and it should be rejected as a double standard.

Here is what I think: We can do it if we do it together. Men can play a constructive role in this opportunity if they are included. This issue does not exist without their role in society. It concerns them equally. Women are our mothers and sisters and we are their fathers and brothers. We care for them and they care for us. We love them and they love us. We cannot do this divided. We either rise together or fall together. Liberation of women in the Third World is directly proportional to the liberation of men.

Nothing can teach us how recklessness and sexism in this reality can hurt society better than what Radical feminism did to the American people. As well, nothing can teach us better about the mistake of taking freedom for granted than the downfall of Western feminism. I hope the UN Women agency will focus on resolving universal human suffering, regardless of gender of course, with great emphasis on women's status in society. As much as democracy separates religion from politics, Third World social order must disconnect feminism from the justice system. This is a prerequisite for *equality for equality* as far as gender relationship is concerned.

I wish my sister, Michelle Blanchet, the best in this challenge as I humbly welcome her with optimistic mindset to lead us using her education and experience to the best of her spiritual fairness. She told her people "estoy contigo" which means "I'm with you," and I believe the motto applies today. In return, I feel honored to tell my sister that we are with her too.